D1605229

DATE DUE

POLICE PATROL

TACTICS AND TECHNIQUES

POLICE PATROL

TACTICS AND TECHNIQUES

Thomas F. Adams

Coordinator, Administration of Justice
Santa Ana College

Prentice-Hall, Inc., Englewood Cliffs, N.J.

Prentice-Hall Series in Law Enforcement
James Stinchcomb, Editor

Current printing (last number):

10   9   8   7   6   5   4   3   2

13–684662–9

Library of Congress Catalog Card Number:
71–138484

Printed in the United States of America

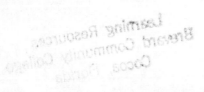

Prentice-Hall International, Inc., *London*
Prentice-Hall of Australia, Pty. Inc., *Sydney*
Prentice-Hall of Canada, Ltd., *Toronto*
Prentice-Hall of India Private Limited, *New Delhi*
Prentice-Hall of Japan, Inc., *Tokyo*

Dedicated to my number one son Tom and his lovely wife Marilyn . . . . who reinforce my confidence in the NOW GENERATION.

LAW ENFORCEMENT

CODE OF ETHICS

As a Law Enforcement Officer, my fundamental duty is to serve mankind; to safeguard lives and property; to protect the innocent against deception, the weak against oppression or intimidation, and the peaceful against violence or disorder; and to respect the Constitutional rights of all men to liberty, equality and justice.

I will keep my private life unsullied as an example to all; maintain courageous calm in the face of danger, scorn, or ridicule; develop self-restraint; and be constantly mindful of the welfare of others. Honest in thought and deed in both my personal and official life, I will be exemplary in obeying the laws of the land and the regulations of my department. Whatever I see or hear of a confidential nature or that is confided to me in my official capacity will be kept ever secret unless revelation is necessary in the performance of my duty.

I will never act officiously or permit personal feelings, prejudices, animosities, or friendships to influence my decisions. With no compromise for crime and with relentless prosecution of criminals, I will enforce the law courteously and appropriately without fear or favor, malice or ill will, never employing unnecessary force or violence and never accepting gratuities.

I recognize the badge of my office as a symbol of public faith, and I accept it as a public trust to be held so long as I am true to the ethics of the police service. I will constantly strive to achieve these objectives and ideals, dedicating myself before God to my chosen profession . . . law enforcement.

Preface

In this day of automation it is not surprising that the service mechanic—or technical representative—should service a highly complex machine when it is operating at peak efficiency rather than when it needs actual repairs. This procedure is quite common and it is known as *preventive maintenance*. This "p m" procedure is not at all unlike the function of the modern police officer, who serves the needs of the people in his assigned district within the scope of his responsibility and authority hopefully when it is at its peak efficiency: when it is enjoying its greatest absence of crimes and accidents, or civil disorders.

As that patrol officer, it is your responsibility to be thoroughly familiar with every part of your police jurisdiction and every one of its fixed and moving parts. The difference between your work and that of the "tech rep" who services the complex data processing machine in your office is that you are concerned with living, vital people who are constantly interacting with one another in a dynamic society. It is your responsibility to determine what is characteristic, or "normal" for your district to make it a peaceful and smoothly functioning entity—if that is what is normal—and to perform your duties in a professional manner to assure the people in your district of maximum protection and crime-free, accident-free, peaceful pursuit of their individual endeavors.

In this book we present in a concise and understandable manner the tactics and techniques that the patrol officer in the field must master in the modern police department. Excluded, of course, are many subjects that are covered in much greater detail in other texts and other courses of instruction. There is always another way to perform any given task, and with experience you will find certain techniques that are more effective for you. I suggest, however, that you start here in the absence of what you consider a "better way," as every one of the procedures and techniques discussed in the pages that follow have been field tested in actual law enforcement situations and they have been proved effective under the conditions prevailing at the specific times of their execution. Consider, please, the material in this text as an eclectic compilation of guidelines, rather than a collection of arbitrary rules that must be followed.

Sources of information and ideas for this text number literally in the hundreds, and most of the credit belongs to those individuals in the *police profession* whose unselfish devotion to our dream of professionalization has motivated them to share their ideas and "trade secrets" with their colleagues. To name a few would be a personal "slight" to those of my colleagues that I would not name. There are two, however, whom I am compelled to mention: Carl Ball of the California Commission on Peace Officers' Standards and Training, and Alex Pantaleoni, Police Science Coordinator at Rio Hondo College. Their incisively critical observations and suggestions concerning what should be done with this manuscript while it was in the making were extremely helpful.

Contents

POLICE PATROL

TACTICS AND TECHNIQUES

Introduction

to

Patrol

CHAPTER ONE   The patrol division is the epitome of police service in the American community. For most members of the community, police patrol officers comprise the only municipal or county police agency within their jurisdiction. The uniformed officer who patrols the streets in a distinctively marked patrol car is on view for everyone to see; he is the hub of the constantly turning wheel of law enforcement. *"The man,"* as he is called by some of the people in his district, is the most visible and direct representative of law enforcement, of the specific department for which he works, and of the entire criminal justice system.

Picture the one-man police department. The town's policeman is the chief of police, the patrol division, the juvenile officer, the identification specialist, and the parking enforcement officer. He performs all of the duties required of the whole police department because he is the whole police department. He devotes the majority of his time and effort to patrolling the city and responding to requests for investigative and various other services. As the city grows, so does the police department. The chief will probably first hire a clerk to handle the paper work, maintain records, operate the switchboard and the radio, and perform other office functions while the chief continues to spend the majority of his time in the field. When the chief hires the first police officer to assist him, specialization of the department begins. Assignments are made on the basis of proportionate needs for the various police services. More than half of the officer's time continues to be devoted to patrol activities.

The police department continues to grow, and eventually it becomes necessary to separate the functions of the department by requiring the chief to devote most of his time to administrative tasks. Some of the officers are assigned to duties that take them out of the "field." As the city continues to grow and the department numbers dozens, hundreds, or thousands of officers, the specialization becomes more well defined, although the patrol function continues to consume the majority of the department's time and manpower. Patrol remains the most important single function of the police department.

OBJECTIVES OF POLICE PATROL

Protection of life and property is the standard and most definitive statement of the police role. Patrol objectives are to the police service what general practice objectives are to the medical profession: all-encompassing. Probably one of the most important police objectives in recent years is what might be called *preventive maintenance*. It is not enough merely to do a good job of "police work." There must be a continual dialogue with many individuals from many segments of the community to discuss and explain the police role, and to exchange views on the merits of law obeisance and enforcement. This dialogue, too, is "police work," and an extremely important facet of it. In the past, all too often this function was given the label "public relations," and was then immediately relegated to the dusty corner of the training library. There it waited in the form of "canned" speeches for an officer to check out whenever called upon to deliver an address to some service club that had a guest speaker cancel at the last minute. Knowing that the police department was always ready to participate in "public relations," the program chairman could always rely upon the narcotics officer or some other specialist to fill the 30-minute speaker's spot and get the program chairman off the hook for another month.

The "canned speech—public relations" approach does not meet the demands of modern law enforcement and the society it serves. The purpose of the *preventive maintenance* approach is to interact; to develop and maintain a rapport with the people.

The patrol officer works an ideal assignment for personal contacts with the many people on his "beat" on a "one-to-one" basis. He should take advantage of every available opportunity to <u>allow these people to get to know him and the law enforcement philosophy of his department</u>. Unfortunately, there are too many people who have developed impressions and attitudes about the police solely on the basis of what they have seen in motion pictures or television, have read in newspapers or magazines, or may have encountered in single and unrelated incidents on occasions when police officers did not exemplify the professional law enforcement concept. Patrol provides an opportunity to strive to overcome such unfavorable attitudes whenever and wherever possible. <u>There is no better way to cultivate favorable attitudes than through personal and informal contacts.</u>

Crime prevention has been frequently defined as that phase of the law enforcement role in which the officer attempts in as many ways as possible to eliminate or reduce the <u>desire</u> of some people to commit crimes. Rehabilitation is the responsibility of probation and parole agencies. They are concerned with the <u>redirection of goals</u> expressed by the criminal law violators who have been identified and apprehended by the police agencies. The patrol officer is involved in the crime prevention process in his contacts with juveniles who commit delinquent acts, and with those whose <u>near-delinquency</u> comes to his attention in the normal course of duty. Through diligent investigation and alert observation, he attempts to <u>locate</u> and detain the first-offender juvenile either before or during the <u>commission</u> of a criminal act and then <u>takes</u> <u>steps</u> to <u>help</u> the <u>child</u> <u>redirect his activities into lawful channels</u>.

As an example of the officer's crime prevention activities, consider the following case:

> Officer Carver is assigned to the foot beat in the slum district, which is composed of old shops, stores, run-down residential dwellings, stores converted into apartments, old mansions converted into rooming and boarding houses, and some newly constructed "redevelopment" dwellings that have already begun to assume the characteristics of "new slums." The department has assigned Carver to this beat because he grew up there as a child. Although his family finally moved away when his father was promoted to foreman, much of his childhood and young adult time was spent in the neighborhood with friends. Carver knew most of the older families in the neighborhood and understood the problems of the community because he had lived most of the same experiences and frustrations.
>
> Carver is well-liked by some of the people in the area, despised by others, feared by some who have learned for various reasons to fear policemen. He is respected by nearly all of the people with whom he has been in contact in his role as a veteran police officer. He is thoroughly sold on the importance of the job that he is doing

and is optimistic about the future. He patrols his beat diligently and handles all of his assignments in a professional manner. Occasionally he stops at the recreation center and "raps" with some of the young men who virtually live at the center. He talks with the youngsters on the playground, shoots a few baskets on the basketball court, and knocks a few "flies" on the baseball diamond; all part of the "extras" that go with his particular assignment.

As he is walking his beat, Carver runs into a situation that is quite typical around the small market, the fruit and vegetable stand, and the corner delicatessen. He observes one of his little acquaintances from the playground "lift" an inexpensive edible item from the display shelf. Knowing that behavior patterns are developed by repetition and reinforced by what may appear to be lack of concern or outright approval by peers or elders, Carver immediately apprehends the youngster. He tells the boy to put the stolen item back where he found it, and suggests to the boy that he should apologize to the store owner. Then he and the boy pay a visit to the boy's home to speak with his parents. On arrival, the boy admits to his mother what he had done (as suggested by Officer Carver) and then Carver discusses the case briefly with the mother, leaving the child in the custody of his mother in hopes that the child will be appropriately disciplined.

Carver has actually performed a crime prevention function. As a result of his apprehension of the boy and some sort of disciplinary action meted out by the parents, the stealing has been followed-up in such a manner that the child will have unpleasant memories of the act of stealing. The child was not allowed to feel rewarded by enjoying the stolen object with impunity.

Officer Carver's role in the situation was merely to apprehend the child and take him to his parents, who arranged for whatever disciplinary action they deemed necessary to redirect the child's future activities. Once is enough for most children. Because of the diligence and concern by the understanding officer, the child will probably not repeat such an unlawful act again. Of course, it takes teamwork. The officer alone cannot hope to meet with the same degree of success that he may accomplish with the cooperation and follow-through by parents who are equally concerned with the behavior of their children.

Crime repression is one of the most obvious objectives of patrol. Their uniforms and distinctively marked patrol cars and other vehicles immediately and unquestionably identify the policemen as the people who are responsible for enforcement of the many laws that have been codified over the span of a few centuries. Actually, the police represent only a small portion of the conglomerate of law enforcement agencies in our system of government. At each level of government, many other agencies also serve as enforcement arms of the executive branch. Health and building inspectors, game wardens, fire marshals, judges, district attorneys, harbor patrolmen, agriculture department inspectors, licensing board investigators, professional standards commissions, and boxing referees are all involved in the enforcement of laws that comprise the police power of the state. Other people responsible for the enforcement of laws and prosecution of violators include social welfare investigators, probation and parole officers, prison guards, school principals and attendance officers, college administrators, highway patrolmen, driver license examiners, animal control officers, weights and measures inspectors, customs inspectors, and border patrolmen. All have one objective in common: crime repression. Hopefully, the people's knowledge that there are such officers with enforcement responsibilities, and compliance with the laws by the great majority of those people at any given time, will make it physically possible for these officers to cope with the violations that do occur. This system presupposes that a peaceful and law-abiding situation exists; if the situation is otherwise, the alternatives are social decadence or a police state.

Crime repression as attempted by police patrol occurs when the opportunity for the commission of crime is reduced in actuality or at least in the minds of the individuals who would otherwise commit their unlawful acts with impunity. In New Amsterdam the night warden, or policeman, walked down the streets and alleyways at nighttime with a noisy staff that made a rattling sound and warned criminals of his proximity. This "rattle watch" was a less sophisticated method of attempting to repress crime. The modern policeman wears a distinctively designed and colored uniform and drives vehicles that are immediately identifiable to everyone, including the criminal. By maintaining a constant and irregular patrol throughout his assigned district, the officer attempts to create a feeling of his omnipresence. This, of course, should be distinguished from what could—without adequate control—become oppressive dominance, a condition not desirable in a free society. The theory is based upon the hope that an individual who intends to commit a crime will not knowingly do so in the presence of a police officer, and is less likely to commit the crime if he is not sure exactly when and where the officer is likely to show up. The policeman's presence may not change an attitude or a habit, but it may minimize the criminal opportunity.

Crime repression is one of the purposes of the field interview program, which consists of making field contacts with certain individuals whose presence at certain locations under particular circumstances gives the field officer reasonable cause to make such inquiries. The following case illustrates how such an activity may repress criminal activity.

> Officer Loya was assigned to the evening watch on beach patrol. The assignment was normally a very cold and lonely one at this time of the winter, and Loya tried to keep reasonably active to

make the time go by faster. As a result he went out of his way to check the security of the beach-front businesses. He stopped frequently and talked to many of the "regulars" who frequented the beach even during the cold season. He became familiar with nearly everyone and everything that seemed to be _normal_ for his beat at that time of year and time of day.

One evening, Officer Loya observed two young men whom he had never seen on this particular part of the beach before. He was not so much concerned with how they were dressed or whether they were well-groomed, as he was with the fact that these two individuals did not seem to "fit" into the scene. Earlier, when the stores were still open, he had noticed that they had been showing considerable interest in some surfboards in one of the shops. Since they had caught his interest, he also noted that they had spent some time standing near the rear exit from the shop. At that time, Loya merely made a mental note of what he had observed and told himself that he would keep an eye on the young men should he observe them later in the evening.

Toward the end of the watch, Loya spotted the same two men. By this time the surfing shop had been closed about an hour and it was dark. The men were loitering near the rear entrance to the shop. Coincidentally, he had observed them loitering inside the same door some time earlier. They were not violating any law, but the circumstances of the moment coupled with his earlier observations of these two strangers, plus his knowledge that surfboards are frequently the object of theft, indicated to Loya that he should contact the young men and discuss his suspicions with them.

Officer Loya walked up to the men and addressed one of them with his usual friendly "Good evening." They immediately separated and ran in opposite directions. No crime had been committed and there seemed to be no apparent reason for their running, but run they did. Loya pursued the closer one and held onto him while he and his suspect (of what, other than running, he did not know) walked to the telephone. Loya called for another unit to help him locate the other person who had fled the scene. About 15 minutes later, Loya had both of the gentlemen in his presence. "Were they under arrest?" they asked. Loya said that they were not at the moment but that he was detaining them for the purpose of finding out who they were and what they were up to.

Both young men identified themselves to Loya's satisfaction, and he requested a record check through communications via the radio in the follow-up unit that had arrived to help him pursue the inquiry. While he was waiting for a return on the record check, Loya asked them why they had attempted to evade him when he merely wanted to talk with them. They said nothing. By this time the record check came back. Both of the subjects had spent some time in juvenile hall for miscellaneous thefts and burglary and were at the time on probation.

Armed with this new information, Loya attempted to talk further with the subjects, and they did establish some rapport. They told the officer that because of their records and the fact that their probation required that they not associate with each other they were afraid that they would be rearrested. Loya again checked the building where the subjects had been loitering and determined that no attempt had been made to enter. They probably had been preparing to commit a crime, but they had not committed one at the time of contact.

Officer Loya filled out field interview cards on both subjects, told them that their probation officer would—no doubt—receive copies of the cards, and stated that he was going to release them. He continued to tell them that because of their obvious intention to commit a crime which he had prevented, they should go to their respective homes. He also advised them that now that he knew who they were and what they had been up to, should some type of burglary occur that evening they could easily be considered suspect. Convinced that they should leave the beach, the young men left. There was no burglary that evening on the beach.

Had the officer not contacted the young men in the case described above, it would seem quite likely that they would have committed the burglary. The officer has no idea whether his contact with them had any influence on their desire to commit crime, but it appears that he at least reduced their opportunity to do so. The burglar relies on his anonymity to avoid apprehension. In this case, the two individuals were merely strange faces until the officer asked them to identify themselves and explain their presence.

Maintenance of order and the public peace in the community the patrol officer serves is one of the most versatile and sometimes most misunderstood of all the police objectives. A free society is characterized by its relatively small number of controls when compared with other types of governed society. Yet, in order that the majority of the 200 million people in the country may enjoy their own pursuit patterns to comfort and happiness, certain controls are intrinsic to such a society. These are accomplished generally through a constant and vigilant patrol, frequent contacts with as many people as possible to serve as a subtle reminder of the police presence, and by responding to calls to "keep the peace."

The patrol officer must attend all places where large numbers of people gather for any purpose to assure the maintenance of order. Most people are peaceful, and the patrol officer is called upon to handle the unusual situation, such as the noisy radio or television, the boisterous party, and the loud and unusual noises, at times and locations when they disturb other persons in the neighborhood.

The "orderly maintenance" process includes many other responsibilities, such as directing traffic to relieve congestion, controlling crowds and preventing panic at disaster scenes, and serving as a referee in a family or neighborhood disturbance. Most of the breaches of the peace are settled merely by requesting that the violators desist and comply with the law. In those cases when the violators do not comply, the officer must take immediate and decisive action, which may include arresting and prosecuting the violators.

The patrol unit of the police department is responsible for the identification and apprehension of as many criminal law violators as possible without capriciously infringing on the constitutional and legal rights and privileges of the many people with whom the officers come in contact. Many offenders identify themselves to the officers who patrol their districts in a variety of ways. Some disobey traffic laws or commit criminal code violations while actually in the presence of the police officer. Others commit their crimes in the presence of witnesses. Most violators commit their crimes out of the presence of the officers and/or witnesses.

To be able to identify and locate the many law violators, the patrol officer must attempt to learn as much as he can about his assigned district and the people in it. Better yet, he should know the entire city in which he works, although that is impossible in large cities. He should make every effort to protect the property in his district against theft, traffic collisions, and malicious mischief; and to protect the people from deliberate or accidental injury. Any people whose unlawful activities pose a threat to the lives and property of the people in his district should be appropriately handled in accordance with the law. This is the patrol process known as *identification and apprehension*.

Another patrol objective is the process sometimes referred to as *judicial assistance*. The officer should always zealously adhere to the Constitution and its amendments, and work according to the guidelines provided by his department, the attorney general and the prosecuting attorney, and the courts. Virtually every step along the way in many criminal cases, the officer must follow explicitly prescribed procedures from his discovery of the crime to the time of his presentation of evidence and testimony in court.

The *due process* provisions of the Constitution and the Bill of Rights have been interpreted by the various courts as controlling influences on such police procedures as field inquiry, arrest, search, seizure of evidence, impounding contraband, and interviewing the suspect. It is the officer's duty to work within the framework of the many laws and guidelines, and to bring his evidence into court for an objective evaluation of the facts and a determination of the guilt of the accused only after the facts have been introduced to the court.

ACTIVITIES OF THE PATROL DIVISION

Routine Patrol and Observation

Basic patrol is usually referred to as "routine," although the object is to avoid any semblance of routine as much as possible. Once an

officer establishes a pattern or any type of schedule for his patrolling
duties, his effectiveness in repressing crime is virtually eliminated.
Many intelligent and wealthy criminals have attributed their phenomenal successes to their apparent ability to work "around" the time
schedules of the field officers. They would learn the watch—or shift—
hours, district assignments, number of units on the street, and time
schedules of the individual officers in the particular districts where
the thieves intended to commit their crimes. The alert and intelligent
officer will study the reasons for such successes by criminal law violators, and change his own patrol tactics accordingly.

When the patrol officer does not have a time schedule for patrolling
his district, the criminal must take his chances against being caught.
If the officer does develop a schedule of any kind, deliberately or
not, the thief can easily adapt his own timing to avoid arrest. The
"routine" of patrol, therefore, is a technique of "routine avoidance."

Preventive Attendance at Public Gatherings

The patrol officer makes his presence known in places where people
gather in any sizable numbers. His presence is for the purpose of
assuring a peaceful assembly and providing protection for those who
wish to exercise their rights to peaceful assembly and free speech.
There is no intention that the officer control or dominate the people
who attend such gatherings. His purpose is to prevent—if he can—any
unlawful activity on the part of the individuals or the crowd as a
whole. Riot prevention is preferred to riot control. Once a riot begins,
everyone loses. Freedom of peaceful assembly is one of the basic
freedoms provided by the Bill of Rights. The field officer visits places
where people are assembled and determines that the meeting is lawful.
His task then is to remain present to assure everyone present that it
will continue that way.

Benevolent and Community Services

Because he is on duty at all times, the policeman is often called
upon to perform many services that do not fall within the list of job
specifications for policemen, but he provides them nevertheless. If
not called for by law, the tasks may be required of him by tradition
and social custom in that particular community. The patrol officer is
constantly called upon to administer first aid to accident victims, to
revive drowning victims, to help persons who are destitute and have
no one to whom they can turn for advice or assistance. The officer will
probably perform as midwife at childbirths, take part in rescue operations, and be asked to give advice on family and marital affairs. He
may deliver death messages, help people who have lost their keys
gain entrance into their homes or automobiles, make emergency de-

liveries of whole blood or body organs for transplant, and inform people about where they may find a family restaurant or attend a motion picture.

A dilemma is created and perpetuated by the traditional acceptance of various nonpolice duties by the police department simply because there seems to be no other government agency geared for the unusual and unexpected. Chauffeur services for visiting dignitaries and certain local officials are obviously a waste of police resources, yet some police officers work as chauffeurs on a full-time basis. To satisfy the ego of an individual who gains a feeling of importance by being taxied in a police car, the department loses the officer and the vehicle for the period of time he is unavailable for calls and emergency services. The local government would save money by paying taxi fare. In the absence of such realistic considerations, which are inevitable if police efficiency is to be increased, the patrol officer will be expected to consider these services as part of his normal and routine duties.

Building and Property Security

The average businessman probably takes great pains in securing his place of business from theft or vandalism. He constructs doors and windows of heavy materials and equips them with expensive locks, although he sometimes neglects the rear doors in the interest of "economy" (the hinges may be on the outside, making it possible to open the door by merely removing the hinges or the pins). He builds other protective devices to cover skylights and ventilation shafts. With all of these precautions, it is not unusual for someone to leave the place for the evening or weekend and forget to lock one of the doors or to close a window. Professional people, such as doctors and lawyers, often work such unusual hours that it is not uncommon for them to leave their offices unlocked and vulnerable to burglars at almost any time of the day. The patrol officer checks the buildings and other property in his district on an unscheduled and frequent basis to determine their security and to apprehend any criminal who attempts to take advantage of such lack of security.

Inspection Service

Inspections for security against theft are immediately obvious responsibilities of the patrol operation. But there are other inspections that the officer performs. One of the most important is to look for fires and fire hazards at the same places that he inspects for security against theft. It would not be feasible for the local government to require another agency to duplicate the police patrol. The officer is already

patrolling this district on a continuous round-the-clock basis. He inspects for various problems or violations and reports them to the
appropriate agency for corrective action.

In addition to reporting fires to the fire department, the patrol
officer looks for and reports outages of public utilities to insure that
broken water mains and downed wires will be quickly repaired and
service resumed. He reports streets and sidewalks in need of repair
before the occurrence of some major pedestrian or vehicular accident.
Health, safety, and building code violations, as well as license infractions come to the officer's attention in a variety of ways, and his reports
to the responsible agencies generate follow-up investigations and
eventual correction of the problem. His initial action may also result
in prosecution of violators of laws other than the criminal codes that
are normally enforced by the police department.

Responding to Calls for Assistance

Virtually every police department study that I have heard of has
shown that the great majority of calls for police service by the people
in the community do not involve matters that lead directly to an arrest
or any other action beyond merely responding to the call and talking
with the people involved. Neighborhood children damage fences or
other property, or the children get involved in a fight that leads to an
argument between their respective parents. One or both of the people
in the debate call the police department and ask the officer to settle
the matter. How the officer is supposed to handle the matter in the
eyes of the adversaries usually differs from how he may actually handle
it within the law. One parent will say to the officer: "Make him pay
for the damages." Another willl say: "Bawl him out and scare that kid
so that he won't do it again." Still another will state: "I don't want you
to do anything but just make a report so that we can sue." And not to
be left out is the request that absolutely surprises the officer whenever
he hears it: "Beat him up and teach him a lesson." The only thing the
officer can do, of course, is determine whether someone is violating
the law and take enforcement action when warranted. Other than that,
he can only advise the people that their problem is a civil one.

The task of responding to calls may sometimes be regarded as a
matter of disposing of *minor complaints*, although none of them are
minor to the parties involved. The problems confronting these people
are obviously beyond their capacity to cope with by the time they
call for police assistance. A tremendous amount of tact and diplomacy
is required for handling such complaints. The child who refuses or
fails to respond to his father's discipline may be a family problem
today, but he will be a police problem tomorrow unless some solution
can be worked out. The unethical, but legal, business transaction in

which the unsuspecting victim purchased a five-dollar "burglar alarm" system for 400 dollars may not in itself be a criminal code violation, but a series of such transactions and accompanying false representations may lead to prosecution of the unscrupulous vendor and return of the money to the people who could use the money far more than the burglar alarms. Many matters of possession and repossession, landlord and tenant arguments, employer and employee relations, property line arguments, poorly constructed dikes and levees, late garbage collection, and simple "gripe sessions" about government service in general are laid in the lap of the field patrol officer. All of them must be dealt with intelligently and with diplomatic persuasion, because the officer usually has no more authority in such matters than the individual who is requesting police response and action.

People commit suicide. The police are called. A woman is having a baby. The police are called. A bedridden, elderly man who lives alone falls out of bed and needs help. The police are called. An explosion destroys a hotel and injures dozens of people. The police are called. A sonic boom rattles some windows. The police are called. The police respond. They act, then resume patrol.

Animal Control

Except when a separate agency has been created for the purpose of caring for animals—sick, injured, lost, and stray—on a continuous round-the-calendar-and-clock basis, the task of animal control is generally relegated to the police department to be handled by a patrol officer. If such a special agency is in existence, but on a limited basis, then the policeman is still responsible for the task on a "sometime" basis.

Traffic Direction and Control

Safe and efficient movement of pedestrians and vehicles throughout the city is the patrol officer's responsibility even when there is another specialized division established strictly for the traffic responsibilities of the police department. Traffic control requires constant attention by all on-duty police officers, and all must be available to deal with unexpected congestion problems at fires, collisions, or disasters. Schools and places where people congregate on a regular or irregular basis should be checked frequently for traffic hazards or congestion, and the patrol officer must take action to relieve any problems. He is charged with the responsibility to take the initiative to step out into the street, direct traffic, call for whatever assistance he needs, then return to his normal patrol activities when he is no longer needed.

Figure 1.1 Traffic Control is an important function of police patrol, whether it is in New York, Delaware, or Hawaii. Courtesy of the Police Department, City of New York.

Figure 1.2 Courtesy of the Police Department, Hilo, Hawaii.

Figure 1.3 Courtesy of the Delaware State Police Department.

    The police officer is the official guide for the jurisdiction he repre-sents. He is expected by both visitors and residents to know approx-imately—if not exactly—where everything is. He is expected to know the shortest way from one place in the city to another, and from his location at any time to other communities and places of entertain-ment. He should know the locations of the all-night service stations and restaurants, the nearest drugstore, the old-fashioned ice cream shop, a book store, a respectable tavern where one could take an out-of-town guest, and just about anything else that the inquirer could be seeking. The patrol officer should also be prepared to answer specific questions about the altitude, population, topography, and history of his community. He should be its goodwill ambassador. To the guest, the uniformed policeman is the direct representative of the community. The officer acts on its behalf.

Developing Contacts

    Developing contacts within the community is a foremost respon-sibility for the total police department as well as for the patrol officer in the field. The officer cannot be satisfied with his own knowledge that he does a good job. Other people must also know how and why he performs his job the way he does and they should be able to evaluate the quality of his work as well. There must be rapport and meaningful interaction between the officer and the people in the community he serves, and he must have the enthusiastic support of most of those people.
    The officer on patrol should develop informants. He will cultivate informants among the criminal ranks, the vice operators who provide information concerning criminal activities of others for various rea-sons, and those who have criminal records but choose to "live it straight" now that they have been rehabilitated. The officer will seek informants among the numbers of people who obey the laws them-selves and who sincerely wish to assist the police in identifying and prosecuting other people in the community who choose to disobey the laws of the community and the state.
    Jewelers are the best informants for leads in locating jewel thieves and their "fences," and for recovering stolen jewelry. People in the construction industry are the best source of information concerning the individuals and companies involved in legitimate and illegitimate machinations of the construction industry. Informants from all oc-cupations, businesses, and professions should be encouraged to par-ticipate in the police business, which probably concerns them more directly than any other business than their own.

Establishing rapport with citizen participants in law enforcement
(*participant* may be a more palatable term than *informant*) should
yield mutual benefits to the police department and the *participants*.
There should never be any gratuities involved in such an association,
but there are many ways the patrol officer may assist the businessman
and merchant. A visit during a lull in other patrol duties may lead
to an informal inspection of the building to see how secure it is from
burglars or shoplifters. The inspecting officer may advise the owner
to place his safe in a location where it can be seen at night by a
patrolling officer from outside the building, and to install a light to
illuminate it. He may suggest that the silent burglar alarm on the
doors and windows is excellent, but that it might be worth the extra
few hundred dollars to also wire the plaster walls between the store
in question and the next door neighbor's seldom occupied furniture
storeroom. Clothing stores may find it to their advantage to alternate
the clotheshanger hooks to slow down the shoplifter who attempts
to take several items off the rack at the same time.

Preliminary Investigations

The patrol officers are on duty and in the field, available to take
prompt action on any incident calling for police response, including
crimes and accidents. Providing that the patrol unit of the police
department is adequately staffed and sufficiently trained, the patrol
division is in the best position to handle the initial phases of the
investigation of all types of crime. Exceptions may include those vice
crimes, narcotics investigations, intelligence operations, and sensitive
cases that require special attention in street clothing instead of
uniforms. Actually, however, in many agencies the majority of vice
and narcotics arrests are made by the uniformed patrol officers.

The first officer on the scene of a crime looks after the safety of
the victim and any witnesses, and apprehends the culprit, if he is still
immediately available. He takes immediate steps to protect the crime
scene from contamination, then establishes communications with the
dispatcher to broadcast the description of the wanted suspect and to
send whatever additional assistance is needed.

Having been on the scene from the beginning and in touch with
all that has been happening, the patrol officer will probably be the
man to continue with the initial investigation up to the point where
all leads are exhausted and any further investigation would take the
officer out of his assigned district for too long a period of time. He
will interview the witnesses, the victim, and any suspects that he
may encounter. He will collect the evidence and catalog and file it,
then he will prepare the reports. At some point the follow-up work on

the investigation may be continued by an investigator and other specialists. The key to the success of the follow-up investigation is usually attributable to the skill of the patrol officer who initially handled the case.

In many agencies, accidents are also handled initially by the patrol officers within their assigned districts, then later followed up by the accident investigators from the traffic division. The reason for the preliminary investigation by the field officer is the same as for crime investigations: the man is only minutes from the scene and will be the first to arrive. He is the logical one to continue to question drivers and witnesses after he has attended to their medical needs and administered any first aid that he finds necessary. Upon his arrival at the scene, he is in a position to observe the vehicles before they are moved, and he is generally in a better position than other officers to conduct the investigation. Somewhere along the way, as with crime investigations, the follow-up investigator may assume responsibility for the continuation and "wrap-up" of the case. In some agencies, the investigation is continued by patrol officers as far as possible up to—and including—the "wrap-up" stages. The primary consideration in determining whether the officer stays with the case is usually the amount of time that it will require him to be away from his district patrol activities.

Patrol officers also conduct investigations into unethical or unlawful business transactions; suspicious persons such as door-to-door canvassers and salesmen who appear to be interested in more than soliciting sales or contributions. In addition, they investigate vagrants, loiterers, and suspected vice operators. The officer conducts field interviews with people whose presence in a particular place, or the circumstances under which they are observed, causes suspicion. He checks out apparently abandoned vehicles to determine if they are stolen, and looks into any other matter that poses a threat to the lives and property of the people in the community he serves.

Collection and Preservation of Evidence

Intrinsic to the investigation process is the proper handling of evidence for the purpose of assuring a fair trial of the accused. From the moment he first arrives on the crime scene until he completes his testimony and presentation of evidence in court, the patrol officer is directly involved in this process. He is careful to avoid contaminating any more evidence than is necessary, such as in cases when he must do so in order to save a life. He carefully assesses the situation when he arrives, then methodically collects the evidence and prepares it for transportation and storage or laboratory analysis. After storing the evidence, or forwarding it to the lab, he prepares the necessary reports. When the time comes for the court appearance and presenta-

tion of the evidence, the same officer usually withdraws the evidence
from storage and accounts for its continuity of custody.

The patrol officer prepares a sketch of the crime scene for many
of the investigations he conducts, using the sketch for orientation
and coordination of his information. Some of the officers assigned to
the patrol division may receive special training in the collection and
preservation of evidence, and work as crime scene specialists with
the other officers who are assigned to the initial investigation. They
take photographs, "dust" for—and collect—latent fingerprints left at
the scene by the suspect, and work as a team with the other officers
in conducting the investigation.

Arrest of Offenders

Another of the many duties of the patrol officer is arresting those
who violate laws. This activity is the officer's primary objective at
the crime scene. Once he accomplishes the arrest, he can use one
of several alternative methods to introduce the arrestee into the
criminal justice system. The methods are prescribed by the laws,
the courts, and the procedural manuals of the various agencies.

In virtually every felony case the officer takes the arrestee to jail,
where he is "booked," or processed, and then given an opportunity to
post bail to assure his later appearance in court. He may be taken
directly before a judge and arraigned prior to booking or bail, although this occurs infrequently. In misdemeanor arrests the violators
are either lodged in jail and processed prior to posting bail, or they
are issued a citation which requires a written promise to appear in
court on or before a specified date. The citation method has been
used extensively in traffic cases for many years, and it has merely been
extended to cover those misdemeanors that the courts, the prosecutors,
and the police agencies agree can be handled in the same manner.

Roll call training sessions and various publications constantly disseminate information about current crimes and wanted criminal offenders. The officer is responsible for diligently searching for those
wanted persons or information concerning their whereabouts and
for seeing that they answer to the courts for their crimes. In many
cases of minor violations the officer also issues written warnings and
oral reminders of miscellaneous violations, particularly traffic situations.

Traffic laws are separated into felonies, misdemeanors, and—in some
states—infractions. The infractions are usually limited to minor, non-
hazardous vehicle and equipment violations that call for correction
rather than punitive action. They are handled as criminal offenses only
when the recipient of the citation fails to take corrective action as
specified in the statement of the nature of the infraction.

Nearly everything an officer does while assigned to the patrol division is ultimately recorded in one or more of a wide variety of reports or written documents. Reporting is usually one of the least publicized tasks of the police officer, but it is actually one of the most important and time-consuming tasks that he is required to perform. The report is used as the basis for determining whether to charge an individual with a crime and, if so, what specific charge will be made. In many cases the officer's report is the only criterion that his superiors have to evaluate his performance and decision-making ability. His report must be complete and accurate, since it is usually the only written record of what transpired.

Testifying in Court

Testifying in court is the patrol officer's final step in the investigation process. He responds to the call, conducts the investigation, arrests the offender, processes the evidence, completes his reports, then presents his evidence and testimony in court. He presents it factually and objectively, then leaves the determination of the defendant's guilt to the courts.

DISTRIBUTION OF THE PATROL FORCE

No one knows exactly how many crimes actually occur, but there is no doubt that considerably more crimes occur than are reported. Nationally, the crime clearance rate for many years has been at about 25 percent, or approximately one-quarter, of the *reported* crimes. Obviously, there is need for considerable improvement. The police department is charged with prevention, repression, and solution of the crimes within the framework of the limitations of funds, manpower, and equipment. Selectivity of assignment seems to be the only realistic approach to the problem short of placing two policemen in every block, and several times that many in high crime areas. Since there is little likelihood that the patrol force will be increased so extensively, other methods must be attempted in an effort to improve the efficiency of the patrol force.

Policy Decisions Concerning Distribution

Prior to consideration of the patrol force distribution on the basis of the more tangible and measurable factors, there must be a series of administrative decisions on many questions, including the following:

1. Which calls for service will be handled completely by telephone, and which ones will require that an officer be sent to the caller's address?
2. Which calls will be "counselled out" by advising the calling party that the matter is not a police department matter and should be handled by another agency?
3. To what extent will the patrol officers become involved in neighborhood quarrels, family disputes, advising children regarding their school attendance and other behavior patterns, giving advice on interpersonal relationships, and peace-keeping functions?
4. What portion of the crime investigations will be handled by patrol officers, and at what point will cases be turned over to the specialists?
5. What is the patrol officers' role in traffic accident investigation and traffic law enforcement? Will the officers be solely responsible, or will there be supplementary assistance and coordination by traffic specialists?
6. To what extent will the officers be responsible for building security in their districts that will necessitate their being away from their patrol units for extended periods of time?
7. How much of the public relations function of the department will directly involve the patrol officer? Will he be required to visit school classes during the day? How much time will be required of him to visit buildings and "burglar-proof" inspect?
8. What will be the reporting responsibilities of the field officers? How detailed must their reports be? Where will they go to make the reports—to headquarters, to a telephone, or to a portable dictating unit in their vehicles? What type of forms will be used—all prose or the checklist type? Who types or writes the reports? How often must the officers visit headquarters to turn in their reports?
9. How will priorities be established to give certain calls precedence over others in case there are more calls for service than there are units to handle them at any given time?
10. How are the supervisors and administrators used for management of the field officers? Are they going to provide field supervision and leadership?
11. What types of forms and other documents must be maintained as supervisory control devices over the patrol officers: daily log, tally sheets, and others?

Factors That Determine Patrol Deployment

How to make maximum use of manpower and material is the tremendous responsibility of the police chief, particularly when deploying his patrol force. There are never enough people authorized to man the police department for the desirable degree of effectiveness.

When arranging working hours and days, vacations, holidays, and days off, the object is to realistically meet the community's demands on the department for police service when it is needed. The chief must study all of the following factors—plus many others that present themselves to him—as they relate to the community, the department, and the personnel available, place them into perspective, establish a system of priorities, and then proceed with the planning. It is imperative that the patrol officer be aware of these factors and their direct relationship to deployment considerations.

1. Resident and transient populations, particularly in business and tourist centers.
2. Amount and types of crimes and arrests.
3. Locations of crimes and arrests.
4. Traffic accident statistics and patterns.
5. Locations of crime hazards, or "frequent incident" locations calling for extra police coverage.
6. Proportionate locations, or displacement of the population. Sparsely populated residential areas versus apartment-business areas, versus industrial centers.
7. Socioeconomic factors. Higher income families may have recreation diversions out of the city, while the less affluent may be captives of the neighborhood.
8. Zoning plan of the city. Relative locations of business, industrial, residential, and other types of zones.
9. Size of the city in square miles.
10. Geography and topography. Are there strips and islands of the city that must be patrolled? Mountains, bays, ravines, rivers, and other natural barriers may separate parts of the city and make them inaccessible although clearly within sight.
11. Parks and recreational facilities. Locations, size, and proximity to residences and access roads.
12. Streets and highways. Total mileage and configurations, traffic flow patterns, state of repair and construction.
13. Locations and number of attractive nuisances, such as rock quarries, abandoned wells, mines, deserted buildings, swimming pools, open holes, woods, sandpits.
14. Age ratios of the population. Juvenile versus adult, and the various age categories: pre-school, adolescent, teenage, young adult, senior citizen.
15. Male-female ratios and married versus single.
16. Homogeneity of the ethnic and cultural backgrounds of the residents.
17. Modes of transportation, and locations of the transportation terminals.
18. Restaurants and theaters. Hours of operation.
19. Residences of persons convicted for various crimes.
20. Maximum number of officers actually available to do the job.
21. Amount of trust and confidence in the department, which may influence the frequency with which the people call for police service and advice.

Taking into consideration all of the preceding factors, the chief must apportion the jurisdiction into patrol districts that can be equitably handled by the assigned officers. With the aid of electronic data processing methods, it is now possible to separate the jurisdiction into very small segments known as "reporting districts," to maintain complete records on each district, to group the reporting districts into contiguous "patrol districts," and then to assign the officers proportionate to the indicated proportionate needs of the districts. Frequent evaluation conferences may cause fluid and frequent changes in the district boundaries to assure maximum utilization of personnel. The days are gone when a city or county can be divided into equal sections, as a waitress cuts a pie, as a basis for work load distribution.

Police patrol is a serious game of chess. The district officers must be armed with current and valid information concerning the crime and other police activity potentialities in their respective districts, then attack each problem through a systematic patrol approach by being at various places in their districts at unpredictable and irregular times. The goal is to minimize the successes of criminals through strategy based upon knowledge and experience.

Rotation of Assignments

In municipal law enforcement, assignment to administrative duties has been traditionally a promotion in exchange for some years of devoted service. Once assigned and given the title "detective," the officer could then plan on spending the remainder of his career in that assignment. The only way out, as long as he "behaved," was to be promoted to a higher rank that necessitated his return to uniform or some other assignment. Many detectives chose not to seek promotion specifically to avoid having to return to uniformed patrol duties.

Lately, however, administrators have begun to realize that many of their better patrol officers are lost forever from the patrol division through this type of promotion policy. In an effort to alleviate the situation, some forward-looking administrators have started to experiment with planned rotational assignments similar to those used in a business management program, in which young business employees are rotated throughout the organization. Certain police officers are rotated throughout the various divisions of the police department, and eventually returned to patrol duty to serve as senior officers, or instructors, to the new men. In departments where this procedure is followed, it is recommended that those senior officers be proportionately assigned to assure the most advantageous use of their talents.

Police patrol should involve as much ingenuity and innovative novelty as possible in order for it to be effective in the aggressive attack on crime. Regardless of how sophisticated it may become, however, its most important function is to serve as the police department's actual field contact with the people—law abiding and criminal alike—on a personal one-to-one basis. The types of patrol refer to the various means of getting from one place to another in the district. None of them are intended to isolate the patrol officer from the people he serves and protects.

Foot Patrol

Foot patrol is probably the original type of police patrol. Although it confines the officer to small areas and limits the scope of his activities, foot patrol is still among the most effective of the various types of patrols. The methods of foot patrol consist of the fixed post, line beat, and random patrol. Foot patrol is restricted to small areas, and is used to deal with special problems of prevention and repression

Figure 1.4   Horses are used by many agencies for various types of patrol. This officer is equipped with two way radio for constant contact with headquarters. Courtesy of the Police Department, Detroit, Michigan.

that cannot be adequately handled by the officers in radio cars.
Fixed foot patrol is usually used for traffic, surveillance, parades, and
special events. Moving foot patrol is used where there is considerable
foot traffic, as in business and shopping centers, bars and taverns, high
crime areas, special hazard areas, and on streets where there are many
multiple family dwellings.

Horse Patrol

Horses may be used for certain patrol problems in cities that contain large park areas or similar places where automobiles either cannot
go, or may be forbidden. Motorized officers cannot be expected to
race across lawns, wooded areas, or pedestrian malls. Horses fulfill
the need for greater mobility in these situations. They also work
quite well for moving crowds of people, hostile and otherwise. Search
and rescue in wild, undeveloped terrain is accomplished with considerable success by a well-trained team of officers on horseback.

Motorcycles

Primarily used for traffic control and enforcement, the two-wheeled
motorcycle has been implemented at times by some agencies as a
fair-weather patrol unit. Speed and maneuverability are outstanding
characteristics of the motorcycle that make it a valuable police vehicle.

Bicycles and Small Vehicles

The bicycle has been used in many countries as a simple and inexpensive means of silent transportation to carry the police officer
throughout his district. Other, newly developed small motorized
vehicles have been employed by various police agencies for whatever needs they meet. Small vehicles may be used for routine patrol
to replace or augment foot or automobile patrol under conditions
when such a vehicle is more practicable than more conventional modes
of travel. Officers may wear casual street clothing and patrol hazardous
areas using these vehicles in order to provide patrol coverage without
being identified as police officers until the crucial moment arises
when an arrest is imminent.

Bicycles and other small vehicles provide the foot patrol officer a
means of carrying radio equipment, foul weather gear, and miscellaneous items that he would otherwise carry in an automobile. The
versatility of the small vehicle makes it an indispensable patrol unit
for covering such places as shopping malls, pathways and trails, and
other places where automobiles cannot travel.

Figure 1.5 Helicopters provide an excellent moving "platform in the sky." Courtesy of the Police Department of Huntington Beach, California.

Helicopters and Airplanes

Except for patrolling long stretches of highway or expanses of inaccessible land, the fixed wing airplane has little flexibility in the congested metropolitan community. Where distances are great and sufficient landing strips are available, the rural police department may find numerous occasions when the airplane will prove itself useful.

In highly congested metropolitan areas, the patrol helicopter has emerged as a true champion. The helicopter has the speed capabilities of the airplane and the advantage of being able to move about easily, free of traffic congestion problems. It requires no long runway for takeoffs and landings. It can operate under marginal visibility conditions at lower altitudes than the fixed wing craft, and its hovering capabilities literally convert it into an observation platform at any desired distance from the ground. The helicopter has been employed by progressive police agencies only during the past few years, but its use in police patrol work is expanding rapidly—thanks to the pioneer attitudes of some police administrators. Utilization of the helicopter seems to be restricted more by financial limitations than by the imagination of the agencies presently using the craft.

Automobile Patrol

The automobile is the most effective means of transportation for police patrol. On the beach it may be an automobile with four-wheel

Figure 1.6   Since its appearance on the streets, the automobile has been an indispensable item of police equipment. Courtesy of the Missouri Highway Patrol.

drive and unusual looking tires. It may be designed like a dune buggy for desert patrol, or like a safari-type vehicle for mountains and forest areas. In the urban community, the vehicle is the distinctively marked late model automobile. For all practical purposes, the police car is a mobile police station. Equipped with the latest in radio gear and various types of rescue and restraining devices, it provides a rapid, safe, and efficient means of transportation under average operating conditions. All modern law enforcement agencies use the automobile as a patrol vehicle and many of them use no other means of transportation.

POLICE DISCRETIONARY PREROGATIVES

In its 1967 report entitled *The Police*, the President's Commission on Law Enforcement and Administration of Justice reported that there is considerable variance in police practices throughout the United States, particularly in tactical field problems and arrest situations.[1] The consensus of many law enforcement observers and critics seems to be that law enforcement agencies provide for their officers

[1] *Task Force Report: The Police* (A Report to the President's Commission on Law Enforcement and Administration of Justice) (Washington, D.C.: Government Printing Office, 1967).

little or no control in the form of operational guidelines in the decision-making processes when so much of the responsibility for making the decisions is delegated to the discretion of the individual officers.

Within the organized structure of law enforcement agencies which are part of the criminal justice system in the United States, there are hundreds of thousands of police officers who function as virtually independent agents when it comes to both routine and extraordinary "in-field" situations that affect the lives of the millions of people they contact during the course of their police duties. It is an operational fact that the personal value systems of the individual police officers determine the actual parameters of law enforcement practices of the police as a professional group.

The broad discretionary powers held by the individual police officer include actions such as dealing with traffic law violators, handling disturbances of the peace involving single individuals or hundreds of people, enforcement of the criminal laws, apprehension and detention of juvenile delinquents and near-delinquents, regulation of public and private morals through enforcement of vice laws, and performance of a myriad of other duties in the course of a normal duty day. He functions with virtually no direction or guidance in many agencies other than that supplied by the laws, and by manuals of regulations and policy. In some agencies there is limited control by higher ranking or senior officers who function as the independent agents and exercise their own discretionary powers. Ultimately, however, there is no way an officer may avoid the responsibility of exercising his own discretionary powers in such matters as determining when to arrest, when to pursue, or when to fire a weapon.

Operational Guidelines for Discretionary Decision Making

The system of criminal justice abundantly provides for broad use of discretion by its law enforcement officers and all others similarly involved in the system. Setting the standard when the new California Penal Code was introduced February 14, 1872, the legislature provided for such discretion by the wording of Section 4:

> The rule of the common law, that penal statutes are to be strictly construed, has no application to this code. All its provisions are to be construed according to the fair import of their terms, with a view to effect its objects and to promote justice.

A leading case that further elucidates the intent of law and those who enforce it has been described in the California Supreme Court's ruling in People v. Alotis, 60 Cal. 2d, 698 (1964):

> When language reasonably susceptible to two constructions is used in a penal law, that construction which is more favorable to the defendant will be adopted. The defendant is entitled to the

benefit of every reasonable doubt as to the true interpretation of words or the construction of language used in a statute.

The police officer has the responsibility and authority within our existing criminal justice system to act or react in a variety of ways when he encounters what in his opinion constitutes a violation of the law or some other incident calling for his official response. He may contact the suspected violator and admonish him with no arrest, or he may arrest and release the violator with no further action because of what he believes to be lack of sufficient evidence or cause for further action. He may issue a citation and release the violator from custody when the latter signs a promise to appear in court at some later pre-designated time and place, or he may take the accused into custody and lodge him in jail for introduction into the criminal justice system. Once introduced, the case is adjudicated according to the system's established procedure with other individuals exercising the discretion. A large percentage of the cases the officer handles will be disposed of informally, and the people involved will never be introduced to the rest of the system. This is the area in which the officer must be most judicious in his use of discretionary power.

Specific sections of the criminal codes involving police discretion include such wording as: . . . searching for weapons on *reasonable cause*, . . . *reasonable* restraint when making an arrest, . . . *reasonable* force to effect an arrest, prevent escape, or overcome resistance. The basic arrest laws state that the officer *may* arrest when he has *reasonable cause* to believe that the person is committing a crime in his presence or that there is *reasonable cause* to believe the subject to be arrested committed certain crimes, although not in the officer's presence, *whether or not such a crime has in fact been committed.*

Wording of other criminal code sections indicate that the use of discretion is in order. Examples of those words are *specific intent, reasonable* or *probable cause* (again), *malicious, unsafe, too close, unfit, unnecessary,* and *reliable.* Every one of these words involve value judgments by individual officers.

Throughout the following chapters, guidelines will be suggested for your consideration as a professional police officer. In many cases, the ultimate decision as to exactly what you shall do rests with you.

EXERCISES AND STUDY QUESTIONS

1. What do we mean when we speak of the "preventive maintenance" aspect of police patrol?
2. Describe how Officer Carver performed what we call the function of crime prevention when he arrested the boy who committed the theft.
3. What is *crime repression* and how is it accomplished by the police patrol officer?

4. How would you explain Officer Loya's justification for chasing and apprehending the two men he saw loitering around the surf shop after dark?

5. Recount a case you worked or one you know of that involved circumstances similar to Officer Loya's experience.

6. What is the patrol officer's *primary* responsibility at the scene of a large crowd of people milling around outside a revival meeting that is about to commence?

7. What do we mean when we say that the officer is responsible for the function known as *judicial assistance?*

8. According to the text, to what do some burglars attribute their so-called "success" in escaping apprehension while committing their crimes of burglary?

9. How would you schedule your eight hours of patrol in your city if you were working a shift from 7:00 P.M. to 3:00 A.M.?

10. How would you define *routine patrol?*

11. What is the purpose of a "running report" that an officer makes on his patrol checks at a shopping center?

12. List and discuss five of the services your department provides that are not actually police tasks. Why are they performed by the police? Who would perform them if the police did not? What is the reason for their continuation?

13. Outline a basic format for the process of developing informants.

14. At what point does a preliminary investigation end?

15. What is so important about the investigation report?

16. Which do you believe is more effective, one-man patrol or two-man patrol? Why?

17. What is the value of foot patrol?

18. List ten factors that should be taken into consideration when the patrol force is distributed.

SUGGESTED SEMESTER OR TERM PROJECTS

1. Write a brief history of your city and make a current file on the vital statistics of your city as if you were going to be the official city host, which the policeman is. Secure the names of all the public officials that the guest will ask about, some information about them, and some facts about your city. List the city flower, average rainfall, mean temperature, altitude, and every available bit of information.

2. Seek permission from the police chief or the sheriff to ride with a field policeman for one full shift. Observe, record, and react. Make a complete running account of your night on patrol.

REFERENCES

ADAMS, THOMAS F., *Law Enforcement—An Introduction to the Police Role in the Community.* Englewood Cliffs, N.J.: Prentice-Hall, Inc., 1968, pp. 135–153.

CHAPMAN, SAMUEL G., *Police Patrol Readings*. Springfield, Ill.: Charles C Thomas, Publisher, 1964.

International City Managers' Association, *Municipal Police Administration*, 5th ed. Chicago: International City Managers' Association, 1961.

Task Force Report: The Police (A Report to the President's Commission on Law Enforcement and Administration of Justice). Washington, D.C.: Government Printing Office, 1967.

WILSON, O. W., *Police Administration*, 2nd ed. New York: McGraw-Hill Book Company, 1963, Chaps. 12 and 13.

Routine

Patrol

Procedures

CHAPTER TWO "Patrol and observation" describes the basic function of the patrol officer who is assigned to patrol a designated district in a distinctively marked patrol car, or any other type of vehicle. He usually wears a uniform that is readily identifiable as that of a police officer. He may be clothed in a slacks and blazer type of uniform with the police emblem embroidered on the breast pocket. Sometimes the patrol officer is assigned to cover his district dressed in ordinary street clothing to avoid immediate recognition. The purpose of the distinctive clothing and vehicle markings is to assure the officer's immediate identification as a peace officer, and to prevent anyone from mistaking him for an employee of some other uniformed service.

Assuming that the great majority of the population is honest and law-abiding, the mere presence of the officer as he makes an appearance at various places throughout his district will remind those who observe him that he is present and that he is present for their pro-

30

Figure 2.1 Formal inspections are morale builders. The uniform is to be worn with care as well as pride. Courtesy of the Police Department of Costa Mesa, California.

tection. The would-be criminal law violator theoretically will not proceed with his criminal intentions, at least not while in the officer's presence. The active criminal is more likely to abandon his plans to commit his crime at a particular location if the officer's frequent visits to the area heighten the criminal's chances of being caught.

The patrol officer makes frequent personal contacts with as many people in his district as he can during the normal course of his duties. He investigates people, crimes, and situations. He performs considerable "police work," which consists of whatever it is that he does in accordance with his own department's regulations and policies. The first chapter defined *what* the patrol officer does. This and subsequent chapters will be more explicit in describing *how* he accomplishes his job of "police work."

PREPARATION FOR PATROL

General Preparation

There are many intangible factors related to an officer's preparation for patrol duty. Some of these factors are attitude preparation, psychological and social maturity, education, physical conditioning, and the officer's personal value system. The officer must bring to work with him an attitude of confidence in the honesty and decency of most of the people who live and visit in his community. Because of the nature of his work and his duty assignment, the patrol officer may not encounter many of the honest and decent majority during some of his tours of duty. Consequently, he must guard against the dangerous impression of universality, the feeling that the majority of the population is criminalistic based upon his personal experiences, most of which are with criminals. The patrol officer is in danger of projecting such an attitude toward the nature of the entire population into his day-long contacts with a succession of petty thieves, burglars, armed robbers, prostitutes, pornography peddlers, and many others of like character that he may encounter. To counteract this feeling, the officer must get involved during his off-duty time with other people like himself who are not violating the law. With this anchor in the normal pattern of society, he is able to maintain a more accurate perspective on life and his fellow human beings.

A broad base of experiences in education, occupations, and social interaction will prepare the officer for his role better than the narrow experiences of a single occupation and continuous living within the same small neighborhood. The police officer must mingle and communicate with people who fill the entire spectrum of social standards, educational and occupational backgrounds, political philosophies, and moral and religious codes. He must be objective, empathetic, and friendly, yet aloof enough that he does not attempt to force any of his personal beliefs on those people, whatever their views. His role is that of diplomat and protector of all the people he serves; a public servant who does not perform with obsequious servitude, but enforces firm adherence to the laws and behavior patterns of the total society he serves. He is a servant to the public, not to single individuals or to his personal needs and wishes. He deals with people on a personal basis, but each situation must be handled for the overall good of the community. To function intelligently and effectively, the officer must continuously prepare for his changing role in our dynamic society by keeping himself informed on exactly how he fits into society as a law enforcement officer.

Pre-Patrol Preparation

Prior to going out on patrol, the officer must arm himself with considerable knowledge and equipment. Only a few of the essentials are covered in this section because they vary among police departments and according to the changing needs from day to day. A medium that is most effective for fulfilling the needs for new information is the 15- to 30-minute session preceding each workday, known as roll call training. Although this "training" session often has no resemblance to what some people regard as training—lecture, notes, test— the training takes on many forms depending on the changing needs of the department. Roll call instruction includes discussions of new and proposed laws, rescinded laws, general and special orders, changes in policy and procedure, and improved techniques in performing the various police tasks.

District and vehicle assignments, lunch and rest breaks, and scheduled duty assignments should be disposed of at this time to avoid later unnecessary use of the radio or telephone. Some departments print and disseminate to their officers daily resumés of wanted people, automobiles, and stolen property. Other agencies prepare master lists of such information and require the officers to copy the information into their personal notebooks and to update them every day. Some departments place the responsibility for keeping current on "wants" and similar information on the individual officer's shoulders.

Frequently new laws and ordinances are passed that directly affect the patrol officer, who is expected to enforce those laws. Most often such laws become effective some time after they are passed to allow for publication, publicity, and education of the people who will be affected by the laws and their application. The police officer should also be included in the educating process. He should be fully informed as to the wording of the law and the intention of the law (sometimes the wording is inadvertently misleading) as articulated by the legislators. His education should also include some clues from the courts as to what they will require in the way of proof to find the accused guilty of a charge. Learning the wording of a new section of the criminal codes is simple. Learning the legislative intent of that section sometimes takes considerable instruction.

If you are the field officer, in addition to absorbing updated information provided by supervisors, you should check the previous day's activity in crimes and accidents so that you will be prepared to apply selective enforcement techniques in your district in an attempt to deter and prevent crimes and accidents. Compile a list of the business establishments and private homes that will be vacated for extended periods of time, such as for annual vacations, so that you may check these places more closely while on patrol. Changes in district or city boundaries, new streets, and new housing tracts or business districts should also be committed to some sort of a list for additional patrol coverage.

While preparing for field duty, the patrol officer is often called upon to complete assignments begun by the earlier shift, but not yet completed. Other jobs have been waiting for assignment to the oncoming shift. These assignments may include follow-up contacts with victims or witnesses to crimes that occurred some time previously. A stake-out of a building expected to be burglarized may call for a relief officer. Special patrol checks of various locations may be made at certain times of the day. Warrants have to be served and the arrestees taken to jail, and subpoenas must be placed in the hands of witnesses to criminal trials. Other assignments may include routine calls that the shift going off duty could not handle because of an extra heavy work load. There should be some coordination of these assignments to assure the officers reporting for duty at the beginning

Figure 2.2 Prior to the tour of duty, the officer should compare notes with the men who have been on duty for some time. Courtesy of the Police Department of Bismarck, North Dakota.

of the shift that all of them are bona fide situations which could not have been handled earlier.

In-Field Preparation

Whenever possible, the officer going on duty should have a conference with the officer whom he is replacing in the same district. If he cannot meet the one he is replacing, there should be an effort to arrange a rendezvous with one or more other officers who are going off duty. Conferences between shifts will tend to assure some continuity in coverage of the district and, hopefully, through a series of similar meetings, continuity in coverage of the entire agency jurisdiction. The officers going off duty have been in their districts throughout their tour of duty. They probably know the traffic conditions, the locations where civil disturbances may develop, the general temper of the people in the community, the locations of loud parties that may develop into disturbances later. They may also have information for the incoming officers about the people and places that involved prior police activity. The conference technique employed in this manner is not unlike the "debriefing" technique employed by research and development teams, military air groups, and numerous other organizations who hope to improve further activities with the aid of the information they have learned from previous performance.

The officer who is ending his tour of duty may have completed

most of his reports prior to the conference with his replacement. He
has probably brought his daily log up to date, and turned in all of
the citations, field interview cards, and reports. What he does not turn
in, of course, is that which is most valuable to the officer who is relieving him: firsthand information and actual experiences. He also
has been making observations and gaining impressions. For example,
the officer going home at 11:00 P.M. knows that a narcotics peddler is
attending a party also attended by several juveniles who are not known
as narcotics users; a station wagon strange to the district at a location
adjacent to a dress shop should be checked out later; two known
burglars were observed cruising near a shopping center and should be
located and observed occasionally to determine if they have really
stopped committing crimes as they had told the probation officer last
week. Some of this valuable information may be learned by the incoming officer only through a personal conference with other officers.
Much of it is gossip and not of sufficient import to warrant a report,
but it may be very significant nevertheless.

Vehicle Inspection

Prior to assuming control of the assigned vehicle for your tour of
duty, inspect it for clean windshield and windows, an adequate supply
of gasoline, and oil. Check the tires and brakes. Start the motor and
listen for any perceptible malfunctions. The emergency nature of your
work requires that the vehicle be performing at peak efficiency. Except under conditions when there is no alternative, do not accept a
vehicle for patrol that is not adequate to the demands of both routine
patrol and pursuit driving. The vehicle is yours for your tour of duty,
and you will be held responsible for its good condition. If you find
any malfunction or deficiency in the vehicle, be sure to follow the
appropriate procedure for filling out "faulty equipment" forms and log
entries to assure its correction.

District Orientation Tour

Once in the field, take a general familiarization and inspection tour
of your assigned district to orient yourself to the sights and sounds
and the "normal" patterns that present themselves to you. Use a different route each time you cross the district and vary your technique
so that no one can predict with any accuracy the sequence of your
tour or see any resemblance to a timetable. Check for streets closed
or under repair and note holes and ruts that may cause traffic accidents
or congestion. During a high-speed pursuit later, it will be good to
know the condition of the streets you will be traveling.
In the initial, cursory tour you may observe many circumstances or
people that arouse your curiosity but not your suspicion that there is

any criminal involvement. Perhaps there is an automobile parked in an unusual location, or a small group of people gathered where such a group has never gathered before. If you believe that you may have stronger suspicions if the situation is unchanged upon your return visit, make notes and plan to return later. Write down license numbers, descriptions of objects, vehicles, and people. These notations may later prove worthless; they may prove priceless.

If you use a daily log, and if your department's policy—and form—provides for such a procedure, notations regarding your initial observations during a district orientation tour may be written directly on your log. In any event, make liberal use of the field notebook for information that you believe may be of some value later. During this initial tour, there will undoubtedly also be some items requiring more formal attention and reports. In such cases, take care of whatever demands your immediate attention, then continue the tour.

There are several good reasons for taking an orientation tour of your district. One is that it may allow you to establish time elements. For example, you may note that a particular location appears normal at 10:13 P.M., but when you return at 11:37 P.M., you find a window smashed out. The initial tour of the district allows you to narrow down the times within which the window was broken considerably more than some time between 5:30 P.M. and 11:37 P.M. Another reason for the orientation tour is to acquaint yourself with the entire district in its current condition to gain an impression of what is "normal" and what appears "abnormal." A third reason for this patrol technique is to put the deterrent forces of your presence in the district to work. Any individual bent on committing a crime should know that you are in the district and that you are likely to show up at virtually any unannounced time or place. The optimum result would be that the would-be criminal does not perform his crime.

PATROLLING THE DISTRICT

There are two basic methods of police patrol: on foot and by vehicle. Both are usually performed in uniform, but either may call for street clothing under unusual circumstances. Use may be made of horses, motorcycles, bicycles, scooters, or aircraft, depending on the individual and special needs of the agency involved. The techniques of patrol are essentially the same regardless of the mode of transportation employed.

The following section deals with police patrol from three primary angles: foot patrol, vehicle patrol and plainclothes patrol. In the discussion of foot patrol, it should be understood that any means of transport may be used to get the officer to the district he will cover on foot. It should also be clear that the discussion of techniques of patrolling a district by automobile may apply equally well to other types of vehicles.

Foot Patrol Tactics

The cop on the beat in the "good old days," whenever that imaginary time existed, seems to be remembered as the sustaining symbol of law enforcement. Depicted in fiction stories and the motion pictures, he was the friendly but firm fatherly type of older man who walked the streets in his small beat, nearly always on duty and always in uniform. He maintained order and control in his district by chiding, scolding, cajoling, and sometimes arresting the violators. He visited the shopkeepers and residents, exchanged anecdotes with the street vendors, and performed numerous benevolent services. Some communities have utilized foot patrol continuously since the beginning of police patrol, but most have discontinued it because of its prohibitive cost and extremely limited use of manpower. During recent years, there has been a trend back to the foot patrolman in an effort to maintain a closer rapport between the people of the community and their police department.

In addition to performing his duties as a professional police officer while on foot patrol, the officer performs community relations tasks for the department. Through his personality and actions, he demonstrates to the young people and others in his district that he is an example of all policemen. By his friendly and understanding attitude, the officer attempts to develop in those he meets a feeling of respect and confidence in their police department and its officers.

Selection of the officer to fill the role in the "foot beat" assignment is a very careful process. The individual should match the image the department wishes to present to the people the officer meets. Although reflecting the desired image is important for all officers, it is especially critical in the case of the foot patrolman. The man assigned has to be adaptable to the neighborhood he serves and he must possess outstanding police officer qualities.

The foot patrol officer should get to know as many people in his district as he can. He should make a deliberate effort to meet and talk with people at every opportunity, and keep a log of the contacts as a normal part of his duties. At the same time he must also perform all of the other functions required of the patrol operation, although on a somewhat limited basis because of his small district and limited mobility. He performs his work for the most part out of touch with his headquarters, although he will carry radio equipment that makes it possible for him to maintain two-way communications with headquarters and other officers. He usually handles citizen complaints and "on-sight" incidents that come to his attention while he is patrolling the district.

Every district has a distinctive personality and it is important that the assigned officer get to know that personality. Wanted persons may live in the area. Known felons and narcotics users may habitually loiter around the local family billiards parlor, which is also frequented by many juveniles and young adults who are not criminals or narcotics users. Certain business establishments fall prey to specific crimes, such as armed robberies and burglaries. These locations should be given close attention in an effort to prevent criminal occurrences or reoccurrences. When you are assigned to the foot beat, get to know it and the people in it, then give it personalized service.

When walking through the district, most experts on the subject recommend that you walk close to the curb during the day and close to the buildings at night. They reason that the objects of daytime foot patrol are to contact and to be seen by as many people as possible, and the objects of nighttime foot patrol are to be seen by as few people as possible and to catch criminals in the act before they are aware of your presence. However, I suggest that for nighttime patrol you consider the time of night and the lighting conditions, evaluate your objectives while covering the particular part of the district in which you find yourself, then work accordingly. There should be no standard place to walk depending on the relationship of the sun to the earth any more than there should be a standard schedule to follow.

Keeping in mind the fact that police patrol means service as well as protection, never hesitate to take the initiative when practicable to offer your services in whatever way is not inconsistent with the purposes of law enforcement. For example, probably no duty manual will be found that requires an officer to give a distressed motorist a little advice on how to start a flooded car, or to call for a tow service for some mother who cannot leave her stalled car containing four preschool children. An elderly lady may have difficulty getting across a busy street because she walks so slowly and no one will allow her to take advantage of a break in a seemingly endless flow of traffic. Stopping traffic to assist the lady across the street would be a typical foot patrol service. These activities are hallmarks of the distinguished police officer who sees his occupation as something more than "just a job."

One of the problems that confronts the foot beat officer, and sometimes comes to the attention of the radio car officer, is the sidewalk showroom. Not having enough room or attention for their products, some merchants move out onto the sidewalk to display their wares. This use of the public walk is unlawful in most cities, and it causes congestion of foot traffic. Maintaining a free flow of pedestrian traffic is just as important as keeping vehicular traffic moving.

When walking the beat, do not develop a routine, yet be sure to give the area adequate coverage. Walk with a purpose and look at the people. Speak with them when it is natural to do so, and encourage them to feel as though they can talk with you. Do not hesitate to

smile when the occasion warrants it. Maintain a professional posture
by being friendly and firm, not aloof and unapproachable. Never
"mooch" by soliciting or accepting special discounts, free merchandise,
or free refreshments. One practice that is absolutely intolerable is paying bills or otherwise tending to personal business while on duty. The
entire on-duty time belongs to the department and the people. It
should be spent accordingly.

Walk from one place to another so that it appears to the observer
that you are *patrolling* the district, not loitering. Stop frequently to
observe the people and the things around you. Change your routine,
sometimes retracing your steps, and do not neglect the alleys or areas
behind buildings when patrolling your district. Determine through observation what is normal for the district, then look for the unusual and
deal with it accordingly.

At nighttime when you are patrolling for possible burglars, approach each building with caution, assuming the possibility that someone may be inside the building, or hiding in the doorway. Stop
momentarily, stand in a darkened area to avoid being seen, and listen
for unusual sounds. At nighttime when there is almost absolute silence,
it is possible to hear the sounds of breaking glass, or walking, or a dog
barking from hundreds of yards away. Sounds seem to be magnified
by silence.

When you are satisfied that there are no unusual sounds, continue
with the routine. Check the doors and windows, feel the glass for
heat that may indicate a fire inside, then move on to the next building.
Watch the rooftops and any means of access to the roofs of the various
buildings. Roofs are a popular means of entry among some professional
burglars. By entering through the roof the burglar delays the discovery
of his crime, and sometimes he is able to work inside without detection even with an officer standing outside.

Vehicle Patrol Tactics

The vehicles used for patrol should not be used as shells, but merely
as means of transportation and protection. When you are on vehicle
patrol, one of the first rules to adhere to is to get out of the car
frequently. Never use it as a means of isolating yourself from your
patrol duties. In fact, you will probably have few opportunities to
remain in the vehicle very long because, due to their high mobility
and access to rapid communications, officers assigned to automobiles
handle virtually all calls for service as well as the bulk of assigned
activities.

For automobile patrol, one-man patrols or two-man teams are used
for various times of the day and types of districts, depending on department experiences. When one-man patrol is utilized, there is a need
for closer coordination of the field officers' activities with communica-

tions personnel, and the field units must frequently follow up to other field units. The one-man patrol concept is not intended to place lone officers at locations where two or more officers are needed. The patrol officers should work in teams for purposes of field contacts, citations, checking open doors, and responding to most calls. Only the patrolling should be done solo.

Operate the vehicle at normal speeds, consistent with traffic conditions. If the traffic is moving faster than you believe necessary for adequate surveillance of the people and places along the way, stop, turn around, or go around the block and retrace your route. If the traffic is too fast for effective patrol, stop frequently and wait, then move on. Patrol in heavily traveled streets is virtually impossible at times. Move around the district on all of the streets rather than just a select few. A patrol officer is of no value when driving at high speeds.

Open the windows of the police car whenever consistent with weather conditions, and turn the radio down low so that the sounds outside are not obliterated by a loud police radio. Patrol the district so that the vehicle will be seen by the greatest number of people, frequently turning corners and covering the side streets as well as the main thoroughfares.

Several types of patrol patterns have been variously described, such as the "zig-zag," "quadrant search," and the "clover-leaf." The design is meaningless as a technique in itself, and merely describes the driving pattern that resembles what the title suggests. Whatever pattern you decide to use should be irregular and unpredictable. Move around the district. Start at one side and work to the other, or work out from the center, or go across the district, turn around, and immediately retrace your route. The entire district should receive attention with emphasis on those places that require special attention because of the frequency of crimes and arrests. Never develop a time schedule for patrolling your assigned district, and always consider the possibility that a burglar or thief will commit crimes in the most illogical places and at the most unusual times of day.

Patrol Driving

Most patrol driving consists of stop-and-start, slow-speed driving with frequent backing. The majority of accidents involving police units occur during this type of driving, and a large percentage of them involve the backing process. Fatigue and inattention to driving are other patrol accident factors.

Keep awake. Driving at nighttime and during the early morning hours often becomes a monotonous routine, particularly when you have not had adequate rest and the patrol routine at that time of the day presents no novelty to you. Open the car window for fresh air, talk out loud occasionally, and move your eyes around frequently while driving along a straight stretch of road. Stop the car occasionally, get out and flex the muscles. Never use any kind of pills or medication to stay awake on the job. It is better to use adequate rest than to use a chemical "crutch" to stay awake.

Set the example by obeying all traffic laws, including boulevard stops, speed laws, and the general rules of the road. The vehicle operated in this manner serves as much of a purpose as the officer driving it by encouraging compliance with the laws by example.

Special skills are required for driving in rain, snow, and slush. In an article entitled "New Facts About Skidding—They May Save Your Life," E. D. Fales, Jr. outlines some excellent suggestions for driving at times when skidding is possible.[1] Fales points out that studies by various agencies have revealed that the front tires of an automobile moving at higher speeds actually leave the surface, or hydroplane, when moving across rain, snow, or slush. At speeds above 30 miles per hour the tires begin to lose contact with the road. At a speed of approximately 55 miles per hour on top of a water covered street surface there is only slight tire contact with the surface, and at higher speeds there is none whatsoever.

Mr. Fales suggests that adding air pressure to the tires and driving more slowly may improve maneuverability. The depth of the tread and the depth of the water on the road surface have a direct bearing on the hydroplaning phenomenon. One other way to reduce the occurrence of hydroplaning in inclement weather is to drive in the tracks made by preceding vehicles, which may be relatively dry because of continuous friction and water displacement.

Skidding occurs under various conditions, and it has been discovered that the skid itself perpetuates the problem. As the vehicle goes into the skid, the tire temperature rises, the rubber melts, and the tire lays down its own thin layer of melted rubber, which makes a slideway. When the vehicle begins to go into a skid, use all of the driver training techniques including braking the vehicle with short and rapid-sequence braking motions instead of the usual steady pushing motion. The brakes are less likely to lock the wheels in a skid when they are applied in this manner.

Parking police vehicles frequently presents problems. Upon arrival in response to an emergency call for service, there may be no readily available space and little time to look for a place to park. The circumstances must dictate the action. There can be no strictly enforced regulations concerning the parking of police vehicles, except that they should always be parked legally unless an emergency condition exists.

---

[1] E. D. Fales, Jr., "New Facts About Skidding—They May Save Your Life," pp. 13–16, FBI Law Enforcement Bulletin, May 1965 (Washington, D.C.). Reprinted from *Popular Science Monthly*. Copyright © 1964 by Popular Science Publishing Co., Inc.

Figure 2.3 Some agencies, including the Pennsylvania
State Police, have comprehensive vehicle operation training for their new officers. Skill development should not be
left to chance. Courtesy of the Pennsylvania State Police.

The vehicle should be parked in a legal manner and the key to the
ignition should be removed. Sometimes it is wise to completely lock
the vehicle to protect it against vandalism. Instead of taking the
ignition key away from the unit, officers working as a radio car team
will take the key out of the ignition and place it in a hiding place that
is convenient and known to both of them. Either officer thus has immediate access to the unit regardless of his partner's location.

Plainclothes Patrol

Unusual conditions may necessitate patrol officers' special assignment to perform their patrol operations in regular street clothing and
to operate department vehicles, or privately owned vehicles, that are
not identifiable as police cars. This type of assignment is particularly
effective for "saturation coverage" of high crime areas. It provides
extra coverage without alarming the occupants or signaling the cul-
prits with an unusual number of patrol units. The burglars or robbers
may possess a false feeling of security because they lack knowledge
of the plainclothes patrol. The result may be successful apprehension
of some "long-time wanted" felons and the clearance of many cases.

For plainclothes patrol, dress to fit the occasion and wear whatever
clothing is the mode of the day and will fit the type of activity you
will ostensibly engage in as a "cover" for your presence in the neighborhood. Use a vehicle that similarly matches the occasion. Sometimes

Figure 2.4   The three people in the foreground are on "plainclothes patrol" covering the uniformed officers on the beach. They also work under cover assignments. Courtesy of the Police Department, Huntington Beach, California.

it may be wiser to use a rented car or borrowed used car than to use a so-called "undercover" unit belonging to the department.

Situations calling for plainclothes patrol vary with current problems. Within the department, it may be used to supplement any existing or "standing" assignment, such as vice or detective assignments, when a particular situation requires more attention than the responsible division can devote to the problem. At the beach or the amusement park in a resort community, plainclothes patrol may be the most effective way to deal with seasonal problems. In the city, there may be several locations where large numbers of juveniles "just fool around" or seek meaningful recreation, and plainclothes patrol may be used to give those locations extra police coverage without fanfare and without giving the juveniles the impression that they are being "overpoliced."

Rallies, sporting events, or other occasions when large numbers of people gather for a variety of reasons may best be patrolled by the police department with an officer or two in uniform and others not in uniform. The latter mingle with the crowd and make themselves available in case of a need for their assistance. A team of plainclothes patrol officers can move about from place to place throughout the city inconspicuously and quite effectively. These same officers may be assigned to check on transient vice conditions, or virtually any other type of problem not requiring uniformed officers. Plainclothes patrol should be a normal part of the patrol division's repertoire of techniques, and it in no way infringes on the privileges or obligations of the other operating units in the department.

One of the many problems you will encounter in working a plainclothes assignment is that of positively identifying yourself as a police officer once the need for such identification becomes necessary. The less you look like an on-duty policeman, the more effective you are on the detail you are working. Suddenly the need arises for you to identify yourself and state "I am a police officer." The revolver displayed by itself means only that the bearer is armed, and may appear to some people as an immediate threat to be overcome. The identification card by itself may look like a driver's license, or a badge carried loose in the pocket may get worn and look like a toy badge when presented for identification. Whatever the arrangement made by your agency for your identification when the need arises, you must make it in a positive manner and the credentials and/or badge should have an official appearing configuration. The individual you are confronting in an arrest situation, or some other form of official business demanding proof of your authority, must know that you *really* are the police officer you say you are.

Whenever you are working a uniformed assignment and you meet another officer who is not wearing a uniform, wait for him to initiate the salutations. Your "Good morning, John, how's the new detail?" may ruin a case that John is currently working which requires that he not be identified as a policeman. In one case some time ago, an officer was working in our department's intelligence unit. He had spent some time on the assignment, and had finally managed to work himself into a position of trust with some rather high-placed members of an organized crime operation, which is not an easy task. While in his undercover role, the officer was walking down the street with a member of the syndicate hierarchy en route to meet a contact, who would open up a new avenue for the investigation. As they approached the building and were about to enter, a uniformed officer was standing nearby and recognized our undercover agent. Not thinking, the officer walked up to him with a warm "Hey_____, How're you doin', ole buddy? Haven't seen you since the academy. Heard you were working intelligence. How do you like that 'cloak and dagger' detail?" Needless to say, the old academy friend did not receive a warm response, and the investigation was completely nullified. It ended at that moment.

DISTRICT RESPONSIBILITY

Your assigned district is the area of the city entrusted to you for a specified period of time to answer calls and to patrol at all times

except while otherwise engaged. During your tour of duty, you may
leave the district to eat lunch, to go to headquarters for reporting or
prisoner transportation, to handle an assigned call outside the district,
or to pursue a known or suspected violator. The reason for assigning
specific units to designated districts is to assure at least minimum
patrol coverage of each district. When you are assigned to a district,
give it your full attention and provide its people with the best possible
police service.

INSPECTIONS ON PATROL

During a tour of duty, the patrol officer performs a succession of
inspections for a variety of purposes, and to assist various other
agencies and individuals as well as the police department. Fundamen-
tally, the inspections of buildings and other places are for the benefit
of the owners and operators themselves, for building security and
early discovery of fires and other hazards. Additionally, the inspections
serve as a crime prevention tool, and there is always an extra deter-
rence factor during the actual presence of the officer. Other inspections
may be for the benefit of building and safety departments, the health
officer, license department, and the public utilities.

Building Inspections

While you are on patrol, get out of the patrol unit frequently and
physically check the buildings. From the front seat of a patrol car
with the aid of a powerful spotlight, it is possible to check windows
and the ground below for broken glass. By getting the right angle of
the light on a space between double doors it is possible to see the
locking bolt where it locks the doors together. One technique used
by officers for building security is to get out of the car and try the
doors and windows of the building, then place a small piece of paper
in the crack above the door. The officer returns periodically during
his tour of duty and shines his light on the slip of paper, assuming
that the building is secure. Some enterprising burglars have been
known to pry open the door bearing the small piece of paper, then
tape the paper to the top of the door, enter, commit their crime, and
leave. The paper never leaves the doorway, but the building security
has been violated. If you use such a device, never take for granted
the security of a building on the basis of such a technique.

Plan to check out the entire group of buildings when you approach
a shopping center or complex of buildings. Although you may use a
spot-check technique, you should be reasonably sure of the security
of the entire area. In most districts it is virtually impossible to provide
all of the police protection that you should because of the heavy de-

mands on your time and attention. To compensate for this lack of complete coverage, work out some sort of unpredictable spot-check procedure, giving the greatest attention to those places most likely to be subject to burglary or similar crimes.

Communications are a problem when you are making building inspections. Unless your department has the good fortune to have a sufficient quantity of radio transceivers to allow you to take a portable unit with you when you leave your unit, it will be necessary for you to notify the dispatcher that you will be away from the radio and for what approximate length of time. If you are not heard from within a reasonable time period, the dispatcher should send a follow-up unit to check on your safety. When you return to the unit, be sure to notify the dispatcher to avoid the unnecessary follow-up assignment.

Park your unit some distance from the building to be inspected and approach the rest of the way on foot. If someone is inside, there is less likelihood that he will hear your approach by foot than by car. Move silently, minus the rattling of keys or tap-tapping of leather heels. Walk quietly, placing the entire foot on the surface to assure less noise. Take advantage of the natural cover of darkness and the shadows. Do not use the flashlight except when absolutely necessary, and then only when holding it to one side away from your body. Walk close to the buildings and avoid silhouetting yourself in doorways or in front of windows.

Plan your approach so that you are not walking in the glare of headlights or other light, or casting shadows that signal your presence. If you work in a team, you and your partner should plan your strategy to complement each other and both of you should know the whereabouts of the other at all times. One effective means of communicating with other officers is by tapping short code signals on the pavement with the police baton. Other methods of communication include flashing a light on a high object that may be visible to officers on two sides of a building, or flashing a signal directly toward another officer with the hand covering all but a small "pinhole" of light emanating from the flashlight. If you must talk, whisper. To reduce the hissing "sibilant explosion" sounds that accompany whispering, first take a deep breath, then let out half of your air before making the first sound.

Some officers profess that every building approach must be made with the anticipation that there is probably a burglar inside. Using that logic, they may recommend that the approaching officer hold his revolver in his hand. In my opinion, carrying the revolver is an extremely poor technique that positively should not be used. The best place for the revolver is in its holster. You already have one hand full of flashlight and the other ready for doorknobs, window latches, and various other objects that you must handle while checking out the premises. It takes very little, if any, more time to draw and fire a

weapon than it does to fire it when it is being held in the hand. If an
armed culprit is inside and intends to shoot you when you enter, and
if you have absolutely no knowledge that he is inside, there is no
reason to believe that you would prevent him from shooting at you
by holding a gun in your hand. Also, consider your situation if you
are turning a doorknob with the gun in the same hand, and a burglar
on the other side of the door suddenly kicks the door toward you.

While approaching the building, look around for vehicles that seem
to be out of place, and sacks or suitcases that might have contained
burglar tools for roof and safe "jobs." Check for footprints in the mud
or loosely packed earth beneath doors and windows that may have
been the point of entry or exit. Inspect the sides of the building where
it is adjacent to utility poles, piles of boxes, ladders, or some other
means of access to the roof. It is possible that the burglar—if there
was one—might have scuffed his shoes on the building when climbing.

Make a serious game out of building inspections, varying your
technique and starting point each time, and generally causing confusion for anyone who might attempt to analyze your methods. The
rear doors and windows are most vulnerable to attack by burglars,
but some burglars prefer the front because they may believe officers
check only back doors. Never overlook the possibility that there may
be some person inside who has a legal and legitimate reason for
being there, but consider everyone suspect until you have completely
checked him out. Also consider the possibility that a lookout accomplice
may be standing, or sitting in a parked automobile, somewhere outside the building, and that he or she may have all the outward appearances of someone who has a perfectly logical reason for being at that
location. The lookout may have some unique method for signaling
your presence to the burglar inside, which may indicate to you his
possible complicity in some type of criminal activity.

When checking out a door, look first to determine which way it
opens. Some burglars close the door just far enough that when someone carelessly grabs it to see if it is locked, the bolt locks into place.
The clicking sound of the bolt serves as a signal device for the burglar.
Do not stand directly in front of the door, since the intruder may
shoot through the door. Standing directly in front has proven a fatal
mistake for many police officers. Hold the door steady, take hold of
the knob and turn it to take up any slack that may exist, then attempt
to open the door in whichever direction it opens. If it is secure, check
for pry marks and then move on to the next door or window.

Inspecting windows usually involves first checking for any broken
glass, pry marks, or latent prints before touching any portion of the
window, to avoid contamination of possible evidence. Make sure there
is actually glass in the window. It may have been completely removed
by some careful burglar. Touch the glass to feel for any unusual heat
inside the building, which may indicate the presence of a smoldering

fire or a faulty heating system. Determine the way the window opens, then attempt to open it by applying reasonable pressure. If there is some evidence of entry, check the wall below for scuff marks, and the sill for dust disturbance. Sometimes the window may prove to be one that was broken earlier but never repaired. At first it may appear to be a burglar's point of entry, but a closer inspection may reveal a substantial quantity of dust and the presence of spider webs, which would have been destroyed if entry had been made recently.

Figure 2.5 Dogs are excellent help for checking the interior of buildings for burglars. Courtesy of the Police Department, Lexington, Kentucky.

If you find the door and/or window of any building open, and there is the possibility that it may be the result of a criminal act, you should check it out in the same manner as if the person in charge had merely left the door open and had neglected to lock up for the night. There is sometimes no way for the patrol officer to determine whether or not a crime has occurred—or is in progress—without investigating further. Assuming the possibility of a burglary in progress, you should use open-door procedures; these are covered in Chapter Seven.

Crime Prevention Follow-up

Whenever there are repeated instances of crime hazards that are inadvertently caused by the potential victims, such as doors or windows left open carelessly, or company trucks parked overnight with the keys left in the ignition locks, ineffective security devices, or other correctable situations, it is the patrol officer's responsibility to attempt to encourage the potential victims to correct the situation.

Because your duty hours may preclude your making personal contacts with many of these people, there should be some provision for follow-up contacts by another officer, preferably during the business hours of the places to be visited. If time does not permit personal contacts, an inspection form may be prepared with notations for suggested improvements in security precautions and it may be mailed to the business in question.

This follow-up procedure serves two purposes: public relations and crime prevention. It is important that we let the public know of the work that we are doing and the attention that is given to their establishments. By expressing our concern over the security of their property, we hope those contacted will follow our advice and at the same time have increased confidence in the value of having such an efficient police department. The crime prevention aspect, of course, will tend to reduce our increasing work load. There is little doubt that the crime rate will increase, but perhaps we may be effective in causing the increase to be less than if we made no effort at all to reduce crime.

Vacation House Inspections

As part of an overall crime repression program, it may be wise to institute a vacation house inspection service if your community does not already have such a service. Some people may be absent from their homes for weeks or months, and a crime committed during their absence may go undetected and unreported for all of that time. The greater the time between the occurrence of the crime and its discovery, the greater is the culprit's chance of escaping apprehension.

Some burglary victims will remember that they actually provided the burglars with valuable information. The wife of a salesman may inform the local newspaper that her husband has won an award for being the salesman of the month, and that he and his family who live at 1327 Lonely Lane will be on a month-long, all-expense-paid vacation in the Bahamas. A society couple whose home is known for its works of art hanging on the walls may let their friends and suppliers know that they are going on a good will mission to a remote Indian village for three months. In both cases, the individuals are indirectly providing burglars with a wealth of information. In the latter case, the burglars may choose to hire a moving van and take the entire houseful of antiques and works of art.

Residents may be asked to report their anticipated absences to the department so that its officers can instruct them on a few methods of burglary prevention. The officers may request that the people announce their good news to the press upon their return rather than at the time of their departure. Arrangements may be made for a college student couple to take up residence during an extended absence, or to have friends or relatives periodically check the house and report to the police department that they have found it still secure. Some plans should be made to eliminate signs of vacation, such as long grass, dry flower beds, accumulated circulars and sales brochures, milk, newspapers, and other objects strewn about the premises. The people should be advised to leave a light or lights on in the house, possibly a radio left playing, and some shades or drapes not drawn all the way, to leave a burglar guessing as to whether there is anyone inside or not. Timers may be installed to electrical appliances and lights and set so that they will turn on and off at normal times rather than continue operating during daylight hours. A friend or neighbor should also be given a key and he should be present to assist the officer in checking out the residence in the event that a crime has been committed.

Figure 2.6 People who leave on vacation often forget at least one item. In this case the family forgot to lock the door. Courtesy of the Police Department, Bismarck, North Dakota.

During the day, vacation house inspections should include a thorough check of the entire premises for security and freedom from vandalism or burglary. Occasional, unscheduled checks should be made during the hours of darkness.

Miscellaneous Inspections

Each jurisdiction has a widely varied set of regulations and procedures for many other inspection services that are required of the patrol officers in their respective jurisdictions. Some cities require their police officers to make quarterly business license inspections. The building codes in some communities may specify that any building department inspector *or* police officer who observes a construction job in progress must check for the necessary permits. When they go into cafes or any place where food is served, officers in some jurisdictions are required to look for unsanitary conditions and to forward a report to the health department whenever they observe violations. When venereal disease may result from some promiscuous activities of juveniles, the health department may require that a form be forwarded to them for follow-up treatment.

Every jurisdiction requires other inspections in various instances and areas. The examples mentioned illustrate the nature and range of these miscellaneous inspection activities.

PATROL HAZARDS

The term *patrol hazard* is frequently used to describe a specific condition or place that requires the patrol officer's special attention. The hazard may be a bar where gang fights occur frequently. It may be an old dump site that has filled up with stagnant water and is now being used as a swimming hole by the neighborhood children. Although this may have no direct bearing on the character of the operators, virtually every place that attracts large numbers of people is a patrol hazard because of the potential problems inherent whenever large numbers of people are thrown together for any purpose.

When you are on patrol, give these "frequent incident" or "hazard" locations more than average attention and attempt to prevent any criminal activity by your frequent and unscheduled attendance. Develop a professional relationship with the owners and operators of the places that require more frequent patrol coverage, and impress upon them the fact that your occasional visits are for their protection as well as that of the other people in the community. Encourage them to call for your assistance if they should need it and generally develop their respect for your ability to perform your duty in a fair and objective manner. Develop informants in the neighborhood, or among the people who work or visit these places, and encourage them to let you know of any potential problems that may be developing so that effective police action may actually prevent the occurrence of any large-scale criminal activity. Maintain a list of these places and continually update your information regarding the names of the owners, operators, and other key people whom you should be able to locate whenever necessary.

SURVEILLANCE AND STAKE-OUTS

Surveillance is the process of keeping under observation a person, a place, or other object for the purpose of obtaining information concerning the activities, identities, and contacts of the people and things that are under surveillance. Surveillance may be moving or fixed. The fixed, or stationary surveillance, is usually referred to as a *stake-out*. *Close surveillance* is a technique that involves constant coverage of an individual or object, and *loose surveillance* is generally considered to be more of a spot check, or occasional surveillance.

A *convoy* is a type of surveillance that is performed either to protect the subject, or to purposefully keep him under observation with his knowledge as a means of letting him know he is being continually watched. This technique is quite effective in cases when a known organized crime "enforcer" flies into town for what you believe to be a secret visit, or to perform a specific task, such as collection or payment of a debt. Although it may seem to be a form of harassment, the "convoy" technique actually involves no harassment at all. It is merely a means of preventive maintenance. While the subject is being watched, there is little likelihood that he will commit any crime; and if he commits no crimes, the officers make no attempt to contact him or to restrict his movements.

Objectives of a Surveillance

These are some of the principal objectives for initiating and maintaining a surveillance.

1. Obtain sufficient evidence to make a physical arrest, or to secure an arrest or search warrant.
2. Locate and apprehend suspects or wanted persons.
3. Locate the residence, hangouts, or other places that the subject of the surveillance and his contacts frequent.
4. Identify the relationships between known and suspected criminals.
5. Prevent—or attempt to prevent—the commission of crimes.
6. Check out informants and the reliability of their information.
7. Prepare for a raid of a gambling or vice establishment.
8. Determine the best way to accomplish an arrest, or to rescue a person being held as a hostage.
9. Locate missing persons or runaways, adult and juvenile.
10. Obtain background information for an interview or interrogation.
11. Locate hiding places, fences, unethical businessmen, relay points for criminal transactions, or headquarters for various criminal or espionage activities.
12. Protect persons, places, or objects.

Preparation for Surveillance

Prior to starting surveillance, secure as much information about the subject as possible. Check the files of your own records system and every other available source of information to help you get to know the subject, his habits, and his acquaintances. If available, secure a copy of a recent photograph of the subject, and familiarize yourself with his general appearance as well as his distinctive features.

If you have any advance information concerning the specific location or general area where you will be maintaining surveillance on the subject, thoroughly familiarize yourself with that area. Get to know the street names, their relative locations, and the tract configuration. Check records and other officers to identify the people in the area who may assist you in the surveillance, or who may assist in the transmission of information to headquarters when regular means are not available.

Foot Surveillance

For an effective surveillance operation, more than one officer must be used. It will be necessary to alternate the sequence and relative locations of the surveillants, or "tails," so that the subject does not become aware of their presence unless they intend that he know they are there. When the subject turns a corner, the surveillant immediately behind him should continue across the street at the intersection, then turn and walk parallel to the subject down the same street. The next surveillant in line should turn the corner and take the lead position immediately behind the subject. If there are three surveillants, the third man can be used for relief or can assume the lead if one of the other officers is identified, or "made" by his subject. This "leap-frogging" technique should continue so that a single officer is not continually following the subject.

When on surveillance, you should work out a signal system with your partner so that it will not be necessary to get together in frequent huddles, or to make obvious signals to each other. If you are conducting a surveillance in street clothing, avoid chameleon disguises. Look natural while operating a "tail." You may find it to your advantage to occasionally wear eyeglasses or sunglasses and to vary the distance between yourself and the subject, but avoid any "private eye" melodramatic actions. The key to your success as a surveillant is to look as inconspicuous as possible and to fit into the surroundings naturally.

Watch out for the subject's methods for testing whether he is being "tailed." Avoid eye to eye contacts, or any other direct confrontation. There must always be some plausible explanation for you to follow the subject for an extended period of time. Frequent alternation of surveillants will ensure that no single officer is following the subject for too long a period of time.

When turning a corner, walk naturally and continue moving at the normal rate of travel. The subject may have stopped immediately after turning. If he has, your sudden appearance around the corner should not be followed by a sudden stop, which is too obvious. Keep on walking, even though it necessitates walking past the subject. If the subject makes a telephone call, you or your partner should also do something natural during the same period of time. There is little likelihood that you will find adjoining phone booths. If you do, perhaps a call of your own would be in order. When the subject enters a building or an elevator, follow suit if it is natural to do so. Otherwise, it may be better to wait until he comes back out before resuming the surveillance.

Testing for surveillance is executed in many ways. The subject may stop suddenly for no apparent reason and look around, or he may suddenly reverse his direction of travel and meet his surveillants head-on. If either of these things happen, the first officer has probably completed his part in the project, and another officer should be put in his place, if one is available. The subject may take a short taxi ride, or get on a bus for a block or two, then get off just before it starts to move after a stop. The subject may watch his "tail" in store windows. To bait the surveillant, the subject may discard some unimportant piece of paper and then watch to see whether the man following him stoops to pick it up.

Auto Surveillance

Before beginning an auto surveillance detail, be sure that you have plenty of gasoline. As with the foot method, it is best to have two or more surveillants (vehicles) so that you may use the same leapfrog technique discussed in the previous paragraphs covering foot surveillance. Be sure not to follow the subject's vehicle too closely. Keep the headlights on low beam, and drive naturally without arousing the suspicions of the subject by attempting to maintain a constant interval between your unit and the subject's. The subject may "test for a tail," as described earlier, and he may also drive alternately fast and slow to watch the car behind him. He may slow down as if to stop at a changing signal, then speed through the intersection just at the moment the light changes to red, leaving his surveillant behind. He may make frequent U-turns, or take other types of evasive action.

The Stake-Out

A stake-out is usually for the purpose of waiting for the anticipated arrival of a suspect who is either wanted for investigation, or who is expected to commit a crime at the location being "staked-out." When working such an assignment, be sure to pre-plan carefully. Get adequate food and rest before entering the place, and take a sufficient quantity of food with you in case it is necessary to spend some time. Arrange for efficient communications with other units and with headquarters.

Deliver your equipment, such as a shotgun, binoculars, or other special equipment, inconspicuously to avoid arousing the least suspicion. Dismantle the gun, and carry it in a case or container that would normally be carried by someone who works at that location. Wear the same type of clothing that would be natural for the establishment.

When working a stake-out in a place of business where other types of crimes may occur that are not related to your purpose, be sure to advise the store owner or other people in charge that they are not to reveal your presence to handle the matter. For example, a stake-out for an anticipated armed robbery will be rendered ineffective if the manager observes a shoplifter and calls to the officer to arrest the petty thief at just about the same time the potential armed robber steps into the store. The manager or others could also destroy the value of the stake-out by announcing to some of the customers that an officer is protecting the place.

Basic Guidelines for a Stake-Out

1. Operate in a business-like manner.
2. Be natural and avoid melodrama.
3. Do not use phony disguises.
4. Be on the alert for a subject "testing for a tail."
5. Be adequately prepared for surveillance, particularly a fixed post where you may have to stay for some time.
6. Prepare a "cover" reason for being in the area while on a surveillance.
7. Keep sufficient money and supplies on hand.
8. Avoid direct eye to eye contact with the subject.
9. Prepare for adequate communications with other officers and with headquarters.

EXERCISES AND STUDY QUESTIONS

1. According to the text, what is the value of an officer's having a broad base of experience and education prior to becoming a police officer?
2. List the various things an officer must do in the office to prepare for his job prior to going into the field.
3. Of what value to the officer is it to hold a conference with the man going off duty?
4. What is the purpose of a general familiarization tour of the patrol district?
5. What is the author's recommendation regarding the use of medication to stay awake? Do you agree with it? Why?
6. What do we mean when we say that a car hydroplanes on a wet street? How does this occur?
7. Under what conditions in your department (where you work or

live) is a "code three"—which involves both red light and siren—automatic?

8. Describe a "district orientation tour" and explain its purpose.
9. What type of entries would you make in your notebook during an orientation tour of your district?
10. List and discuss two types of inspections the patrol officer performs to assist other government agencies.
11. List at least three purposes for a plainclothes patrol.
12. Define "patrol hazard" and give at least three examples.
13. What is the difference between "public nuisance" and "attractive nuisance"?
14. What is the recommended procedure for checking out the security of a building in an industrial district?
15. What is the police responsibility at a fire scene?

SUGGESTED SEMESTER OR TERM PROJECTS

1. Prepare a set of guidelines for a security inspection of a medical center, a department store, and a light manufacturing building in your city. (Or do a similar project for any other combination of three types of buildings.)
2. Devise a workable daily log and an accompanying set of guidelines to explain its use and to assure maximum utilization of the log.
3. Devise a vehicle inspection sheet and a system for keeping an accurate log of the condition of the vehicles maintained by your department.

REFERENCES

California Vehicle Code

CHAPMAN, SAMUEL G., *Police Patrol Readings.* Springfield, Ill.: Charles C Thomas, Publisher, 1964.

FALES, E. D., JR., "New Facts About Skidding—They May Save Your Life," *F.B.I. Law Enforcement Bulletin* (May 1965), pp. 13–16. Copyright 1964 by Popular Science Pub. Co., Inc.

HOLCOMB, R. L., *Police Patrol.* Springfield, Ill.: Charles C Thomas, Publisher, 1964.

Los Angeles Police Department, *Daily Training Bulletins,* Vol. 1. Springfield, Ill.: Charles C Thomas, Publisher, 1954, Chap. 10.
————, *Daily Training Bulletins,* Vol. II. Springfield, Ill.: Charles C Thomas, Publisher, 1958, Chaps. 7, 9, and 10.

WILSON, O. W., *Police Planning,* 2nd ed. Springfield, Ill.: Charles C Thomas, Publisher, 1958, Chap. 6.

Various training bulletins and related materials from the police departments of Glendale, Los Angeles, Riverside, Santa Ana, California Highway Patrol, and others.

Communications

Procedures

CHAPTER THREE   In recent years, law enforcement advances in some areas have been phenomenal. Innovations in communications techniques and equipment provide the most vivid examples of such advances. Not many years have gone by since the lone police officer on the beat had to rely on the tap of another officer's nightstick, or the blinking light on top of the tallest building in the block, for a signal that his assistance was needed by an officer in the adjoining beat or back at the station house. Radio was not available to the majority of law enforcement agencies until the 1930s, and the only means of contact with the station prior to that time was via the call-box telephone. Today it is possible for the beat officer working on foot to maintain constant communications with headquarters by means of a portable, miniature two-way radio. It is also possible to communicate by teletype and radio directly with the central crime information clearing house located at FBI headquarters in Washington, D.C., and to virtually any other police agency in the country.   **57**

Figure 3.1

With increasing use of electronic data processing systems, there is no doubt that tomorrow's communications system for law enforcement will undergo revolutionary changes which will make today's methods and systems obsolete.

ESSENTIALS FOR A POLICE COMMUNICATIONS SYSTEM

The police department is an emergency operation. All forms of communication must be geared for emergency conditions and completely operational at all times. In addition, secondary systems must be ready for immediate implementation without loss of time or manpower. Under most conditions the actual routine of meeting the emergency and routine demands upon the various forms of communication will function smoothly and efficiently. However, plans should exist to cover all of the potential, "unexpected" situations that can be foreseen as well as those situations that occur frequently. To assure maximum efficiency in carrying out those plans, certain criteria must be met.

1. TRAINING.   As much as possible, most types of messages should be committed to standard handling procedures. Any conceivable type of situation should be worked out in hypothetical "role play" sessions and communications procedures worked out accordingly. Once standard operating procedures are established, they should be made well-known to all operating personnel, and these personnel should be instructed and rehearsed in as many different types of situations as possible. The training must coincide with the planning, and both must be constant in the dynamic environment of the law enforcement milieu.

2. DEPENDABILITY.   The police communications system must be totally dependable under both emergency and routine conditions. Secondary systems must be available on a stand-by basis, and they must be totally operational. Frequent inspections and tests should be made as a matter of routine. For example, an auxiliary radio transmitter should be occasionally used for a short time to test its efficiency.

3. SECURITY.   The police communications system must be secure from attack in the event of any criminal action directed toward destruction or neutralization of any part of the police agency's vital functions. It must also be secure from any foreseeable natural or accidental disaster, such as fire, flood, earthquake, tornado, hurricane, or airplane crash.

4. ACCESSIBILITY.   All operational units of the organization must have convenient access to every type of communications medium that is essential to its efficient operation. Mail delivery and extension telephone systems usually accommodate most of the basic needs of a police organization, but there may also be a need for radio broadcast and monitoring equipment at remote locations, and for teletype units in locations separate from the battery of units maintained in a communication center. It is also quite feasible to install remote terminals for electronic data processing systems that tie in with centralized information storage banks. Access must be commensurate with utilization.

5. SPEED.   Radio and telephone provide immediate access to other persons or agencies, assuming the line or air is clear to transmit the message. One method to assure maximum utilization of all forms of communications for law enforcement agencies is to develop a language that is clearly understandable to all its users but that can appreciably shorten the time it takes to deliver the message. Radio codes are primarily designed for such brevity as well as clarity and, to some small extent, possibly some confidentialness. Redundancy in police correspondence or teletype messages should be avoided.

6. SECRECY.   Police communications should not be made public as a matter of course. Much of the information in possession of the

police agency is private and personal as it relates to suspects and victims, and it is essential that this information be guarded to protect the innocent. Although radio codes are known by virtually anyone who is involved in law enforcement, there is some degree of privacy in using the codes because they are not universally known. Teletype systems used by law enforcement agencies are on private lines with accessibility only through coordinating agency authorization. For some transmissions by radio or telephone, it may be feasible to use scrambler systems which transmit what sound like unintelligible, garbled sounds and "unscramble" them at each end. For certain types of unusual police operations, unpublished frequencies may be utilized. Of course, it is possible to monitor such calls, but the intended listener must have some advance knowledge of the exact frequency to cover; otherwise, finding the signal on the receiver will be purely by chance. By the time the hopeful eavesdropper finds the frequency used by vice officers, for example, the officers could change frequencies and continue their private discussion.

INTRA- AND INTERDEPARTMENTAL COMMUNICATIONS

Two other aspects of police communications that should be defined are intra- and interdepartmental communications. Intradepartmental communications involves the formal and informal transmission and exchange of information throughout the various divisions and subdivisions within the agency. The interdepartmental communications system involves the interchange of information among the members of two or more agencies. Both of these systems will be briefly reviewed.

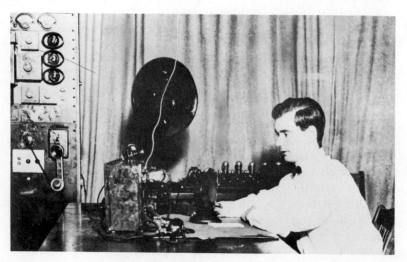

Figure 3.2 The first police radio broadcasting station. Courtesy of the Police Department, Detroit, Michigan.

Within a quasi-military organization such as a police department, there are several methods for the formal transmission of directives, orders, ideas, and information to be conveyed through the various levels of the organizational structure in a downward, upward, or lateral direction. There must also be provisions for an informal interchange of ideas and information in all directions throughout the department. Without this informal flow of communications, there is the danger that incentive will be destroyed, mediocrity will be perpetuated, and eventually the effectiveness of the department will be totally neutralized.

Figure 3.3 One of Detroit's first radio-equipped cruisers. Note the "antenna" on the roof. Courtesy of the Police Department, Detroit, Michigan.

For the purpose of presenting to the public an image of unanimity within the agency, all news releases and general information emanating from the agency should "clear" through the office of the agency head—the chief of police or sheriff. Correspondence should be over his signature or by his authority. All incoming material or information should be directed to a central mail room to be re-routed to the appropriate offices and individuals once it reaches the department.

General and special orders usually originate in the office of the chief. *General orders* are long-lasting policy statements or standardized procedures that affect all members of the department. *Special orders* have a shorter effective length, or they involve matters of interest to some number of employees rather than the general membership. A variety of other types of directives or information bulletins may emanate from the chief's office or other divisions within the department in accordance with the system established by the chief and his staff. Conformity to some sort of system assures consistency and predictability.

In addition to the written message that the chief or sheriff must continually originate and update, there should be a more informal system for the interchange of ideas as well as the delivery of orders. The chief usually meets with his immediate staff on a daily basis, sometimes several times during the day. The immediate staff consists of those ranking officers who are in the direct line of command in the organization and report directly to him as indicated on the organizational charts. The chief holds less frequent meetings on a formal and informal basis at irregular or scheduled times with command and supervisory officers. The general purposes of such staff and command meetings are to articulate policies, to maintain some uniformity in the interpretation and execution of the department's responsibilities, and to provide for a continual, free flow of communications and feedback essential to the management process.

Following the lead of the chief, all supervisory employees and ranking officers should have both formal and informal meetings with their subordinates to discuss the same general policies, philosophies, and ethics, but also to work out ways and means to perform their jobs with the greatest degree of efficiency. There should also be provisions within the organization at all levels of supervision up to—and including—the chief for an open door into that person's office to discuss any personal matter that directly affects the department. Naturally, it is not possible for the chief of police or the sheriff of a large agency to personally visit with each of the members of his department, or his entire time would be consumed by such visits and he could not accomplish the other responsibilities of his office. However, there must be some system of unstifled flow of information to allow feedback and also to provide a safety valve for the officers and other employees to communicate their emotions, their ideas, and their complaints.

Within the ranks and between the various working units in the department there must also be an established system for the free flow of information without the unbending restriction that everyone go through the "chain of command" to exchange information. There is a particularly acute need for such a continuous flow of information between the patrol officers and the investigators, for example. A patrol officer may develop some good leads on a case and pass them on to the investigator assigned to the follow-up investigation of that case. It is imperative that the investigator later send back word to the officer who originally uncovered the leads, preferably by telephone or a personal note in a department mail box, to let him know his lead aided in the case. The investigators should frequently visit the patrol roll call sessions to discuss their cases and to seek assistance in locating wanted individuals or information that the patrol officers may be in a better position to find because of their continuous presence in the field.

Accident investigators may ask for patrol assistance in a hit-and-run case in which the only leads they have are that the suspect drives a light blue car and that he might drive on a certain street every night at about the same time. Vice detail officers may request that a particular house be watched for unusual activity or more than the average number of automobiles in the vicinity. These are just a few examples of the many instances when the cooperative efforts of two or more operating units are enhanced by informal communications.

Rumors will usually fill the gaps left by the lack of information, and police departments are not exempt from rumor-passing situations. In order to counteract the dissemination of rumors, it may be necessary to openly point out the true facts of a situation, such as the purpose for disciplinary action. Rules and regulations should be published and distributed. Policies, procedures, and other types of information should be passed on to the employees. Additionally, there should be some provision for the release of information that is newsworthy to the many members of the department. Although there are some items of information that must remain confidential, they should be kept to a minimum to keep the air clear of intrigue and rumor-producing conditions.

Interdepartmental Communications

There is an acute need for a free flow of communications between the various law enforcement agencies throughout the country and, in many cases, with other law enforcement bodies in foreign countries. Nonpolitical and nonreligious organizations that are directly involved in the law enforcement or investigative process serve as one means of assuring this interdepartmental exchange of information and ideas. Through his membership in national and international organizations the chief meets other chief administrators from the United States and the rest of the world. He and his intelligence detail and community relations officers also develop valuable contacts outside their own jurisdictions. These contacts facilitate the flow of information that is essential for the successful operation of police units in cases having national and international aspects and far-reaching effects. They may be extremely useful, for example, in cases involving safe burglars or clothing store burglars, who often work many cities across the country.

Another instance of interdepartmental communications is when the officer-specialists in several different departments meet under formal organization meeting situations. Through such organizational relationships they form friendships that facilitate frequent informal contacts for social reasons as well as for discussion of cases in which they are mutually interested. It is not unusual for the officers from several departments in contiguous jurisdictions to jointly solve a series of cases through the medium of their organizational ties. Otherwise, they might solve only those crimes that a culprit commits in one jurisdiction.

Isolation is not a favorable situation for any single segment of society, and the police officer should avoid developing an insulated barrier between himself and the other members of his society. He should make a diligent effort to diversify his associations among as many different special and general purpose organizations as possible, consistent with his work schedule and other responsibilities. These include school parent organizations, church clubs, fraternal organizations, youth groups, and others that he encounters in the course of the many life roles that he plays. If he focuses all of his attention on those organizations related to law enforcement, there is a danger that he will compartmentalize himself and subconsciously develop a narrow, ethnocentric type of outlook. Such a phenomenon occurs whenever an individual isolates himself in this way.

The question of religious and political activism is often cause for debate when a police officer is involved. As a private individual he should be encouraged to take an active part in exercising his right to vote and expressing his freedom to worship in any way that he chooses. When on duty, however, the officer should be as objective as possible, and he should remain aloof from religious or political discussion so that he does not become identified as an officer who attempts to foist his own point of view on others under the color of authority. On duty, he should never be so overt in his beliefs that it can be said that he arrested an individual, or used his official position to coerce another person to comply with a certain request, because of their differences in religious or political beliefs. A police force should not be used as a tool to extort votes for a particular individual, or the people have a political police force, which is contrary to the American system of government. Keeping this neutral attitude on duty is a must, but the officer should take an active part in his private life to affiliate himself with a church and political party of his own free choice as a first-class citizen. He relinquishes his right for public expression in his role as a public servant, but retains it in his private role as a citizen.

COMMUNICATIONS MEDIA, BASIC GUIDELINES

United States Mail

Mail is one of the oldest and most durable forms of communication used by law enforcement. Virtually every type of police business

is transacted by mail, from the routine letter of verification for delivery
of a shipment of ball-point pens, to a special delivery, airmail letter
to the detective division advising them of the whereabouts of a possible robbery suspect. Individual patrol officers may not be directly
involved in the routine use of the mails; but whenever it is necessary
to send a letter related to the department's business, it should be in
accordance with an established procedure. Outgoing mail should be
sent over the signature of the chief of police or the division head,
never the individual officer, and returns should be requested in the
same manner. The primary purpose of this procedure is to present
the image of a single agency rather than a haphazard conglomeration
of individual operators.

Whistles and Night Sticks

Prearranged signals with either or both of these standard items
of police equipment may be used for a variety of worthwhile purposes. At nighttime a night stick rapped on the sidewalk pavement
may be heard with a distinctive sound for several blocks. Short blasts
of the whistle may likewise be heard, yet be considerably less notice-
able than an officer's voice shouting a command or call for assistance.
Whenever working with other officers under conditions when it will
be necessary to be on foot, set up two or three distinctive signals.
These may be particularly effective when attempting to surround a
building in order to apprehend a burglar who is hiding inside.

Recall Signal Devices

In the absence of portable radios that can be carried on the belt,
over the shoulder, or in some other manner, there is almost no way
for the home station to get in touch with the lone officer on a foot
beat except to wait for him to go to a telephone and call in at prearranged times. Prior to the advent of portable two-way radios, some
police departments set up systems of signal lights located throughout
the areas covered by officers on foot beats. The lights were connected
directly to the station houses, and messages were sent to the beat
officers by means of coded combinations of light flashes. In other
cities, small signal lights were installed atop a building in the center
of town, and they signaled the officers downtown to report immediately to the station to take out a car for a service call in the outlying
areas, or to come in for lunch relief.

The signal light system has been replaced by more sophisticated
equipment in large urban areas. However, variations of the signal
method are still being used with more modern equipment. One device
is a small sound signal mechanism that the officer can wear inconspicuously on his belt or some other part of his uniform. A very faint
signal that can hardly be heard by anyone but the wearer signals

him to go to the nearest telephone and call in to his office. Another device is a small light on top of the car, or a connection to the auto lights, that are activated when a radio signal is beamed from headquarters. An officer out of the car is signaled to return by means of the light signal, and when he returns to his vehicle he calls the station. The most widely used recall device today is a portable receiver, which the officer carries with him whenever he is out of the vehicle.

Telegraph

Before the implementation of the teletype, one of the more common means of police communication was telegraph. Telegraph wires were linked to the police headquarters and the various precinct stations. They were also wired from one police department to another. Telegraphers were employed for the purpose of maintaining communications between stations. One disadvantage to the system was that police officers had to be specially trained in operating the telegraph equipment and using the Morse code, which consists of combinations of clicks made by activating an electromagnetic key. The alternative was to employ trained telegraphers for the specialized job, and to keep them on duty around the clock, which they apparently did. The system was used for many years, but it is now virtually obsolete.

Teletype

Automatic teletypewriters on telephone lines connecting headquarters with substations in the various precincts, and connecting police departments throughout the various states in a nationwide network, are now fully operational. Most of the major cities in the United States are linked together through the facilities of the various coordinating agencies. The past few years have seen the marriage of teletype and computers to create a highly efficient system of information storage and retrieval, which holds great promise for the future. Centralized records of stolen automobiles, criminal records, pawned and stolen items are maintained in state clearinghouses, and the teletype networks make it possible to inquire and receive replies regarding whether or not an item is stolen or a person is wanted within a matter of microseconds.

In addition to the statewide teletype networks and information systems, the U.S. Department of Justice has established a central computerized information clearinghouse that will eventually provide instantaneous information retrieval and storage services for virtually every police agency in the country. Known as the National Crime Information Center, or NCIC, the system is operational and functioning as an integral part of the police information system.

Secretaries, stenographers, and other clerks regularly employed by the various police departments may be easily trained to use teletype equipment because of its utilization of the typewriter configuration. Established uniform message formats should be followed closely to assure brevity, clarity, and maximum benefit from the exchange of information in accordance with a uniform sequence and style.

Speed-Photo and Facsimile

By means of cables, telephone lines, or microwave radio signals, it is possible to send as many different types of messages as the imagination can concoct. An individual can write a check in a San Francisco bank on a bank account that he has in Miami, can have it cleared through a central clearinghouse in Chicago, and can cash it in about the same amount of time it would take to merely write the check. As the check is being written at one location, it is simultaneously being duplicated by means of sound signals at the location where the signature will be verified and the account checked to verify the existence of a balance that will cover the check being written.

Devices of this type can be used quite effectively by police departments to compare handwriting samples with writings on anonymous letters, kidnap ransom notes, forged documents, and virtually any kind of document requiring a signature. Many variations of the image transmission technique are used by law enforcement agencies, and have proven quite effective. For example, photographs are sent to remote receivers within seconds after they are developed and printed, making it possible for photos of wanted felons to be widely disseminated within only a few minutes after they have been identified. Latent fingerprints collected at the scene of a crime in Macon can be sent to Cleveland for comparison with the rolled fingerprints of a suspect in custody, or to the central clearinghouse of fingerprints at FBI headquarters to be checked against their massive collection of fingerprints on file.

Television

Sight and sound transmissions by means of television are an excellent adjunct to the other communications media employed by police departments. Television's use is gaining considerable popularity because of its economy and ease of operation. As employed by the field officer in the patrol division, it is possible for the investigating officer at the scene of a crime to take with him a television camera and to record the entire scene by means of videotape, or to transmit the signal to a remote transmitter that in turn will relay it back to headquarters where it may be monitored and taped for future reference. The most practical method is to use a portable camera and videotape combination that can be carried with a shoulder strap.

Use of television makes it possible for lineups to be held at a central location while witnesses who are unable to travel view the suspects at some other location. The chief of police, the sheriff, or other ranking officers may address a maximum number of officers and other employees who are located at various places throughout the jurisdiction either "live" or on videotape, thereby assuring the greatest possible coverage without interfering with normal operations or the off-duty time of the many employees.

Remote television cameras and transmitters carried in a helicopter, or located at various key places in a city, such as a heavily used intersection of two major arterials, make it possible for officers to view many places simultaneously, providing greater patrol coverage. A single officer can visually observe as many places as there are television cameras, and can dispatch a patrol unit to whichever one of the various locations requires the physical presence of a police officer. Using television to supplement patrol, it is conceivable that a single officer will be able to observe on a continuous basis as many high hazard or high crime areas as he possibly could visit once or twice a day for only a few minutes at a time.

Telephone

The most common means of communication between police departments and the people they serve will always be personal contact. The first contact—and sometimes the only one—usually consists of the telephone call requesting advice or assistance from the policeman. No type of police operation is transacted without frequent use of the telephone. Many members of the department literally spend their entire duty time on the telephone, answering questions for information or advice, questioning people concerning their identities, where they are, and their reasons for calling the police.

The telephone is not new to law enforcement. Since its inception, it has adapted quite naturally to the needs of the police as well as the people they serve. It is a convenient, economical, and rapid means of communicating with others. Because the telephone is so intimately involved with the role of law enforcement in the lives of people during times of great need and tragedy, every department member must be constantly mindful of the sensitive part he plays in that role. It is just as important that the representative of the police department answer every call with a pleasant attitude as it is that the representative of an insurance company respond to each call as if it were from a new customer.

Every phone call must be answered with a pleasant voice, never a brusque or gruff-sounding voice that might be intended to impress someone with the "manliness" of the policeman at the other end of

the line. The word should be "gentlemanliness," and it is not a sign
of weakness to be empathic and polite.

Cultivate a good telephone voice: clear, distinct, evenly paced, pleasant, and natural. Always answer the phone promptly, or transfer the call to someone who can answer. Be attentive to the caller and attempt to determine from the tone of his voice the urgency of his call for the services of a police officer. Keep the length of all incoming calls short. Be polite, but discourage the marathon conversation. If the caller must talk longer than you have time for, perhaps it may be possible to transfer the call to a clerk who will advise the caller that the officer was required to move on to another call and inquire whether there is additional information that should be passed on to the officer. Such a tactic should not be designed to discourage callers, but it is necessary if the lines are to be kept reasonably clear for an emergency call that may come in at any moment.

Any incoming phone call to the police department may be a request for help in a life or death situation. It may not be such a call—most calls are not—but law enforcement is an emergency service organization and must be geared for emergency at all times. The next call may be the most important call of the day, and a minute saved may mean the difference between an individual's life or death. The phone must not be allowed to continue ringing unanswered, and there should be a standard procedure for immediate response when the telephone operator is busy. One method for handling all incoming phone calls is to have the principal operator respond to as many calls as she can, and immediately connect any calls that she cannot answer to other persons who have desk assignments in the building. The call may be handled by that person, or if it is a nonemergency call for service or a request to speak with a particular individual within the building, it can be returned to the operator when the earlier surge of overloading calls has subsided.

One effective method for handling many calls at once is to answer each call with "Police Department. Is this an emergency?" If the person at the other end of the line states "No," the operator goes to the next call. Handling only the emergency calls, the operator then goes back to the calls that were not in need of immediate attention. By using this method it is possible to give all callers the attention they expect of their police department and at the same time give them priority attention. If you use this procedure, the key to success is to wait for a reply when asking, "Is this an emergency?" Otherwise the purpose is defeated.

Another technique is to utilize a complaint board and tape recorder combination. Any request for service can be switched to the tape recorder on a delayed action arrangement which allows the complaint officer to switch to the extension after the caller has already begun talking. The officer can listen to the recorded conversation

Figure 3.4 Telephone switchboard and complaint desk arrangement work well for larger departments. Calls requiring response at the scene are indicated on assignment sheets and sent to the radio or "mike" room for assignment. Courtesy of the Police Department, Los Angeles, California.

at high speed and catch up with the slower speed of the caller. The recording may alert the caller that he is talking into a tape recorder, or the phone operator may so advise the caller. When the complaint desk is operating at normal load conditions, the officer may answer the call directly and assume the conversation with the caller immediately. He may use the tape recording to replay for clarification or study.

Whatever means are used to answer the phone, once a call has been transferred or placed on "hold," there should be a frequent check to ascertain whether the intended recipient of the call did respond when signaled. Next to having to wait for the phone to ring a score or more times before it is answered by the department's operator, the most exasperating experience for a caller is to be greeted with "Police department. One moment, please," followed by a click and then unbroken dead silence for an interminable waiting period.

Incoming calls of an emergency nature should not be referred to another phone number. The operator should take the information and relay it to the agency that can respond to the situation by virtue of jurisdiction or nature of the requested service. If the call is for some type of service or information that does not require immediate attention, the caller should be referred to the correct agency and

Figure 3.5 The "mike" room where all radio transmissions are handled for the department. Each frequency has a separate operator. An experienced police officer is on duty at all times. Courtesy of the Police Department, Los Angeles, California.

provided with the correct name, address, and telephone number. "It's in the phone book" is not an appropriate retort.

Some agencies have an excellent incoming phone call arrangement called the *hot line*. Whenever the telephone operator receives an emergency call that involves several different units within the department, such as an armed robbery in progress, she simultaneously rings the "hot line" on all the phone extensions carrying it as one of their numbers. The operator immediately connects the call and an unusually loud bell or signal sounds. The officer in charge, the investigative unit, dispatcher, and anyone else to whom the call is directed can listen simultaneously. Only one person, usually the dispatcher, carries on the conversation with the caller to get pertinent information. The others listen and handle whatever assignments or other arrangements they deem necessary.

Alarm companies frequently call concerning silent or audible alarms that are triggered in burglary or robbery situations. They are also set off accidentally by tellers and clerks, and by conditions during windstorms, by shorted connections, and a variety of other malfunctions. When an alarm system is activated, the alarm company follows a prescribed procedure to check the system, then calls the police department for response. All of these calls must be treated as potentially dangerous "in-progress" crime situations, and should be connected to the "hot line."

Whenever a private person takes the time to call the police department about some need for police service, it is usually one of the most important events in his life at that particular moment. Very few people call for police aid with any regularity, and they are sometimes unfortunately referred to as "chronic complainers." With due respect for the officers who use this term, we would agree that there are some persons who fit that category somewhat appropriately because their requests are for the police officers to perform false arrests or to "put a scare into" someone. On the whole, however, most callers are sincere and justifiably want the police to perform some action that falls within the purview of our responsibilities. When such is the case, it should be a matter of routine courtesy to take a few extra minutes when possible after responding to the call to phone the caller back or pay him a visit to bring him up to date on the action you took. There is no need to disseminate tidbits of gossip for the rumor-mongers; just state what is sufficient to satisfy the caller that you did perform your duty.

Police Radio

It is difficult to imagine a modern, efficient law enforcement agency without the use of radio. Now it is taken as a matter of course, with little thought to the fact that police radio was nonexistent until about 1929. The first radios were quite cumbersome and considerably different from those in use today. The transmitter was located at head-quarters and the police cars were equipped with receivers only. In many agencies there was no transmitter and it was necessary to send emergency calls to the police cars in the field by using the facilities of local broadcast stations.

By 1938 the use of one-way radio in police cars had become rather widespread, and it was during that year that some departments began installing transmitters in their vehicles, making two-way radio communication possible. The system involved use of a common frequency for all transmissions from both the station at headquarters and the mobile units. This simple configuration is called a *simplex system*. The next step was to provide separate frequencies so that the station was using one frequency and the mobile units another. This double frequency system is known as the *duplex system*. As it progressed, police radio added a third frequency for car-to-car transmissions, and the triple frequency system was named the *triplex system*. Variations of all three systems are presently in operation.

GUIDELINES FOR RADIO OPERATION

Introduction

Utilization of the radio frequencies for many purposes by hundreds of different types of organizations and individual operations has made it necessary to have very strict limitations on frequency allocations and on the actual use of those frequencies that are allocated. Along the spectrum of sound wave frequencies, only a portion of the frequencies may be used by radio. Other frequencies are used for ultraviolet and infrared transmissions, for X-ray, diathermic, and ultrasonic therapeutic devices, and for television and both private and commercial radio. As a result of all of these demands on the existent frequencies, which cannot be expanded, the frequencies are constantly being narrowed and exploited more efficiently through the use of highly sophisticated equipment.

Air time on the police frequency is as valuable to the police officer as the most valuable gem is to the jeweler, and it should be handled and used accordingly. Even though there may be silent gaps in the normal day, it is just as desirable for the officer to save the silent moments as it is for the jeweler to preserve every scrap of the precious gem or metal and get maximum use of the leftovers in producing other items. With the radio, the object is to use only that time which is necessary to deliver the message, no more. Each transmission must be brief, but not so brief that it must be repeated for explanation or clarification, and it must be accurate. Through the use of standardized radio codes it is possible to cut sentences down into numbers, such as "Code Seven at 14," which means, "I am going to stop for a few minutes for lunch at the coffee shop that we gave the number '14' sometime previously, and I may be reached at that phone number—also listed previously—if you need to get in touch with me while I am eating."

Operating Laws and Regulations

The Federal Communications Commission is charged with the responsibility for the legal and efficient use of the radio frequencies. Profanity, obscenity, and superfluous transmissions are unlawful and are prosecutable offenses. The patrol officer's responsibility is to follow the recommended procedures discussed in this chapter, and to avoid the use of profanity, obscenity, and superfluous transmissions. All other matters will be handled by the engineers and those people who are appropriately licensed as the principal operators for the various radio stations. Most field officers are not licensed. Some are holders of lifetime or provisional permits, but very few are licensed commercial radio operators.

Microphone Technique

Prior to broadcasting by radio, depress the button to turn the microphone on and wait for a brief moment to allow the transmitter to be at full power when you are speaking. Hold the microphone about two inches from your mouth and in such a position that the sound is going past the microphone rather than directly into it. Using this technique will reduce the distracting sounds that occur when spitting the P's and hissing or whistling the S's. Some high quality broadcast microphones filter these sounds out, making it possible to speak directly into them, but the standard vehicle microphone is not so equipped.

Use radio codes as much as possible for clarity and brevity, and speak in an evenly modulated tone of voice, slowly and distinctly. Exaggerate the diction slightly, such as the consonants at the end of the words, and the vowel sounds. For example, the word "police" should sound like "po lees" rather than "plece." As much as possible under the circumstances at the time of broadcast, try to make every transmission free of emotion. Any expression of anger, impatience, rudeness, or excitement may be exaggerated during the radio transmission and its contagion will negatively affect most of the people who are listening to that particular frequency.

Volume control is essential. Keep the volume evenly modulated and at an even volume. Shouting will cause a distorted transmission, and an important request for help may be so distorted by shouting that it is unintelligible. Outside noises from sirens, racing motors, overhead aircraft, and other sources all interfere with the transmissions, but shouting over the noise will not correct the problem. If at all possible, time your broadcasts so that they occur at times of least interference.

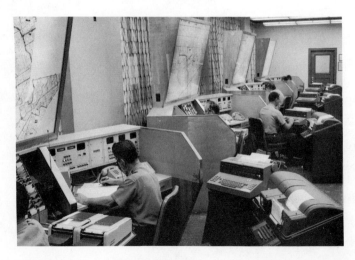

Figure 3.6 The modern facilities of Detroit are a vast improvement over their system of four decades ago. Courtesy of the Police Department, Los Angeles, California. Photo by Edward Hall.

Listen to the radio for a minute or two before broadcasting to be sure that you are not interfering with another exchange of transmis- sions. Use this time to quickly think out your message before you send it. Depress the microphone button and begin talking immediately after a brief pause, keeping the transmission "moving." If you must stop to think or secure additional information, clear the air and return a minute later rather than stutter or stammer as a stall for time. The air time is valuable; use it as if it were gold dust.

If the transmission is long, stop occasionally and secure an acknowledgment of the message so far before continuing. The break will ensure clear communication, and it will also permit another unit with an urgent message to interfere when essential. Wait briefly for an acknowledgment before repeating the message or asking for an acknowledgment. The person at the other end of the message may have received the message, but he may have been momentarily called away from the microphone by some other matter. If you do not wait, you may be broadcasting at the same time he is broadcasting his acknowledgment, and with both transmitters on simultaneously, neither of you will hear the other. Unfortunately, impatience for a response sometimes causes considerable confusion.

Do not repeat messages unnecessarily, as occasionally portrayed on television or in the movies. A well-executed message given once may be sufficient, and usually is. If the receiver did not get it all, he will ask for a repeat of that portion he missed. There is no need to transmit a message then ask for an acknowledgment in the same manner as the individual who asks after every sentence, "Do you understand?" or "Did you get that?" Whether he is asked or not, the receiver is required to acknowledge a transmission. Therefore, the request for acknowledgment is superfluous.

Pay attention to other transmissions on the radio that do not directly affect you, such as open-door discoveries or car stops. Although the officer may not request a follow-up unit, it should be a matter of course for the nearest unit to follow up to assure adequate protection for the lone field officer. When another unit calls in a license number and auto description when he makes a car stop, copy it down. In the event that the officer is attacked or the vehicle flees the scene, or both, you already have the essential information and do not have to wait for a general broadcast to take action.

Acknowledgment of Calls

Respond to all calls as quickly as possible to avoid the need for a repeat or a second call to ask you if you received the first one. When acknowledging a call, respond with the appropriate code, but also give your location. The dispatcher and the other units that are listening to your transmission will know the distance you will have to travel to respond to a call and they can estimate your probable route of travel. Follow-up units, if necessary for the occasion, will know how they should proceed. In some cases, it may be possible to reassign a call to a closer unit, which is particularly important for injury accidents and "crime in progress" calls. If you are operating the follow-up unit and intend to respond, broadcast your intentions and the location from where you are responding.

Station Broadcasting

Although the radio operator at the base station usually is not a ranking officer, he broadcasts with the authority of the chief of police. The operator does not have that power as an individual, but is merely relaying that authority, and he should avoid any attempt to assume an attitude of personal control of the authority he is merely relaying. The radio is often the field officer's only contact with headquarters; the operator is his partner in most of his field activities that involve use of the radio, and the dispatcher must constantly operate as an efficient partner. The field officer relies heavily on the dispatcher to provide him with assistance and protection whenever he needs it.

Most assignments of field officers are by radio. They must be as clear and understandable as possible. Avoid any display of emotionalism to avoid transmitting undue anxiety. The radio is no medium for transmitting a scolding, or impatience, anger, or any other emotion to the field officer. The transmissions must be impersonal. They are station-to-station messages and have no relationship to personal, face-to-face conversations. The radio is not licensed for personal messages. It should be standard operating procedure to limit transmissions only to essential transmissions that are directly related to the official business of the police department.

General Broadcasting Rules

Whenever using the police radio, use the following rules as guidelines for effective broadcasting results.

1. Practice courtesy. It is contagious and will make their work much easier for everyone who uses the radio as well as those who must listen to it constantly during their entire tour of duty.
2. Broadcast station-to-station only. "Mike to Joe" transmissions are not allowed and should be held for personal meetings or telephone calls.
3. Humor and horseplay have no place on the police frequency. Rude sounds and sarcastic comments emanating from anonymous users of

the radio frequency may sound funny for the moment, but they are immature, unlawful, and they may someday interfere with a transmission that could mean the difference between whether the officer lives or dies. Leave the humor to the commercial broadcasting clowns, who are employed specifically for the purpose of entertainment.

4. Avoid any use of the radio for personal conflicts, such as "chewing out," arguments, or sarcasm.
5. Keep all transmissions brief and to the point. Use the telephone for lengthy messages.
6. Profane and indecent language are unlawful.
7. Transmit only essential messages. Avoid asking for the time of day just to hear the radio, and secure routine information, such as time to eat lunch and other scheduled matters, either before going out in the field or by telephone.
8. Be completely familiar with your department's radio procedures and the individual items of equipment.
9. Assume a personal responsibility for correct and intelligent use of the radio by your department.

EXERCISES AND STUDY QUESTIONS

1. Six criteria for an efficient radio system were presented in this chapter. List five.
2. What is *intradepartmental* communication? How can it be improved in your own police department?
3. What is a "recall signal device" and how does it work?
4. How do speed-photo and facsimile aid law enforcement?
5. Of what use is videotape in the field?
6. How would you handle incoming phone calls when they are coming in faster than you can handle them?
7. Of what value is a "hot line" and how might it be used by your department?
8. In approximately what year did police radio become a reality?
9. Define simplex, duplex, and triplex radio systems.
10. What is the basic purpose of the radio codes?
11. What is the radio code for _____ (drill yourself on all of the codes for your jurisdiction).

SUGGESTED SEMESTER OR TERM PROJECTS

1. Study the electronic data information system in your state and show how it links with NCIC in Washington, D.C. to give local police departments access to nationwide information in a matter of minutes.
2. Study the feasibility of your police department's using videotape and closed-circuit television and prepare a report of your findings.

REFERENCES

ADAMS, THOMAS F., *Training Officers' Handbook*. Springfield, Ill.: Charles C Thomas, Publisher, 1964, Chap. 5.

Federal Communications Commission Rules and Regulations.

Los Angeles Police Department, *Daily Training Bulletins*, Vol. I. Springfield, Ill.: Charles C Thomas, Publisher, 1954, Chap. 9.

————, *Daily Training Bulletins*, Vol. II. Springfield, Ill.: Charles C Thomas, Publisher, 1958, Chap. 25.

Los Angeles Sheriff's Department, *Communication Procedure* (Daily Training Bulletins 1 through 8), Vol. 1. Los Angeles: Los Angeles Sheriff's Department, n.d.

WILSON, O. W., Police Administration, 2nd ed. New York: McGraw-Hill Book Company, 1963, Chap. 18.

Observation

and

Perception

CHAPTER FOUR "As unreliable as an eyewitness" may well express a viewpoint of many experienced police officers who have had to rely entirely upon eyewitnesses to identify and locate some of the suspects in crimes the officers were assigned to investigate. Most people are not trained observers. They observe many people they encounter without actually perceiving their physical characteristics and other traits. If the observer likes or dislikes, or recognizes something in what he sees, he is more apt to be able to describe that object than if it has no meaning to him at the time of perception. One of the most important aspects of seeking accurate identifications by imperfect witnesses is to capitalize on those imperfections and seek descriptions that will more closely describe what it is that the officer must look for on the basis of those descriptions.

On several occasions I have had the opportunity in the classroom to experiment with descriptions, and I have been involved in investigating cases critically involving personal identifications. Following are some examples of those experiences.

One day during a patrol and observation class at the police academy, attended by about 40 new officers, a man from my office in street clothing and a very attractive young woman came into the classroom to visit the instructor. They were in the room during the break, and continued visiting with the instructor while the student officers filed into the classroom past the place where all three (instructor, man, and attractive woman) were standing. The officers were instructed to take their seats while the conversation continued for about another two minutes. The plainclothes officer and the attractive woman then left the room. Many sets of eyes followed her while she and her companion took the long way out of the room. Immediately after their departure, the instructor said: "O.K., gentlemen, take out a clean sheet of paper and write a complete description of the man and woman who just left the room." One almost immediate, humorous retort was, "What man?"

The officers all individually wrote out complete descriptions (complete as best they remembered the subjects, that is) of their subjects. Actually the officer was male, Caucasian, about 24, 5'10", 175 lbs., dark brown wavy hair, blue eyes, and medium complexion. The woman was female, Caucasian, 23, 5'3", about 125 lbs., medium brown hair, blue eyes, and fair complexion. From their written descriptions we attempted to make a composite set of descriptions on the chalkboard. The members of the class only vaguely remembered the officer, and about the only thing they all agreed on was that he was male Caucasian. Their estimates of his age ranged from 20 to 40, and their guesses as to height varied from 5'8" to 6'3". They described his hair as being several colors, and almost to a man, called his complexion ruddy. No one had any idea of his eye color.

Our young lady was defined in several superlatives that would be more appropriate in the locker room than in a patrol text. She was described as female, Caucasian, from 17 to 22 years of age. Her height was guessed at 5'1" to 5'5", weight from 110 to 130 lbs., and her combination of height and weight were again described in superlatives by some of our student-officers, in approximate "bathing beauty" measurements by some of the others. Her hair and eye color were described as being several colors of the spectrum, and her skin color was described as fair. The descriptions of the young lady were far more descriptive than those of the man, who had spent the same amount of time in front of the class.

Clothing and accessory descriptions were vague, but the students were able to give better descriptions of the man's suit and tie than of the young lady's dress. They were fairly accurate as to *how* she wore it, but their descriptions of the dress itself would have been more accurate if she had been wearing a flour sack. The instructor made liberal use of suggestions to "help" the students in their descriptions, and met with an unusual degree of success in gaining agreement that the man was wearing a sport coat and slacks rather than a business suit, and various items of jewelry such as a tie pin (actually none), lapel pin (none) and wrist watch with silver band (actually black leather). The woman wore no jewelry, but the class agreed with the instructor that she was wearing earrings, a pin on her dress, and a bracelet. Their guesses, they explained during the later discussion, were based upon what they thought a girl who looked like her would wear.

Situation Two: Actual Case

One December morning several investigators brought copies of a report to the polygraph examiner and requested that he subject a particular individual to an examination. The problem was that there had been a series of street "muggings" and molestations of women of all ages occurring in the downtown area along the dark side streets of the city. In all cases, the attacks had been made on women who had been shopping and were leaving the stores at nighttime en route to their cars. In each case, the suspect would approach the woman, walk past her, turn just as she had passed, then ask a question, such as, "Do you know what time it is?" As the woman would turn, the culprit would strike her along the side of the head, knocking her senseless, but not entirely unconscious. The culprit would then grab the woman's purse, extract valuables and the wallet, take whatever merchandise the woman had been carrying, then run. In about three of the nine cases, the culprit also sexually abused the woman in addition to committing the acts of theft and assault.

The investigators working the case recognized the method of operation ("MO" or "modus operandi") as being quite similar to that of one subject they had encountered some months earlier, who had been convicted. He was out on probation at the time and the investigators checked into his activities on the dates when the crimes were committed. The suspect looked "good," but they had no evidence to connect him with the case. They secured a recent jail photograph of the subject. Taking about a dozen similar photographs of other persons together with the photograph of their suspect, the officers individually contacted their victims. Of the five or six they contacted, only three were able to give even an approximate description. When handed the dozen "mug" photos, each of the three victims stated something to the effect that one of the photos looked like the man who had attacked them. All three women picked out the photograph of the individual the investigators believed to be their best suspect. The three identifications made by the women separately, without knowing that the other two had made similar choices, led the investigators to believe that they now had more of a case against their suspect.

Armed now with tentative identification of their suspect, the investigators brought him in for questioning. He freely discussed his actions of about a year earlier, stating that he had been convicted for one count of forcible rape, but he adamantly denied any involvement in the current series of crimes for which he was now under suspicion. He was prepared for a lineup. The investigators collected several other persons from a variety of sources to stand in the lineup with their now number one suspect. The lineup procedure was fair. The subject chose his own place in a line with several other subjects, and in all respects it was handled in an objective manner. The three victims were asked to make individual identifications and not to talk to each other about their decison. Then each of the three victims separately pointed out the suspect to the officers. At this point one has to be very cautious about a lineup identification. The question must be asked: Did the victim identify the suspect from the scene of the crime, or did she merely recognize him from his photograph, which *resembled* the suspect?

With their suspicions reinforced by the photo identification and the lineup, but still lacking tangible evidence, the investigators continued their investigation. During their questioning of the suspect, he denied his guilt, but refused to discuss his whereabouts on the nights when the crimes occurred. Finally, after one questioning session, the suspect said, "All right. If you want me to confess to your crime, I will if it will make you happy. But I didn't do it." The officers did not want it this way. They had to be convinced that he did commit the crime, and there was some doubt. By now, of course, the three victims were convinced that the officers had located the right suspect and they demanded that he be brought to trial, stating vehemently that they would testify to get such an evil person placed in prison where he belonged.

The investigators brought the case to the polygraph examiner. They wanted to determine in their own mind whether their suspect had committed the crime. The polygraph examiner accepted the case. During his pre-test interview with the suspect, the man confessed to an atrocious type of crime that he had repeatedly committed with his sister from childhood until about four years previous to the time of his examination. The statute of limitations had run out on the case, and it had occurred in another state. He told the polygraph examiner that perhaps if he were able to be judged guilty and punished for the rape of those three women, his sentence might be his punishment for committing incest with his sister. Of course, the examiner pointed out to him that this was legally impossible and stressed that it would be unethical to settle a case in this manner. He explained that the suspect had been arrested for some specific offenses and that the polygraph examination was to help determine his truthfulness about those cases in point. The subject was allowed sufficient time to recover from the trauma of confessing about his earlier crimes, then he underwent the polygraph exam. His charts showed "no deception." The examiner's opinion was that he had not lied about his innocence of the crimes for which he had been arrested.

The investigators were advised of the polygraph examination results. Their investigation to date led them to believe that perhaps the polygraph examiner had made a mistake. Their eyewitnesses were more positive than ever now and they wanted to go to trial. They went to trial. The suspect was charged with armed robbery and forcible rape. The jury acquitted him and he went free.

There was an end to this story. Eleven months later, the same type of crimes started occurring again. The locations were the same. The modus operandi and description of the suspect were the same. Officers maintained a "stake-out" and apprehended the subject in this new series of crimes. He was not the same man that had been arrested the previous year, but there was an uncanny similarity in their appearances. The only differences were in their ages (about four years) and their heights (about six inches). While the suspect was being interviewed, he confessed to the crime for which he had been apprehended, but added that he might as well clear up the crimes that he had committed the previous year for which he had avoided apprehension. He was subjected to a series of polygraph examinations. The man's responsibility for the earlier crimes was verified by the polygraph, another look by the victims (who apologized for their earlier mistake), and conclusive evidence that he had committed the crimes. It took 11 months to clear an innocent man who had been *positively identified* as the criminal by *three eyewitnesses*.

Keeping these cases in mind, consider the problems involved in observation and description. You must make every effort to separate fact from fantasy, and to put a witnesses' testimony in perspective.

BASIC REQUIREMENTS OF A WITNESS

Three facts must be determined about an eyewitness when considering the information he has to offer.

First, the witness must have been present. "Presence" may be defined for the purpose of this discussion as being at a place of vantage to gain knowledge of a particular fact through perception with one or more of the senses: sight, sound, taste, smell, touch. Some witnesses have been considered "present" when they have (a) observed a game law violation through binoculars in which the offense occurred across a ravine several miles of walking distance away, (b) smelled marijuana smoke through the cracks in a locked door, (c) heard voices in a bookmaking operation through a thin wall, (d) heard lewd remarks by an individual who was telephoning from several miles across town, (e) felt something that was wet or cold, (f) tasted something that was bitter, and (g) saw a murder committed in the same room. All qualify for presence, and the annals of the courts abound with similar examples.

Second, the witness must have been conscious of what he is expected to have perceived. In other words, he must have been actually aware of the event he was supposed to have perceived. An individual may be present in the same room as an old friend and frequently look in the friend's general direction, yet never actually be conscious of the friend's presence because of his own occupation or preoccupation with some other phenomenon he is observing. Two officers may have been sitting in a patrol car parked near an intersection when one officer said: "Say, did you see that violation? That yellow Oldsmobile went through the stop sign." The second officer may have looked up immediately and seen the yellow Oldsmobile traveling east across the boulevard. Only one element is missing: he did not see the actual violation at the moment it occurred and he cannot testify to that fact. He can, however, testify to the identify of the driver of the car and all other circumstances surrounding the pursuit and citation, providing he perceives all of the rest of the activity.

Third, the witness must have been attentive at the time he observed the event about which he is testifying. To have been present and to have seen something may not be sufficient for an individual to actually have been cognizant of what took place. A witness may actually observe a man holding a revolver up to another man's chest during the commission of an armed robbery and be so inattentive that the action seems to him to be some form of friendly play among friends. When asked about the event, the man who observed the crime may respond, "Yes, I saw it, but I wasn't aware of what was going on." As described earlier in this chapter, the police students who observed the man and the attractive young woman in the classroom, were certainly not attentive to everything they saw.

FACTORS IN PERCEPTION

When considering the perceptive faculties of a witness, many factors must be taken into account. These may be divided into two broad categories: (1) external factors and (2) internal factors.

External Factors

DISTANCE, OR PROXIMITY. The closer an object or event is to the observer, the greater likelihood there is that he will direct some of

his attention toward it. Something that occurs nearby more directly
involves him than something that may occur in a remote location.

PHENOMENA THAT MAY AFFECT PERCEPTION, SUCH AS DIFFERENCES
IN LIGHTING, VARIOUS WEATHER CONDITIONS, AND SOUNDS. The eyes
function differently under different lighting conditions through the
medium of the cones or the rods, and colors appear quite differently
under different kinds of light. Some people are night blind. Artificial
lighting in darkness causes shadows, which may appreciably affect an
individual's powers of perception. Rain, snow, wind, and fog may cause
a significant difference in an individual's perceptive abilities. Distortions
of vision are not unusual. Noises directly affect one's perception. Loud
and unusual noises may cause distractions that divert the observer's attention completely away from an object he may be looking at. An event
may be meaningless without sound, but pleasant or frightening with
the appropriate sounds. For an example of this phenomenon, watch a
"thriller" motion picture on television with the sound off, then turn
it on and compare your reactions. Certain illusions also occur when
color is introduced. For example, compare a red object with a blue
object of the same size. The blue object will appear smaller. The
object that makes more noise will appear larger. An object speeding
toward the observer will appear larger than the same object speeding
away from him.

INTENSITY AND SIZE. If something is louder and larger than other
things about it, it will receive the attention of observers more rapidly
and with greater intensity than the things around it.

CONTRAST. Something unusual or out of the ordinary will receive
more attention than common or ordinary things. For example, the
golfer in a funeral home will receive about as much attention as the
tuxedoed undertaker on the golf course.

REPETITION. An individual or object that appears—under certain
conditions—more than one time will attract much more attention than
if he or it appears only once. This factor is probably one of the reasons why an individual who appears to be loitering attracts more
attention than the individual who seems to be moving with a purpose
and a destination.

MOVEMENT. A stationary object will soon appear as if it belongs
where it is and will blend in even with contrasting objects. The moving
object attracts and holds the attention. For example, consider the
attention that a running man on a downtown street receives as opposed
to all of the other walking men.

SIMILARITIES. A woman who looks like Cousin Dalmation is likely
to receive more attention than one who is completely strange. For
example, when a witness with missing teeth observes a suspect with
missing teeth, that characteristic will probably be the most outstanding one the witness will remember having noticed.

PERSONAL CHARACTERISTICS ABOUT THE WITNESS. The individual's perceptive abilities depend on his physical condition. Eyesight is one sense that is relied upon most heavily, and the individual's capabilities with respect to acuity and perception should be the subject of inquiry. Some people should wear corrective lenses but do not for reasons of vanity, as in the following case when an identification depended entirely upon the single eyewitness.

One evening after dark, the witness arrived home and was walking along the corridor of the semidark apartment house approaching his front door. At that particular moment a form that appeared to be a man pushed past the witness and hastily departed down the corridor and down the stairs. The witness only glanced at him for a moment, commenting to himself about the rudeness of some people. As he started to enter his apartment, the lady from the apartment across the hall screamed that someone had been attempting to break down her door. She did not see the culprit.

The witness was the only person who saw the suspect. The woman called the police department and reported the attempted entry, and the gentleman witness described the suspect. Shortly thereafter a young man was stopped for questioning in the neighborhood and he was invited to return to the scene of the crime for a possible elimination as a suspect. The witness looked at the young man and stated that he could not be sure, but that there was a strong resemblance to the suspect he had seen in the hallway. The young man's name and address were recorded and he was allowed to continue whatever he was doing. Two days later, an investigator contacted the same witness and asked him to look at some photographs of suspects. He replied that he would be glad to, then took out a pair of glasses with lenses that were as thick as coke bottle bottoms, indicating an obvious case of myopia. The man could not help with the identification. The investigator asked him if he had an eyesight problem, and he replied, "Oh, yes, I'm blind without my glasses." The investigator asked him if he had been wearing them on the night of the crime, and he replied, "No, I never wear them when I'm driving. I usually leave them home."

Although the case just cited is unusual, there are many degrees of disability that people experience and do not talk about. Some people have no night or peripheral vision, some are color blind, and others have difficulty with depth perception. People who are tone deaf cannot hear some sounds, and even someone who hears well can have his perception of sounds to which he is listening altered by distracting noises. Taste, touch, and smell are similarly affected.

EMOTIONAL AND PSYCHOLOGICAL CONSIDERATIONS. Under various types of stress, people react differently than when they are in complete control of their faculties in a relaxed state. Some senses may be

sharpened by the increased state of agitation of the body functions,
and others may be rendered ineffective because of preoccupation with
a single incident, such as a suspect pointing a gun at the victim.
Exaggeration and elaboration are commonplace. A revolver pointed at
the face may actually be a .22 automatic, but take on the appearance
of a .45 automatic. A boisterous and belligerent attacker may appear
to be taller and heavier than he actually is. A crowd of five may appear
more like 25.

The personal drives of sex, hunger, and comfort may actually play
a part in a witness's perception, as indicated by some events that seem
to occur at various times which are described in minute detail. For
example, a man who has just eaten a meal may not remember any
food odors, while a hungry man may recall them precisely.

Some people who suffer from handicaps such as a malformed or
missing finger, harelip, missing teeth, or some congenital birth defect,
are naturally more sensitive to similar problems experienced by others
and would be better qualified to describe such irregularities. Personal interests in occupations and hobbies stimulate greater attention
in objects and events that may be peculiar to those particular interests.

EXPERIENCE AND EDUCATION. The witness's conditioning to certain
observation experiences through learning help him to perceive, remember, and communicate his observations and impressions. Conversely, his lack of experience or training may cause problems in communications, such as difficulty in interpreting what he sees into meaningful symbols and expressions. There may be a language barrier.

PREJUDICE OR BIAS. Most people tend to see what they want to
see. Strong feelings toward or against an object tend to influence the
amount of attention one pays to any particular event or object. In his
role as the collector of information from the witnesses, the officer's
task is not to change such attitudes, but to be aware of them and their
effect on the ability of the witnesses to recount a reasonably accurate
and objective picture of what actually took place.

POINT OF VIEW. When considering the statements of witnesses,
ask yourself this question: Could they actually have observed what
they purport to have seen from their respective vantage points? Some
well-meaning people may actually be lacking bits of information and
will sometimes fill in the gaps with what they *believe* happened rather
than what they *saw*. All people see things through different sets of
eyes and experiences, interpret with different combinations of interpretation processes, and then communicate differently using their own
unique methods of conveying thoughts and ideas. The police officer's
function is to coordinate all of these bits of information and interpret
them into terms that are meaningful to his superiors, to the prosecuting
attorney, and to the courts in order to assure the accused of due
process of the law.

DESCRIPTIONS OF PERSONS

Standard formats have been established and are in general use for the purpose of communicating brief but accurate messages regarding descriptions of people and property. When asking a witness to describe an individual, it is usually a good procedure to ask him to first describe something about the suspect that "stood out," or to recall some similarity between the suspect and anyone that the witness knows. This technique calls into play the witness's ability to recognize objects that are familiar. After he has recalled the familiar features, go back and obtain as much detailed description as possible, using the following format.

1. Name, if known. Include the nickname, or "monicker." List also all aliases, or "aka" (also known as). Include first, middle, last name, plus any additional designation, such as junior or III.
2. Sex.
3. Race and nationality descent, if known. "W" for Caucasian, "N" for Negro, "O" for Oriental. Except when representatives of other racial origins are indigenous to the area, spell out the origin to avoid misunderstanding. The nationality descent tends to reduce the field of suspects by identifying hair and eye color and certain similarities in facial features, and it should be used when known.
4. Age. Either an estimate or exact age, if known. If such information is available, list date of birth.
5. Height. Exact, if known. A male suspect is short if he is less than 5'6", medium if 5'6" to 5'10", and tall if over 5'10". Women are proportionately less: short if less than 5'2", medium if 5'2" to 5'6", and tall if over 5'6". Victims and witnesses will usually overestimate height.
6. Weight. Men are light up to about 150 lbs., medium if from 150 to 180 lbs., and heavy if over 180 lbs. The weight and height ratio largely determines the body build. Women are similarly classified. In addition to the approximate weight, indicate whether "slim," "stocky," or other general build.
7. Hair. Color, type of hair style, length, and any baldness.
8. Eyes. Color, shape if other than Caucasian configuration, and any distinctive characteristics.
9. Complexion. Color and shade, plus any other characteristics, such as freckles, pockmarks, acne, birthmarks, blotches, suntan or burn, skin grafts.
10. All other features and accessories. Describe facial hair and sideburns, unusual shape or appearance of some facial feature, any disfigurement, scars, marks, or visible tattoos. Include any unusual characteristics about any other visible part of the body.
11. Eyeglasses and jewelry, if any. Although eyeglasses may be worn as a partial disguise, the wearer may be required to wear them. Look for any distinctive characteristic about them, such as extra thickness or unusual appearance caused by the way they are ground.
12. Clothing worn. Start at the top and work down in the following

order: headgear, shirt, tie, jacket, coat, dress or trousers, shoes and socks. Include style, color, material, and any characteristics that will identify the clothing article. On headgear, indicate whether it is a hat, cap, uniform cap, helmet, beret, or mantilla. The necktie is usually most distinctive and the shape, style, design, and colors should all be described. The shirt should be described by color and style, such as sport, dress, uniform, and the material should be given if it can be determined. On the coat and trousers, or dress, describe the material, design, and the colors. Sweaters or other overwear are quite distinctive and can often be described in detail. Shoe style and color should be indicated, if known, also any heel pattern, if known, for possible surface prints.

13. Personal characteristics. Anything about the subject that will tend to distinguish him from any other person should be listed, such as a speech impediment or accent, or a distinctive tonal quality or pitch of the voice. Note any habits or unconscious movements he may be making, such as twitching, chewing fingernails, scratching the face, cracking knuckles, whistling, making unusual sounds with the teeth, picking at any part of the body or clothing, and generally any other observation about the individual that would aid in later identifying him.

IDENTIFICATION BY MEANS OF A PHOTOGRAPH AND LINEUP

Identification of a suspect by means of an eyewitness may be the only means possible, or it may tend to corroborate other information and physical evidence. It is a method frequently employed by police officers. To be certain that your use of this means of identification will withstand any test of validity, adhere to the following guidelines which have met U.S. Supreme Court requirements.[1]

1. Each witness should view the photographs alone or under circumstances such that other witnesses will not be influenced or open to suggestion.

2. The officer should explain to the witness that:

(a) . . . the fact that a photograph is shown to him should not influence the witness's judgment.

(b) . . . the witness should not conclude or guess that the photographs contain the picture of the person who committed the crime.

(c) . . . there is no obligation to identify anyone.

(d) . . . it is as important to exonerate the innocent as it is to identify a suspect, not only to prevent miscarriages of justice, but also to help the police find the true criminal.

3. The photographs shown to the witness should be selected to insure fairness and impartiality to the suspect.

[1] See Wade vs. U.S., 358, U.S. 257 (1966).

4. The fairness and impartiality of identification by photographs depends upon the circumstances. As much as practicable, photographs should be selected using guidelines similar to those involved in the selection of persons appearing in a formal lineup. Similarity of features of the suspect(s) and other persons appearing in the photographs, inclusion of photographs showing persons other than the suspect(s), and similarity of the type of photographs shown are all important. For example, if a picture of the suspect is shown to the witness, pictures of persons having similar features should also be shown; if a group photograph showing the suspect is used, there should be several similar group photographs used. What is a fair and impartial selection of photographs depends upon the reasonable availability to police of photographs which would lessen the risk of misidentification.

5. Any photographs shown to witnesses as part of a procedure should be retained for any subsequent criminal proceedings.

6. A lineup should be conducted pursuant to departmental regulations or policies (consistent with Supreme Court rules as to right of counsel) after the suspect has been apprehended and placed in custody. If a witness who has made a pre-custody identification by means of photographs appears for the lineup, he should be advised that he should try not to be influenced by his identification by means of photograph, and that he should not assume that any person to be shown in the lineup is necessarily the same person he identified by means of photograph or the same person who committed the crime.

7. When there are several witnesses, only one or two witnesses should view the photographs and the rest should be "saved" for the formal lineup. This procedure must be at the discretion of the officer in charge, as such a "saving" may not be advisable for the specific case under investigation.

8. When the suspect is in custody, identification by photograph should not be made if a formal lineup is possible. If the suspect, for whatever reason, refuses to cooperate in the conduct of the lineup, he should be advised that his failure to do so can be used as evidence against him and that the legality of the lineup can be decided by a judge if the case goes to court. If he still refuses (or is instructed to refuse by an attorney) to cooperate, identification by photograph would be permissible because a fair and impartial lineup is impossible unless a suspect cooperates. The fairness and impartiality of identification by photographs will be more closely scrutinized by the courts in the case of a suspect in custody. In no case should lineup witnesses be shown photographs of the suspect after the lineup.

STANDARD FORMULA FOR DESCRIBING PROPERTY

Many people in law enforcement and its related agencies have devoted considerable time and effort to developing a uniform method for describing property. The following material represents some of their work toward establishing such uniformity. For maximum results in the effort to return stolen property to its owner, the formula presented here should be followed as closely as possible when preparing reports, teletypes, and in any other way describing lost, stolen, pawned, purchased, or sold property.

A. Number of the Article in the List.

In each itemized list, use a numbering system to facilitate references to a specific item for teletypes or correspondence.

B. Quantity of the Article.

Example: 1. (3) watches . . .
2. (1) television set . . .

C. Kind of Article.

1. Watch (or ring, or tire, or . . .).
2. For whom or for what purpose the article is designed.

Example: watch, man's (or woman's, or child's)
saw, keyhole
tire, bicycle

3. Trade name and manufacturer.

D. Identifying Serial and Model Numbers.

E. Material or Type of Metal.

Example: Yellow metal. Indicate the kind of metal claimed by the victim, such as "WM, platinum claimed." The officer's report does not verify the actual material or its value. His report merely reflects the claims and statements of the victim.

1. Gold.
Solid gold is 24 carat gold. Carat, when used to describe gold, is a unit of quality. In 24 carats of gold, there are 24 grains of gold to the pennyweight.
Filled gold and *rolled gold* are both veneers of gold on a base metal. The processes involved in applying the gold are the same, however, the gold used on a filled gold article is of greater carat value than that used on a rolled gold article. A filled gold article has gold of .03 carat or more, and a rolled gold article has gold of .015 to .03 carat.
Gold-plated or *gold-washed* articles are electroplated with gold of below .015 carat value.

2. Other metals or minerals.
In the case of jewels, follow the same procedure: Red Stone, Green Stone. Indicate the kind of stone claimed by the victim. Diamonds are designated as white stones.

3. Other materials.

It is necessary to question the victim closely in order to get the correct material.

"Silk" may be rayon, bemberg, taffeta, pongee, shantung, satin, crepe, or nylon.

"Leather" may be artificial leatherette, cowhide, horsehide, sealskin, ostrich, alligator, snakeskin, calfskin, or a number of others.

"Wool" may be all wool, half wool, virgin wool, or reclaimed wool.

F. Physical Description.

1. Model, size, shape, color, pattern, measurements, style.

A picture of the article from a catalog or from advertising material is useful.

A sketch of the article may be drawn by the victim.

Clothing size may be determined from the owner's height, weight, and build.

2. Identifying marks.

These include initials, marks put on by the owner, dents, scratches, and damage repairs.

In the case of watches when the numbers are known to the owner, find out what jeweler last repaired the watch. If it has never been repaired, find out where and when it was purchased and whether it was bought on credit. Every jeweler keeps a record book of the work he has done. In the book will be found the date the work was done, a description of the watch, the owner's name and address, the watch case and movement numbers, and the jeweler's own number. If the watch has never been repaired, the dealer may have a record of its sale.

Flat silver, or table silver, has a pattern name. Specify which company made the set, since there are duplications of names among the various lines. List whether the set is sterling or plate. If the silver was in a chest or box, include a complete description of it as well.

Silver services, silver dishes, and silver trays have a number on the bottom and usually a hallmark or trademark. Their patterns will also have a name.

Expensive jewelry will often have a jeweler's scratch mark.

G. Age and Condition.

1. When purchased, whether new or used when purchased.
2. State of repair.
3. Shabby, dirty, worn, mended, patched, clean, new, etc.

H. Market Value.

The current market value should be determined by an expert in the values of the specific items stolen. The value may distinguish the difference between petty or grand theft.

ORDER FOR LISTING ITEMS IN THE REPORT

1. Articles bearing numbers.
2. Articles bearing initials or personal marks.
3. Articles bearing identifying marks.
4. Articles bearing identifying characteristics.
5. Articles without market value.

DETAILED DESCRIPTIONS OF COMMONLY STOLEN ITEMS

A. Jewelry.

1. Novelty jewelry.
   Figures, charms, scatterpins, bracelets, necklaces, rings, etc.
   Of little value, usually gaudy and set with cheap rhinestones of various colors.

2. Costume jewelry.
   Generally the same as for costume jewelry except that the material and workmanship are better and the value is somewhat greater.

3. Jewelry as such.
   Pins.
   > Kinds: Breastpins or brooches.
   > Lapel pins.
   > Scatterpins.

   Clips.
   > Same as for pins, but clip-on rather than pin-on. May be in sets with earrings, necklaces, and/or bracelets.

   Earrings.
   > Kinds: Clip.
   > Screw.
   > Hoop.
   > Latter two may be for pierced ears.
   > Styles: Teardrop.
   > Dangle.
   > Petal.
   > Button.
   > Novelty.

   Cuff buttons, cuff links, and studs.
   > Note difference between cuff links and cuff buttons.

   Necklaces.
   > Kinds: Chain (size and design of links).
   > Snake.

Lariat.

Pearl (simulated, cultured, seed).

Crystal (artificial, tin cut, rock).

Stones (artificial, synthetic, genuine).

Note number of stones and space between stones.

Number of strands and length.

Knotted.

Choker.

Lavalieres (on necklace).

Lockets.

On chain, fob, pin, or bracelet.

Bracelets.

Kinds: Expansion.

Link.

Bangle.

Settings.

How mounted.

Distance between sets.

Number of sets.

Kind and color of sets.

Rings.

Parts: shank, mounting, and set.

Size.

Engraving.

Outside and inside.

Trademark and carat designation inside.

Scratch marks.

Kinds:

Man's, woman's, baby's.

Emblem (lodge, fraternity, class, school).

Signet (initials and type of letters).

Dinner rings.

Number, kind, and size of settings.

Baguettes, chip and cut stones.

Ornamental colored stones.

Wedding rings.

Width, engraving inside and out.

Styles: Diamond (how many, size and spacing).

Antique.

Modern.

Unusual (chain or two that fit together).

Mountings.

Belcher: an old-type mounting, 8 to 12 prongs, deeply scalloped.

Bezel: may extend all around or be on corners or sides only.

Gypsy: set directly into ring with bezel.

Tiffany: set high on 6 or 8 prongs. Named after jeweler who
designed it.

Claw: any prong set other than tiffany.

Basket: filigree work around the stone.

Diamonds.

Color.

Shapes and cuts.

Size has no bearing; may be small, decorative, or the large main stone.

Facets.

58 on brilliant, round full cut, emerald cut marquise.

24 to 32 on Swiss cut.

18 on single cut.

Chips.

Just what the name implies.

Used for decoration.

Cameos and intaglios.

Cameo is a carved, raised figure, usually a head; intaglio is a figure carved *into* a stone.

Cameos and intaglios are used in earrings, pins, fobs and cuff links, as well as in rings.

Birthstones and other colored stones.

Garnet, amethyst, bloodstone, aquamarine, emerald, moonstone, ruby.

May be genuine, synthetic, or artificial.

B. Clothing.

1. Suits.

Men's and women's.

Women's tailored suits and coats have the same general identifying characteristics as men's suits and overcoats. The word "tailored," when applied to any article of women's wear, means plain, or without decoration. Men's suits come in three lengths—short, medium, and long—plus a size number. For instance, size 40 will be found in short, medium, and long.

Color and material.

Be as exact in color as possible.

Get a description of any pattern in the weave.

Whipcord, serge, gabardine, flannel, tweed, broadcloth. Most other materials are known as worsted.

Labels.

Manufacturer's inside of inside coat pocket.

Retailer's outside of inside coat pocket or at nape of neck.

In women's suits and coats, the labels may be any place, so the location would be an identifying feature if it was out of the ordinary. Women's skirts sometimes have labels also.

Tailor-made frequently has the owner's name or initials on the inner coat pocket. Also, many tailors and furriers have the customer sign the inner lining of the coat near the front; it is necessary to loosen the lining to see the name.

Coats (suit coats, overcoats, topcoats).

There is a difference between a coat and a jacket. Retailers have fallen into the habit of advertising sport coats as sport "jackets." The difference between a coat and a jacket is that the latter is of waist length. Casual or leisure coats are also erroneously referred to as jackets.

Single or double breasted.

Number of buttons.

Lapels.

Peaked, semi-peaked, and notched. Wing on women's coats.

Cardigan (on men's sport coats and women's suit and top coats).

Shawl (on tuxedos).

Button holes in one or both lapels.

Pockets.

Patch or inset. With or without flaps, or piped.

Extra cash pocket.

Number and locations of inside pockets.

Lining.

Color and type of material.

Full-, half-, or quarter-lined.

Back.

Box (with or without seam).

Conservative (slightly formfitting).

Formfitting (pronounced form fit).

Drape (extremely formfitting).

Lounge (hangs from shoulders to hips, where it is snug. Wedge-shaped, not formfitting at waist).

Sport back (half belt with pleats; may or may not have "free swing" or vent. May have two vents).

Stitched or welted edge.

Trousers, men's and women's slacks.

Men's trousers and women's tailored slacks, in many cases, are similar even to the front fly.

Waistband.

Regular, with waistband and belt loops at the top.

Drop belt loops, with waistband and belt loops, one end of loop on waistband and the other end below.

French waistband, with no visible waistband and belt loops below top of trousers.

Extended waistband, with waistband continued beyond fly and buttoned.

Cuff (or none).

Pleats (number and whether turned in or out).

Men's overcoats, women's tailored topcoats.

Same as suit coats as far as lapels, pockets, linings, single and double breasted are concerned, but with the following additions:

Slash pockets.

Collar (wing lapels, cardigan).

Sleeves.
    Split.
    Cuff (adjustable cuff tabs).
    Leg-of-mutton (women's only) fitted to elbow or all the
        way. 1' length of sleeves, i.e., short, elbow, ¾, or long.
Trim (women's only).
    Different material or color from rest of coat, or fur.
    Collar, cuffs, bottom, tuxedo.
    Pleats, front or back.
Length.
    Rarely important in men's coats; however, women's coats
        come in: full, ¾, fingertip, shortie, jacket, and cape.
Fit.
    Wrap-around in both men's and women's.
    Flared, in women's only.
    Full, or "new look," in women's only.
Fly front.
Vent.
Removable lining, zipper or button.
Reversible.
Raglan shoulders.
    Hang from shoulders. Usually have split sleeves and slash
        pockets.
Chesterfield.

2. Women's clothes generally.
    Size.
    Labels.
    Material.
        Kind.
        Color (figured, colors and design of figure).
    Trim.
        Color.
        Buttons.
        Braid or piping.
        Embroidery or cut work.
    Skirts.
        May be part of a suit.
        Length.
        Fit (flared, full, or tailored).
        Slashed or slitted (location and length of slit).
        Pockets.
        Number of panels or gores.

3. Jackets, men's. Waist-length coats. Although a type of man's coat
    is advertised as a sport jacket, for the purpose of description of
    property, it should be referred to as a sport coat.
    Size.
    Material.
        Gabardine, melton, leather (kind).
        Color and design of weave.

Pockets.
  Number (inside and outside).
  Kind.
    Slash, inset, patch, muff type, flap.
    Fastenings (zipper and button).
Front fastenings (zipper or button).
Collar.
  Knitted, also cuffs as in leather jackets.
  Fur, pile.
  Lapels.
  Detachable.
  Parka hood.
Lining.
  Color.
  Rayon, quilted, sheepskin, blanket.
Back.
  Plain, half-belt, swing shoulders.

4. Sweaters.
   Kind.
     Man's, woman's, child's (size).
     Coat (button or zipper).
     Pull-over.
     Neck (crew neck, turtle neck, V-neck, roll collar).
     Sleeve or sleeveless.

5. Furs. Furs are hard to recover because their appearance can be
   easily altered. It is necessary to get as complete a description of
   the piece as possible. Furs are seldom pawned; they are more
   often sold in the street, in bars, in houses of prostitution, or flown
   to another part of the country to be sold on consignment.
   Kind.
     Generally the name of the animal, but may have a more exotic
     name to correspond with the price.
   Color (dyed or natural).
   Lining.
     Material: dull or shiny, color, bindings or pockets.
     Pockets.
     Labels.
     Wear and repairs.
   If custom-made or if ever repaired, the owner might have written
     her name on reverse of skin.
   Length.
     Measured from bottom of collar down back.
     ¾, fingertip, chubby.
   Fasteners.
     Frogs (size).
     Hook and eye (size).
     Buttons (kind and size).
     Snaps (number and size).

If a neckpiece, number of skins.
    Heads and/or tails sewn on.
    Fasteners.
Any repairs, and what furrier used.

6. Hosiery.
    Kind.
        Brand-new or used.
        Full-fashioned or circular knit (show difference between full-
            fashioned and circular knit).
    Material.
        Silk, nylon, rayon, silk and wool, wool.
    Size.
        Foot size.
        Length.
    Weight.
        Sheer, medium weight, service weight.
        Run-proof weave (denier, or gauge).
    Color (clocks or heel decoration).
    Cotton tops and/or feet.

7. Men's shirts.
    Color, pattern, brand, collar style.
    With or without collars.
    Size.
        Collar and sleeve length.
        Sport shirts come in small, medium, and large.
    Kind: sport, dress, work, cowboy.
    Material.
        Cotton, wool, rayon, rayon-gabardine, nylon.
        Oxford weave.
    Buttons.
        Number on cuffs if more than one, as on cowboy shirts.
        Button-down collar.
        Number of buttons down front.
    Pockets
        Number.
        With or without flaps.
    Cuffs.
        Regular.
        For cuff links (both collar attached and without collar).
        French cuffs.

8. Handbags.
    Style. Women's handbags are of five basic styles: pouch, box,
        envelope, underarm, shoulder strap.
        Frame.
    Handles.
        Pannier and double pannier, cuff, wrist, plastic, chain.
    Fasteners.
        Zipper, turn lock, lift lock, snap lock.

Material.
    Leather.
        Patent leather, suede, sealskin, ostrich, calfskin, cowhide (any of which might be imitation).
        Plastic (may look like patent leather or enamel).
    Cloth.
        Corde, petit point, moire, knitted, metal mesh, etc.
    Reptile.
        Alligator, lizard, snake.
Inside.
    Lining (material and color).
    Label.
    Number of divisions.
    Attached or loose coin purse and/or mirror.
    Accessories (comb, lighter, lipstick, lipstick holder, address book).
Contents.
    Complete list.

C. Radios and Televisions.

Kind (portable, table model, etc.).
Brand.
Dials.
    Horizontal or vertical slot.
    Round.
    Slide.
    Half-circle.
Bands.
    AM, FM.
    Short wave.
Number of control knobs.
Color and material of case.
    Measurements.
Phonograph or stereo.
Television.
    Size of screen.
    Control knobs.
Description of case and cabinet.
Serial numbers (do not confuse with model numbers).
    On small radios, the serial number is usually inside, out of sight, and on the outside of the carton.

D. Tools. Tools are frequently the objects of theft. Since there are so many kinds, types, and manufacturers, it is necessary to depend upon the victim for details.

Private marks.
Damage.
Description of the chest or box if one was taken, and of the tools inside.

Serial numbers on certain tools.
Electrically operated tools.

E. Luggage.

Suitcases.
 Gladstone (suitcase-size bag that opens flat).
 Club bag (box bottom with top the apex of a triangle. Closed
  with zipper or locks).
 Two-suiter.
 Week-end case (may be fitted).
 Fortnighter (small trunk carried like a suitcase).
Describe inside.
 Lining and color.
 Number of partitions, pockets.
Material.
 Top grain cowhide, split cowhide, rawhide, plastic, canvas.
Handles and fasteners.
Trunks.
 Foot lockers (with or without tray).
 Steamer or wardrobe trunk (number of hangers, drawers).
 Box trunk.
  Describe material, inside, fasteners.
Brief cases and brief bags.
 Describe material.
 With or without straps.
 Single or double handles.
 Fasteners.
 Number of compartments.

F. Cameras. Two numbers appear on the more valuable cameras, one
 on the lens and one on the camera itself. Camera lenses are inter-
 changeable. Speed of the lens is important. Owner's description is
 usually dependable.

G. Binoculars.

Power and size. First number indicates power, and the second num-
  ber indicates the size of the lens in millimeters (8x30).
Type of focusing (central or single eye).
Hinged or solid bridge.
Barrels (length and covering material).
Coated lenses.
Carrying case.

H. Firearms.

Make, caliber, and serial number.
 Hidden numbers and parts' numbers.
 Foreign guns without serial numbers; they also have proofmarks
  as a rule.

Complete description.
Finish.
   Nickel-plated.
   Blue.
   Anodized.
   Rough or sandblasted.
Length of barrel.
Grips.
   Material and color.
Condition.
   Marks.
   Damage.
   Repairs.
   Signs of wear.
Loaded or unloaded.
Where and when purchased.

I. Musical Instruments.

Kind, make, and serial number.
   Pitch. Most wind instruments are made in varying pitch, e.g., saxophones are in C, E flat, B flat, tenor, and B flat baritone. Clarinets are in A, B flat, tenor, and bass. The same applies to many stringed instruments.
Finish.
   Brass, silver, or gold.
   Rough or sandblasted.
   Gold or brass with silver design or vice versa.
   Silver with gold bell.
Condition.
   Signs of wear.
   Dents and scratches.
Case.
   Complete description.
   Attachments and other articles in the case.
Where and when purchased.

EXERCISES AND STUDY QUESTIONS

1. After you have spent one session with your instructor, sit down and write a complete description of him. Compare your notes when you see him the next time.
2. How might you have handled the actual case of mistaken identity recounted in the first part of the chapter to avoid the result that the officers encountered?
3. What are the three basic requirements of a witness?
4. Describe *presence* as it refers to that of a witness?
5. List three of the external factors that influence perception.
6. List three of the internal factors that influence perception.

7. Describe the lineup procedure outlined in the text.
8. Using the recommended format, describe the wrist watch or some other item of jewelry you are wearing.
9. Using the recommended format, describe a suit of clothing that you own but are not wearing.
10. List the proper format for describing a revolver.

SUGGESTED SEMESTER OR TERM PROJECTS

1. For your department, set up a "mug book" type of file on various basic items of jewelry and jewelry designs for description purposes.
2. Establish a lineup procedure for use by your department.

REFERENCES

California Bureau of Criminal Identification and Investigation, *Modus Operandi and Crime Reporting*. Sacramento, Calif.: State Printing Office, 1955.

Los Angeles Police Department, *Daily Training Bulletins*, Vol. 1. Springfield, Ill.: Charles C Thomas, Publisher, 1954, Chap. 4.

Reporting

and

Records Utilization

INTRODUCTION

CHAPTER FIVE The novice often looks upon the preparation of reports and the maintenance of records as an unimportant part of the total police role. These tasks do not hold much interest for him. However, as experience creeps in, and as cases are won and lost in court, personal evaluations are discussed with superior officers, commendations for outstanding performance of duty are awarded, and reports are sent back for rewrite, the tremendously important part played by officer-prepared records becomes quite evident. They are vital to the continued efficiency of any police agency.

This chapter covers the subject of reporting and records maintenance in three parts. The purpose of this format is to emphasize the relative importance of each of the three parts with respect to the other two. Basic to all three sections is the premise that no police action is performed correctly unless the report accurately recounts such action exactly as it happened in clear, concise, and objective language. Part One deals with field notetaking. This is where it all begins.

Figure 5.1 Computers are a national adjunct to the police records system. Instant recall aids in clearing cases and, in some states, reduces the hazard factor for field officers. Courtesy of the Police Department, St. Louis, Missouri.

Accuracy at this stage will often set the tone for an entire investigation and will be the determining factor in the eventual success in prosecution. Part Two covers basic report writing techniques, including report dictation, which is actually the most logical method for recording reports. It also presents a series of forms that can be completed by checking the appropriate statements concerning routine calls that have been handled in accordance with standard operating procedures. Part Three, "Getting the Most Out of Records," is intended to stimulate the field patrol officer to do just that: get the most out of the police records system. It is a gold mine of information providing, of course, that it has been filled previously with "gold" as indicated in Parts One and Two in this chapter

SECTION ONE:
FIELD NOTETAKING AND CRIME SCENE RECORDING

INTRODUCTION

Of all the various types of notes the field officer makes regarding his day-to-day activities, the most important are his field notes. He is making them specifically for the purpose of compiling facts in the order in which they present themselves to him. As viewed by the observer at some later time, it is apparent that the officer making the notes has no reason, no desire to alter the notes in any appreciable way. They are likely to be highest on a credibility scale, if there were to be such a measuring device. It is probably for this reason that the rules of evidence provide that a witness may refer to notes while giving testimony if those notes were made by the witness himself or by someone under his direction at the time the fact being recorded was actually occurring, or was still fresh in the memory of the person recording it.

Field notes should be limited to names, addresses, and other pertinent data relevant to the identities of persons mentioned in reports and their relationships with the incident, and short succinct statements relating elements of the situation being recorded in the sequence as they occur and come to the attention of the recorder. Any opinions should be clearly explained and substantiated by facts, and kept to an absolute minimum. Departure from facts should occur only when inferences could be made by any other reasonable and prudent person with the same collection of information.

WHAT CONSTITUTES FIELD NOTES?

Field notes are actually the index to an officer's memory. They are generally limited to brief notations entered into some type of book, or a collection of notes on cards or papers habitually carried by the officer for the purpose of recording notes. They may include letters or diaries, log books, or complete reports prepared in the field as the officer completes the call. Principal characteristics of field notes are accuracy and proximity in time to the actual incidents recorded.

NOTETAKING

The officer's field notebook may be used for a general collection of notes concerning the many aspects of his job, such as new orders or policies emanating from the administrative sections of the department, work schedules, court appearance calendars, notices of changes in laws, and any other bits of information that the officer wishes to have at his immediate disposal in his pocket. The key to maintaining a good notebook, it would seem, is to determine what notes *not* to keep. Selectivity is necessary to insure that only essential data is recorded.

When to Take Notes

At the beginning of the workday, it is advisable to start a new page, list the date and time worked, partner—if any, unit number, and district worked. It should be a matter of routine to jot down notes on each incident as soon as possible after arriving on the scene. It would not seem appropriate for an officer to approach the calling party with notebook in hand, or to approach a suspected law violator with his

hands full. His initial approach should be made with his hands free
to respond to any immediate need for his action, such as rescue or
apprehension. Once he has taken whatever immediate action is necessary, it should then be a practice for him to take out his notebook
and start recording brief but succinct notes.

The date and time of the incident, weather conditions if relevant,
location of the incident, including not only the street address, but also
the character of the neighborhood (industrial, residential, transitional)
if the incident and the neighborhood for some reason should be
recorded. The officer making the record may find it an excellent adjunct to his memory to write down any impressions he may have to
indicate reasonable cause to interview an individual at a particular
moment. He may later find himself hard put to define his impressions
at the time of the interview. When walking into a crime scene, he
may detect a peculiar odor, hear unusual noises, or see something that
just does not seem right for that particular place or time of day. Such
an impression is a fleeting one, and will almost as quickly be forgotten
if not recorded as it is perceived.

When taking information concerning routine complaints, the notes
the officer may enter in his notebook may later prove quite important.
Such a situation might arise from a routine neighborhood quarrel.
The officer responds to the call for his presence. After contacting the
calling party and serving as a referee while the several persons present
settle—or at least air—their differences, the officer determines that no
crime is being committed in his presence and that nothing seems to
have occurred prior to his arrival but hot debate. He records in his
notebook the names and addresses of all the people he contacts and
jots down a few statements concerning the actions he observed and
whatever action he took or advice he offered, and then leaves. Some
time later he is dispatched to return to the same scene to investigate
an aggravated assault or worse. Armed with the notes he made at the
earlier incident involving the same principals, the officer will be far
better prepared to handle the investigation through to a successful
conclusion.

When the officer first arrives on the scene of a crime, the most ideal
arrangement would be for him to have at his disposal a portable television recorder with attached microphone. As he walked up to the
scene he would simply record the scene visually while simultaneously
narrating his observations, pointing out and describing each item of
evidence, and generally attempting to reconstruct the crime as it
probably occurred. The next best arrangement is for the officer to
immediately begin preparing a rough sketch and jotting down notes
in his notebook in the same manner as if he were going to later nar-
rate his investigation from start to finish. He should then continue to
record all statements made by victims, witnesses, suspects, and anyone
else whom he questions concerning the incident, and generally record

brief notes on everything which he will later commit to more formal reports. When should he take notes? He should take notes when the information presents itself to him, so that he may later refer to his notes for the accurate preparation of reports, and for the reconstruction of the facts as he knows them in the courtroom.

Value of Field Notes

There are many valuable aspects to the officer's field notes and his notebook, some of which we have already covered. Consider a few more. In the officer's busy day, he responds to many demands for his service. It is impossible for him to remember all that he should about each incident that involves him. His notebook serves as his memory bank, and the brief entries serve as his index of "landmarks" in his memory.

The notes provide valuable leads for investigations, data about certain items of evidence that should be checked out more thoroughly, and invaluable bits of information necessary to conduct an intelligent interview with witnesses or suspects. The notes actually serve as a self-discipline tool for the officer, forcing him to be accurate and thorough, and to organize his thoughts in logical sequence.

Because of their admissibility as "best recollections recalled," the set of well-prepared notes provide a medium whereby the officer may quote exactly entire statements by the principals in his investigation, rather than fragments and sometimes inaccurate bits of statements. Good notes thus prepare the officer to deal in specifics rather than generalities. The notes will "remember," whereas the human mind may not remember efficiently. Needless to say, testimony based upon an excellent set of notes will make a more favorable impression in the courtroom, and will be weighed against testimony presented by persons who did not take notes, and whose memory on key points is very vague and may be sprinkled with "I don't recalls" and similar excuses for not having all the facts.

What to Record

Selectivity is essential for field notes. Experience in the field and in the courtroom will be the principal teachers in this important matter, however both take time. Foremost in the recorder's mind should be the elements of the corpus delicti if the officer is investigating a crime. All of those elements are going to have to be substantiated if he is to lead the case to a successful conclusion. The five W's and the H of every case—When, Who, Where, What, Why, and How—whatever they may be, must be satisfactorily answered. While compiling the experience in the field and the courtroom, the officer will have to attempt to anticipate all the questions that will be asked by the report forms that have to be completed, the supervisors, the prosecutor, and the court, and then he must set about recording the answers to all those questions in his notebook.

The Notebook

Although some departments are quite specific about the type of notebook the officer purchases and carries, the type of book is secondary to what he puts inside. Some "experts" recommend that only looseleaf books be used, allowing the insertion or removal of pages in any desired sequence. I prefer the bound or spiral notebook, because it is immediately apparent that no pages have been inserted, and it is just as immediately apparent when a page has been removed. Most legally required log books and ledgers are bound in order to avoid the problem of "page juggling." The least efficient type of notebook is the standard clipboard with a collection of loose sheets of paper held together only by a spring clip at the top of the board.

The argument against the bound notebook is that when an officer once refers to his notebook in court, the defense attorney may inspect the book, presumably to challenge its authenticity. The argument then points out that the rest of the book is laid bare for the inspection of the attorney, and that he will go on a "fishing expedition," reading passages from other cases, and perhaps reading aloud in the courtroom some statement that might prove embarrassing to the author, thereby serving as a means to attempt to impeach the officer's reference to the notes in question. If that is the case, where is the prosecutor? The officer who plans to refer to his notebook in court should make that fact known to the prosecutor, and show him the portion of the book that includes notes relevant to the instant case. Any other portion of the notebook is "off limits" because it is totally irrelevant and immaterial to this case. Introduction of any of that extraneous material to the case by either side would be inadmissible, as would be any other extraneous material.

The book should bear some identifying data on the cover, such as the name and badge number of the officer, and perhaps a notebook number. After the book has been filled with information, it is a good practice to keep it for a reasonable period of time. The book should be numbered and maintained in some semblance of sequence for quick retrieval in the case of a call to court to testify in some case whenever it comes up for trial, or retrial. To reduce the possibility of any charge of "doctoring," the pages can be numbered.

Format of the Book

The specific style of keeping notes should be a personal matter; notebooks will be distinctively different from one officer to another.

As a guide in developing your own style, consider the following format.

The style of notes will vary with the situation, and several styles may occur while recording facts in a single event. The narrative style is a shortened version of the events as they are going to be recounted in the more lengthy report. It may include information that is only indirectly related to the incident and is included because it provides a series of memory "landmarks." For example, when a suspect states that he was attending a motion picture, it may be immaterial to the case at hand, but it will be significant to the investigation if the suspect is asked about the title of the picture and the story line. Other people he saw, or incidents that may have occurred during his attendance at the theater, such as the traffic accident that occurred just outside the theater as he and his date were en route to the ticket booth to purchase tickets, may be necessary for inclusion in a narrative account recorded in the field notebook.

Another notetaking format is the question-and-answer method. An excellent example of this format provided by the officer who develops the habit of recording verbatim—or as nearly as possible—the advisement of a suspect's constitutional rights against self-incrimination and to an attorney before and during questioning, and the suspect's verbatim responses to both the admonishment and his exercise or waiver of those rights. Exact words used by the subject to tell the officer that he knows exactly what his rights are and that he still chooses to confess may prove quite significant when later referring to those notes in court, leading up to the introduction of the actual confession. Use of the question-and-answer format in this instance may make the case because it demonstrates the professional approach of the officer to a delicate situation involving an individual's constitutional rights in our democratic society.

A third format for recording notes is the chronological approach, which may consist of a series of notes, each preceded by a letter or number to indicate the exact sequence of events as they occurred and as they presented themselves to the recorder.

Numbering pages in the notebook is a matter of choice for the keeper of the book. The advantages have been pointed out, but there may be no actual need for this extra procedure. As a general guide, I recommend that when you come to the end of information concerning one case before reaching the end of the page, you draw a line or several lines from the bottom of that information to the bottom of the page to clearly indicate that there is no more information to be entered. The lines also show to the observer that nothing has been added since the drawing of the lines.

Each new case or incident should begin on a new page in the book, with the identifying data somewhere on the page. Using a fresh page makes it easier to keep information on several cases separate, and it will also serve to keep the nonrelated material out of the courtroom. The data on each case should include the date and time the notes are being entered, the weather conditions (if relevant), the location, names and addresses of persons contacted or mentioned, and their respective relationships to the incident. It may later serve to the reporter's advantage if he also writes a brief description of each individual named to serve as an additional memory jogger. This description should be followed, of course, by whatever information is provided about or by each individual named.

Techniques in Notetaking

One of the predominant pitfalls in recording statements by various persons contacted during the course of an investigation is to represent paraphrased information provided by witnesses or victims as exact quotations. A simple rule to follow is to identify quotations with quotation marks, and then record the verbatim statements in precisely the same words used by the subject.

Whenever questioning people for the purpose of securing notes, be sure to separate them and secure individually thought-out information. This is particularly important when securing descriptions of suspects, since the differences between descriptions may lead to a quicker apprehension. The individual with the stronger personality may be wrong and yet be able to convince his fellow witnesses that he is right and they are wrong. Be sure to get facts, not suppositions, about what might have happened.

Too much information in the notebook is better than too little, but completeness in compiling field notes can be overdone. This factor must be borne in the mind of the recorder, as any effort to define guidelines that are too restrictive may render notes valueless. Use all the room you need for the notes, but keep the language understandable and the writing legible. One instructor may say that you should make your notes illegible and use a shorthand that is understandable only to yourself, so that you can testify in your own style without having to slavishly stick to your notes. Use of such a system seems foolish and unnecessary. If there is some question as to the veracity of your notes, then perhaps they should not be used at all. Deliberate efforts to keep notes are difficult enough without the added complication of deliberate illegibility.

There should be some sort of general uniformity throughout your notebook that will develop as you identify the elements that are essential to good reporting. Consistency in your reporting format and style will make it much easier for you to use your notes intelligently for later testimony and report preparation.

In addition to the field notebook, it is essential that you maintain a daily log or some form of accounting system to keep track of your on-duty field patrol activities. With a data processing system, it may be possible to maintain accurate records without a log by using "activity record cards" that are made out and time-stamped for every accountable activity in which you take part. In lieu of the computer method, which will doubtless become standard with law enforcement agencies throughout the country within a few years, you must keep a log.

The purposes of a log are manifold. One obvious purpose is that the log actually serves as a chronological diary of the field officer's working day. The officer may use it for reference at some later date to supply specific information, it may serve him as a memory jogger, and it can be relied on to show where he was and what he was doing at particular times of the day. In addition, supervisors use the log as a control device, for guidance in counseling an officer on the types of activity with which he concerns himself, and to discuss the officer's work in general with him. The log can also be used for cost accounting, tabulating actual time spent on various types of activities and interpreting the information in matters of actual cost for each activity. Other uses for the log are as a source for tabulating volume of work, and percentages of time devoted to various tasks on the job.

The daily log should contain columns for each of the following entries for each separate activity: source of call (radio, supervisor, private person, or observation by officer), time started, time completed, and time consumed in performing the activity. Next in line should be a space for a brief statement of the nature of the call and names of principals. The disposition is next, and the final space calls for any numbers related to the incident, such as case, citation, or warrant numbers.

If necessary for management or planning purposes, the various amounts of time could easily be totaled at the end of the day. The breakdown would vary with individual department needs, such as criminal versus noncriminal activities, time spent on incidents observed at the officer's own initiative, miscellaneous time spent in delivering or servicing vehicles, actual patrol time, and reporting time. The recapitulation portion at the top of the log could include spaces for tabulating such activities as citations issued, field interviews conducted, open doors investigated, vehicles recovered, and any other type of activity for which a number count would aid in supervision or planning.

Each log should be maintained for a separate day, with the officer's name, his district assignment, unit number, and any other pertinent information. If it would serve a purpose, a space for starting and ending vehicle mileage could be provided, as well as a place for statements on the condition of the vehicle and any conditions on the beat requiring some attention but not a separate report.

INTRODUCTION

Reports and other police records provide the basis for the many different activities carried out by the field officers, the investigators, the many specialists in the organization, the supervisors, and the administrators.

Nearly every service you perform, each crime or accident you investigate, and any other police operation you participate in calls for the initiation of a permanent record of some type or other. The record may range from a single terse entry on a line in a daily activity log to a detailed document several pages in length.

Your skills as a police officer are evaluated largely on the basis of your reports. How you do a job or perform a service is of tremendous importance and is actually the real test of your abilities as a police officer. How you report what you have done indicates your skill not only in doing the task, but also in transmitting that information to your readers. To the majority of people affected by your actions, your report is accepted at face value as an accurate account of what you did. A supervisor may have been present when you performed your task, but probably was not (at least during the majority of occasions he will not be). The ranking officer in the office who reviews your reports and passes judgment on your abilities through his in-office contacts, and through your reports, will not have been present. The various people to whom the report is sent for appraisal, action, or filing will have only the report to go on.

Your supervisor checks the report to make sure that you operated in conformance with department policies and procedures. Follow-up investigators of your department and other agencies determine what you have done on the case to date (based upon what you relate in your report), and what they must do next in order to bring the case to a successful conclusion.

For example, assume that during a routine crime investigation you collected evidence, interviewed witnesses, and performed hundreds of minor related acts, thoroughly investigating the case. During the investigation, several of the people whom you contacted had nothing of material value to add to the case. Several leads resulted in dead ends. When preparing the report, you omit the information that led to dead ends because it is of no evidential or material value to the case; and you also omit any mention of the names or identities of the many persons you contacted who had no information to offer. By omitting this information you have streamlined the report. However, when the follow-up investigator gets the case and sets out to wrap up the many loose ends, he will probably go out and go through many hours of wasted motion. He will retrace your footsteps without knowing it, come to the same dead ends you did, and gain the same lack of information from the many nonwitnesses you had contacted earlier. What a tremendous loss of time! It would have been of far greater value to the investigator if your report had been a page or two longer, and had included all the negative information—which is also essential to an investigation—as well as the positive.

In an office far removed from the scene of the crime, the prosecutor reviews the report and the many factors which constitute the circumstances surrounding the crime: dramatic moments of confrontation between officer and suspect, weapons, sounds, and other factors. The prosecutor must use the report as the sole criterion for determining whether the elements of the crime are all reflected accurately and firmly so that the charge will be sustained. "Is there sufficient information to show that the evidence will prove the case?" he asks himself.

A confession or admissions by the suspect are valueless in themselves. If they are to be of value, certain other factors must be shown in the report: Was the suspect admonished regarding his rights to remain silent and to have an attorney present while questioned? Did he intelligently waive those rights? What language was used to admonish him and what langauge did he use to convey his waiver? Was the officer acting on reasonable cause when he made the stop or conducted the search of the suspect? What were the circumstances? What was the exchange of dialogue between the officer and the suspect?

The prosecutor can assume nothing. He must have accurate facts so that he can plan his strategy for the courtroom. All of his decisions concerning the preceding questions must be made in the absence of the reporting officer, and be based exclusively on the officer's report. If any questions remain unanswered, the prosecutor must act on the premise that the reporting officer probably did not perform a specific function, such as admonishment of rights, if the report does not indicate that he did. Absence of information in the report indicates absence of action in the field.

After conviction of a defendant, the judge must determine the most appropriate punishment within the framework of the law. He relies upon a report from a probation officer, who investigates the background of the accused. That background includes information from the many police reports he may review and summarize for the judge. The judge may also review the actual report itself. Even though the defendant may have been found guilty, if the judge finds that the report is an extremely poor one, he may determine that the investigation was equally poor. His punishment may then be lessened because of his sympathy for the defendant, who apparently has not been handled by a professional police officer.

When the guilty party is sentenced to prison in states having the indeterminate sentence, a committee of responsible citizens may review all the facts surrounding the subject and the crime he committed, including a copy of the reports, from which they make their determination as to whether or not they will schedule an early date when the subject may apply for parole. The police report may or may not be used. What type of impression would it make upon them if they were to find the report full of misspelled words and grammatical structure reflecting a sixth grade education, although the officer preparing the report is alleged to have attended college for some time? If the report also lacks critical information about the crime and the criminal, it will be virtually worthless.

Figure 5.2 Lt. Glenn Pauly applies his technique of personnel assignment on the basis of computer indicated needs, the result of accurate reporting methods. Courtesy of the Metropolitan Police Department, St. Louis, Missouri.

Many other situations may present themselves when the officer's reports are reviewed in an effort to know the man preparing them. Transfers into choice assignments may be on the basis of how well an officer can express himself in the written and spoken word, and promotions may also take into account the officer's ability to prepare reports. Policies are formed, police action is planned, command decisions are made, and cases are won and lost on the basis of single police reports.

The report file and all of its related indices serve as the memory bank for the police department. This file provides for the members of the department a compilation of written records of all department transactions for which policy requires that reports be made and maintained. How extensive and detailed the system must be is a matter for the administrator to decide. What you expect to get out of it is, of course, the determinant as to what is going to have to be put into it.

Figure 5.3 Chief Curtis Brostrow of the St. Louis Police Department relies heavily on records and statistics to efficiently perform his duties. Courtesy of the Police Department, St. Louis, Missouri.

Allocation of Resources

Reports are administrative tools. Budgeting decisions are made through a series of interpretations involving translating manpower and materiel needs into realistic money amounts. Various types of plans, long and short range, are made on the basis of compiled reports. Most plans involve establishment of a system of priorities for the order in which certain police operations will be performed, or the amount of stress to be placed upon each operation. Officers' reports of past experience in performing those various tasks will be used as the basis for planning future activities. In some cases, certain types of police service traditionally relegated to the police for no apparent reason,

particularly those involving noncriminal matters, may be discontinued.
The decision to discontinue the service will be backed up by a collection of reports involving police officers' actions in that type of situation
in the past.

Manpower will be distributed to the various shifts, or watches, of the day, days of the week, and even the various separate operating divisions, on the basis of the reports compiled by the department and its members. If there is not sufficient manpower to cope with the problems confronting the agency, or if the existing force is performing in substandard fashion because of insufficient manpower, the reports should also indicate a need for the decision as to whether additional manpower is to be added, or whether certain services are to be discontinued.

Policy Changes

Long-standing department policies often go unchallenged because of apathy, lack of interest, a desire to avoid conflicts with stronger personalities, or a "don't rock the boat" philosophy. Properly prepared reports recounting department activities utilizing means prescribed by department policies may actually point up the need for revision, or at least review, of those existing policies. In defense of tradition, I might add that some long-standing policies are still quite valid and workable; often, however, the officers may have developed habits and actually be performing in violation of the existing policies. The officer's lack of efficiency may actually be due to the fact that he *is not* abiding by policy. Any change in procedures will be long-lasting and affect a great many people. Such change must be for improvement, not merely for "furniture rearrangement.

Statistics and crime trends are indicated through the medium of police reports. Data is compiled as well for annual or semi-annual reports.

Investigative Source

The reports serve as an information exchange device between the officers in different divisions and between the officers on different shifts in the same division. They provide leads for investigation, and a common pool of information available to all who have access to the files. Compare this method of relaying information to a system in which each officer has his own series of information sources and resources. In order to find what information he has, you must first guess that he is the one with the information you are seeking. Once you have found him, then you must seek him out at your mutual convenience, considering days off, sick leaves, vacations, holidays, and work schedules. The common pool of information is instantly available regardless of all those considerations. The reports, if kept current, will accurately reflect work that has been done and things still to be done. It serves as an aid to preparation for court and prosecution.

Figure 5.4   Cathode Ray Tube (CRT) device utilized by the Los Angeles Police Department is part of an automated want and warrant system. Courtesy of the Police Department, Los Angeles, California.

Information Resource for Other Agencies

Police reports provide prosecutors and the courts with a ready source of information regarding current or past cases. Probation and parole officers make decisions and recommendations regarding their probationers and parolees, using every possible source of information, including police reports. Even innocuous types of reports may have an appreciable influence on their actions. The press makes use of police records to assure accuracy in reporting.

The various press media have access to most police files for the purpose of assuring accuracy in reporting. Cases under investigation usually are not open to anyone, but some agencies find that by frankly presenting considerable information to the press concerning a specific case, then pointing out how the release of certain information will hinder the investigation, ethical press men will respect a confidence and are less apt to release critical information.

Although police records are generally private records of a public agency, much of the information they contain is relevant and useful to other agencies. An individual agency may be given access to that information which affects its operation.

PREPARATION OF REPORTS

Background Preparation

Before proceeding with the actual preparation of a report, spend a few minutes gathering and arranging the information in a logical sequence, thus outlining the report before you start. Although it takes more time in the initial stages, preparing a rough outline is more than worth the time, and actually results in a net saving of time. Working from an outline reduces the likelihood of your finding it necessary to later insert out of sequence statements such as "It should be noted that . . ." or "We failed to mention in the preceding paragraph. . . ."

Arrange all your notes, evidence, and exhibits in the same order as you intend to present the information in your report. When you come to the part of the report in which you refer to a certain item of evidence, you will not need to look for it. You can simply pick it up or otherwise examine it, determine how you are going to discuss it in the report, and then continue with the report.

Before starting with the report, also eliminate any superfluous information and excess verbiage. Mere words to fill space have no place in a police report. This does not imply that valuable information should be sacrificed for space purposes, but merely that the report should be used as a medium for transfer of information and not as an entry for a literary award.

If there is to be more than one officer taking part in the preparation of the report, in one continuous document, or if each officer is to prepare a summary of his own part in the case, be sure to correlate the information before beginning your work. In addition, be sure that the reports refer to each other and that they are correlated in such a way that readers will have no difficulty in maintaining continuity of thoughts when reading the reports and taking follow-up action on them.

Report Style

Use a free-flowing and uncomplicated reporting style to describe the action and investigation and other information in logical sequence as it presented itself to you. Be sure to write to express, not impress. If you use the same language you use in normal conversation, and know the meaning of the words you use, there will be little likelihood of confusion. The reporting style should reflect your individual personality.

Resist temptations to exaggerate or to model a report on someone else's work. There is sometimes a desire to prepare an outstanding report on an individual's physical appearance, as when someone is under the influence of narcotics or dangerous drugs. The temptation is also great to memorize the case number of a report that was brilliantly executed by another officer at some time in the past, to refer to it for guidance in preparing similar reports, then to either consciously or unconsciously plagiarize the material because it reads so well and can be used to apply to the specific case at hand. Incongruity between the officer and his reports will indicate whether this may be the case.

Follow a logical sequence when preparing the report. The sequence of events as reported to you will probably be the most common method of presentation. In a very complicated case, the events that occurred may be presented to you entirely out of sequence through several disconnected accounts from a series of people. If that is the case, it will be necessary for you to reconstruct the information, and the various bits and pieces of information, and report it in logical sequence without showing a lack of continuity in the investigation. It may be necessary to list the many people who provided information, describe briefly what each person had to offer to the case, and then bring together all the information in the report.

If you are reconstructing the crime on the basis of your investigation as it progresses, you may have to step back briefly, look at the entire sequence of events, then attempt to reconstruct the crime as you believe it *probably* occurred. If you use this method, be sure your report reflects a statement to that effect.

Use variety in your vocabulary. It will reduce reader fatigue as well as the possibility of each of your reports developing into a carbon copy of each preceding one on a similar matter. A person may state, he may reiterate, retort, reply, say, or do any number of things when he responds to a question. The English language is designed to express many shades of meaning when appropriately used.

Unless your own department head has established a policy that prohibits it, try using the first person singular when reporting what you did, whom you questioned, what you observed. It seems more sensible to write that "I" did something than for you to write the "undersigned" or "officer" did this or that. Suppose that you and another officer jointly investigate a case, and one discovers a piece of evidence while the other questions a witness. The alternatives might be: "Officer Jones discovered a crowbar with a 2-inch bite under the left front seat of the suspect's car while I was questioning him. He told me that he had used the crowbar to force entry into the drugstore just a few minutes before I had observed him running down the alley." or, "Undersigned and Officer Jones conducted a search. Officer Jones (who is also undersigned, by the way) found the crowbar while the suspect told the undersigned that he had used the crowbar just a few minutes before he was discovered by the undersigned." Which way do you talk when recounting the situation to your supervisor or how will you relate it in court?

There are some proponents of the traditional third-person style who will say that third person makes the case more impersonal and unbiased. They also feel that it reduces the possibility that personal aggrandizement will creep into the account of the story, maintaining that too frequent use of the word "I" does not belong in a police report. I say that this argument is invalid. The personality of the reporting officer, and not his style of writing, will determine whether or not he will let bias creep into the picture. An egotist will not be stifled by mere elimination of his use of the word "I." He will use it in court, why not in the report?

If you have prepared in advance and have arranged the sequence of events in the report, it will seldom be necessary to use statements such as, "It should be noted," and "We failed to mention," or to preface a statement with "The information gained was substantially as follows." If the information substantially follows, why preface it with worthless words?

CONSTRUCTION OF THE REPORT

Many police reports have been reduced to forms and filling in numbered boxes or spaces with single words, symbols, or checks. This is ideal for the common types of reports, when it is necessary to report only that certain procedural requirements have been met by the reporting officer. The time saved by maximum utilization of this type of form amply justifies the creation of the separate form it may require.

Most reports, however, demand that the officer recount the information in prose form and in longhand fashion. As in an essay or other form of written communication of succinct ideas and information, the report should have an introduction, a body, and a conclusion. The introduction usually consists of a synopsis of the report and an announcement of what the reader may expect to find in the body of the report. The conclusion consists of a reiteration of the body of the report in capsule form and some recommendation for further action, or a statement that this particular case requires no further action. The following deals with these basic components in more detail.

The Synopsis, or Introduction

Designate the type of report according to the agency's classification system. List all the names of persons mentioned in the report for whom there are no specific "boxes" in the standardized portion of the form, if there is such a section. Be sure to indicate the relationship to the case each named person plays. Enumerate and describe any evidence, exhibits, or other information you intend to bring in during the body of the report. In a paragraph, summarize briefly the information you are going to recount in more detail in the following paragraphs.

The Body

Describe the sequence of events and information in concise and understandable terms. Either recount the events as presented to you, or, if necessary for continuity and if possible without compromising the authenticity of the report, lay out the body of the report in a logical sequence either as the events occurred or as you believe they might have occurred.

Be completely honest and objective. Be sure to include all information developed, even though some of it may be detrimental to the case from your point of view. The purpose of the report is to accurately report information as it presents itself, not to distort it to make a more convincing case against anyone named in the report. When taking and recording statements by various informants, bear in mind the fact that victims and witnesses are not always unequivocally correct. Suspects may offer rationalizations and defenses that may be wholly or partly true. Any opinions you may have to advance as the report progresses should be clearly identified as such, and they should be included only when the opinion has a substantial bearing on the case. Never express an opinion as fact. It is more appropriate to label and recite observations and impressions that present themselves to you, and to leave any opinion-making to the reader. Whatever reporting method you choose, be sure that you do not employ any device that serves to communicate any prejudice or bias that you may entertain about any of the persons named in the report.

When recording statements made by the many persons in the

report, identify verbatim statements with quotation marks and correct punctuation. Never paraphrase a statement and present it as a direct quotation.

Answer all the questions that must be answered in any police report, or at least all those to which you can obtain answers. The five W's (who, what, when, where, why) and How should be the object of your investigation, and as many as possible should be answered. Sometimes the absence of certain answers are just as significant as their presence.

Report all of the investigative leads you have followed, including those that did not bear fruit. It is just as important to report that you contacted five named potential witnesses and gained no information, as it is to enumerate only the names and information provided by those who present positive leads and information. Without the unsuccessful leads, the follow-up investigator will be placed in a position where he will unknowingly have to pursue leads that you have already checked out. If you obtain identical information (or lack of it), it is correct to summarize by reporting that witness Jones stated substantially the same as Izenthall, if that is the case.

Use of Names

The first time you use a name in a report, list it in full, including the title, such as Mr. Jonathan Quincy Forthright. During subsequent references, use the last name only. If there are two or more persons with the same name, such as Mr. and Mrs., or John and Georgia, it will be necessary to use the different first names or titles to continue to distinguish the two different players. Avoid the use of labels, such as "victim number one" and "witness number thirteen." Such labeling adds to the confusion that is already prevalent in what is usually a complicated case, and the reader has to prepare a cast of characters for himself so that he can continuously refer to it while reading your report. Use of the names lessens the confusion.

The tenor of your report should indicate the nature of the follow up necessary. Sometimes the results you achieve will be far more productive if you provide the reader with sufficient information to determine the need for urgent action as a result of his own thought process, rather than tell him that he should perform his job in the manner you suggest. The message is the same, but the method is more effective. If there is an urgent reason for following a certain lead, the wording of your report should indicate the priority it should receive. In most agencies, cases are handled in accordance with some system of priorities. The priorities are usually established by the follow-up officer on the basis of the information he gleans from the reports, except for those cases which fall into specific report classifications.

Before preparing the conclusion of the report, go over the synopsis and body at least cursorily, then "wrap it up" with your conclusion. If the case is cleared or closed, indicate same so that record-keeping requirements may be fulfilled. Any unfinished work should be listed and presented in such a manner that the reader can make his decision to pursue the investigation according to his own priority system. Generally summarize what you have done and what is left to be done on the case. In some cases, policy may require that you make a recommendation for further action. If that is the case, any recommendation you make should be based upon information that the reader may find in the body of the report.

Abbreviations

Some standardized forms make it necessary to abbreviate in order to get all the relevant data in the undersized space provided. Only in that case is it wise to use abbreviations. Too often the time that may be saved by using them is lost in later attempts to decipher some of the abbreviations that may be employed by the economy-minded reporter. If in doubt, do not abbreviate except for use of the very commonly accepted forms that are listed in any standard dictionary.

Destroy Used Notes

Any notes, outlines, or other information you may have generated for the purpose of completing your report in addition to those in your field notebook, including partially typed reports that were discarded because of errors, should be destroyed. Before placing such material in the wastebasket, tear it into shreds. Also destroy any used carbon paper. Intelligent criminals know that a good source of information is the police department's trash.

Dictating the Report

An encouraging trend during the past few years has been the attempt to reduce the time required for report writing without reducing the efficiency of the reports. Short forms have been developed for many of the "routine" reports, such as miscellaneous service, calling for insertion of a series of X's in appropriate boxes on the form. Other forms have been streamlined and designed so that the officer may write or print out his report in its entirety while still in the field, and turn it in at his convenience when he returns to headquarters for some other purpose. Some reports have been virtually eliminated, and the information they once contained is now recorded in a terse statement as a single line entry on the officer's daily log. Despite such developments, however, many reports cannot be streamlined by use of any of these methods. The crime report must include a detailed narrative account of exactly what took place during the commission of the crime and during the investigation. In cases when the report must recount actual words used and verbatim accounts of things done by the principals, the narrative report is still the only efficient method for recording the necessary information.

Stenographers have been introduced into the police reporting system, as well as several types of dictating and transcribing equipment to be used by reporting officers and clerical assistants as a team. The results have been rewarding in many cases. Reports have improved, and officers have increased their ratio of field time to report time. In other cases, the results have been tremendously disappointing. I suggest that the concept is sound, but that the system must be well planned and executed. The people using it must be willing to sit down together and work out the details of how to make it work.

Individual department needs vary, as well as their financial resources and facilities. However, every department must have some provision that will allow the officer to occasionally stop and listen to a partial playback (or readback in the case of an in-person stenographer), so that he may edit when necessary and maintain continuity in his reports. This practice should be kept to a minimum, and should not be used as a substitute for pre-planning a report. Whether you dictate your reports in person to the stenographer in the office, telephone in the reports to her or to some sort of dictating instrument, or carry your dictating unit in the field with you, there are a few basic rules that must be followed in all cases.

1. Organize your thoughts in advance. You should have developed the report from start to finish before you begin dictating. Random notes may suffice, but an outline may prove more useful.
2. Dictate the report in clear, concise language. Exaggerate the consonants so that they are heard, and avoid slurring words together. Whenever there is any possibility of misunderstanding in the pronunciation of a word, particularly when listing, spell it out. The person transcribing the information you dictate cannot be expected to guess what it is that you meant to say, or how a particular name should be spelled.
3. Dictate the report in the same language and style you would use if you were telling it in person. First person singular reads most naturally, and I recommend its use.
4. Avoid redundancy. Do not ramble on and on, repeating yourself in several different approaches. This is one of the most common pitfalls to be avoided when dictating a report rather than typing it yourself.
5. Have all names, addresses, and phone numbers to be included in the report close at hand.

6. Do one thing at a time. While dictating, be sure to avoid performing other tasks at the same time, such as making out a log, shuffling papers, or carrying on a conversation with another person.
7. Make maximum use of your field notes, which should provide a good foundation for accurate and complete reports if they have been compiled as recommended earlier in this chapter.
8. Keep your sentence structure simple and correct.
9. Never expect the person who is preparing the actual typewritten draft of the report to alter it in any way from the way in which you dictated it.

THE MISCELLANEOUS INCIDENT REPORT

Every agency has a standard procedure for reporting actions and incidents for which there is no specific form. In fact, such a miscellaneous classification may have a standardized form. There are two basic kinds of formats for this type of form. One consists of a series of statements with adjacent blocks for insertion of X's or check marks for indicating basic information which is so standarized that no value could be derived from narrative response. For example, an officer might respond to a call on a family disturbance. Upon his arrival he determines that no law had been broken. He contacts the principals in the case, separates them, and gets a brief account of the nature of the problem. He determines that the matter is entirely civil in nature, and that if he were to give advice it would be unethical and extralegal. He arbitrates the matter because his role is to prevent crimes. After calming the people down and making sure that the likelihood of a crime's occurring after his departure is not apparent, he leaves.

In this case, the officer might use a forced choice type of form. He merely has to fill in the date and time of the incident, the names and addresses of the principals, the identity of the calling party, and the location of the incident. He then goes down the list of choices and marks the boxes adjacent to the statements to the effect that the call was a neighborhood dispute; it was noncriminal in nature; the people were advised to contact attorneys in any civil law question; he, the officer, kept the peace and advised the parties that someone could be arrested for any law violation.

The second type of form for miscellaneous incidents is more common. It calls for brief statements concerning the nature of the call and any action taken by the officer, a summary of the circumstances leading up to the demand for police service, and a synopsis of any other relevant data that might later be of some value in criminal investigations.

In completing this report, indicate the names of all principals involved in the call, and indicate by a brief statement the relationship of each named individual to the call, such as ". . . requested presence of officer to keep the peace," and ". . . involved in neighborhood disturbance." The report should briefly recount the facts in an informative fashion and contain only relevant data. What occurred while en route to the call and the fact the officer "resumed patrol" are examples of irrelevant data.

THE ARREST REPORT

Many departments use a form that serves as a combined booking slip and arrest report. The information required is mostly self-explanatory, and only a very small space is reserved for any narrative that may be necessary. Listing the name of the arrestee may seem relatively unimportant because it is so routine. Yet this is probably the most important part of the report. When spelling out the name, be sure to check all the identification materials and documents the subject has in his possession. Ask the arrestee to explain any discrepancies, and be sure to record all different spellings as aliases. Many times a name has not been assumed at all; it has merely been misspelled.

Of the many sources of information about the identity of a subject, the arrest report is—or should be—the best. Take extra care to fill out the form completely. Add any items of information that come to your attention, such as various organizations and unions in which the subject holds membership cards, and physical deformities or other distinguishing characteristics, that would later help identify him even under an assumed name or after an attempt at altering his appearance.

THE CRIME REPORT

Usually the crime report form consists of a series of standardized, required bits of information to establish jurisdiction for the case, questions that must be answered to reflect all of the elements of the corpus delicti—or body—of the offense, and all of the required data to serve as a base for the investigation and, ultimately, the successful prosecution of the perpetrator.

The heading of each report calls for a title. In a crime report, the title includes the specific law that has been violated. The balance of the report must substantiate that fact. When more than one law violation is listed, the report must also reflect all of the elements of each separate offense.

The date and time of the occurrence and the date it is reported may provide clues to the investigator as to the possible motive of the reporting party, particularly in cases where personal animosity may be involved. The occupation and age of the victim, and the location and type of premises where the crime occurred, might lead to a specific suspect who specializes in some type of crime. Every question has a purpose and should be answered as thoughtfully as possible.

Spaces are provided for the name, address, and phone numbers of the victim, the person reporting the crime, the person who originally discovered its occurrence, and other witnesses. When listing this information, be sure to secure additional information concerning where each of these persons may be contacted when they are not at their places of residence, such as business addresses and phone numbers. If they are planning to be absent from the area for some period of time, be sure to include that information in the summary portion of the report.

The crime report should include a "modus operandi" section for recording in easy-to-locate spaces certain distinguishing characteristics about the crime that provide keys to the investigatory leads and to the possible identification of the culprit. At times the criminal will say and do certain things during the commission of his crimes that are almost as effective in identifying him as his fingerprints. The experienced investigator can sometimes compare the reports of two different crimes and see similarities in the "M O" section that indicate to him that both crimes may have been committed by the same individual. Filling in those spaces in the report should be done very carefully.

In crimes against property, such as burglary or breaking and entering, and in some crimes against persons, the point of entry and the point of exit must be identified and an effort should be made to reconstruct the crime as it probably occurred. In some cases, the nature of the force—or lack of it—used to gain entry serves to prove intent. This is particularly important in specific intent offenses.

The weapon or tool used should be identified. If not known, marks made by tools may serve to indicate the type of weapon probably used. Be sure to include in the report a statement that the weapon or tool was *probably* whatever you believe it was if you do not know for sure. A positive statement could be disastrous to the prosecution if it later developed that an error had been made. Only when you have positive facts should you make a positive statement.

The location of the property stolen or damaged is always significant, but it is more so when the property had been in a concealed or out-of-the-way location. The apparent ease with which the culprit found the item may indicate that he is familiar with the place. The nature of the object attacked, such as a safe, may indicate the skill of the thief.

It is never necessary to prove motive to prove the elements of the case or to establish the identity of the culprit. In a crime of property gain, the motive is usually to gain possession of the stolen object.

The motive in a sex offense may be satisfaction of sexual desires. An
attack with a deadly weapon may be for the purpose of committing
another crime, such as robbery or rape, or it may be a matter of
revenge. When attempting to determine the motivation for the crime,
it is sometimes possible to come up with one or more suspects. To
know the motive is also an insight into the personality of the perpetrator.

Each crime report calls for a "trademark." Whether it is discernible
depends on the case, but most criminals do something that is just a
little unique which distinguishes them from all others. Some individuals make a habit of using exactly the same words each time they
assault a victim; others use a specific technique that seems to work
each time they force entry into a place of business. The "trademark"
thus becomes as distinctive as the person himself, and it may immediately identify a known criminal to the follow-up investigator. An
example of a burglar's trademark is found in the case of the thief
who steals an item of some value from a teacher's drawer in a classroom and then causes so much destruction that it appears to be the
act of several juvenile vandals. One case that I worked presented such
an appalling sight that I immediately approached the investigation
from the standpoint of malicious mischief. It was just by accident
that we found a pried drawer that was usually kept locked and discovered that some prescribed medication the teacher had kept in that
drawer had been stolen. Because of the outrage, the teacher herself
had actually overlooked the theft. Several trademarks may be present
in this case of robbery: The bandit walks into the savings and loan
office precisely at 12:15 P.M., walks up to the cashier, hands her a
brown paper bag, orders her to place all the money she has in the
drawer into the bag, then smiles and apologizes for the inconvenience,
and leaves through the front door. Both the time and the brown paper
bag may be significant. Another unusual factor is the smile and the
apology. The eventual solution in a similar case established that the
robber always committed his crimes during his lunch hour and that the
bag was actually the one in which he brought his lunch to work.
Unusual? So is the idea of committing armed robberies.

SUSPECT

Whenever you describe, or name and describe, a person in the
"suspect" box of the crime report form, there must be sufficient sub-
stantiation of the subject's responsibility for the crime to justify an
arrest. If there is enough information in the report reflecting evidence
pointing toward an individual as the culprit, and if a judge would
issue a warrant on the basis of that information, the individual should
be listed as a suspect. If there is some doubt, or if there is no proof

but circumstances indicate that a particular individual's possible relationship to the crime is more than casual, list and discuss him in the narrative portion of the report as a possible suspect.

DESCRIPTIONS OF PROPERTY
AND OTHER RELEVANT INFORMATION

Additional spaces in the crime report form call for complete descriptions of the property stolen, the vehicle used by the culprit, and any evidence collected during the investigation. Several spaces are also provided for administrative handling of the report and its accompanying material. In addition to these special information spaces, there is usually a substantial portion of space for the narrative account of the crime as reported to the officer, as he observes it, and as it is developed during the investigation. This section often continues on a second page. It is in the narrative portion that the entire case should be explained in narrative form.

SPECIAL REPORTS

In addition to miscellaneous incident reports, crime and arrest reports, and traffic accident reports, each department has a wide variety of special forms. Some departments create separate forms for every conceivable type of incident, while others have a few basic forms and instruct their officers to adapt the information in each situation to fit existing forms. A few of the items for which special forms are often used are missing persons, dead body, lewd or annoying phone calls, impounded vehicle, evidence report, checks, intoxication, advisement of rights, and abandoned vehicle. Other special forms may be made to fit virtually any need of some unit within the department with a special interest.

DISCUSSION

Every agency has a different set of reporting policies. For a crime report to be prepared, all of the elements of a corpus delicti must be evident and reportable. For a traffic accident report, the vehicle must be moving, or there must be a minimum value damage. For a missing persons report, the person who is allegedly missing must have been absent for some time in excess of two or three hours past dinner time on pay day. The responding officer will prepare some type of report, but it may not be on exactly the same form the reporting party would like to have it on. Some people may request that a specific report be

made, such as a theft report for the benefit of an insurance or tax de-
duction claim. Exactly which form the reporting officer uses is strictly
a department matter and should be of no concern to the complaining
party. It is of absolutely no value to the overall effectiveness of the
department to tell a distraught wife "sorry but your husband has not
been gone long enough for us to make a 'missing person' report."
What matters is that you have taken the information, that you will
make some sort of report, and that you and the department will take
some action on the basis of that report.

INTRODUCTION

The records system is the nerve center, the memory bank, and the
control center of the police department. The nerve center characteristic of the records system is seen in the fact that virtually all of the
functions of the department involve maintenance of records, constant
reference to them, and sometimes total dependence upon them. The
memory bank aspect is apparent. As with any other memory system, it
is only as accurate as the information fed into it, and its indexing system must be as comprehensive and as easy to understand as possible
to assure complete and instantaneous access to the contents of the files.
The control center aspect is best illustrated by the fact that the personnel responsible for the system will not accept faulty or incomplete
records for inclusion in the system—whenever they receive it through
channels—because it "does not compute." Reports prepared by field
officers constitute the majority of the records for the system. Accuracy
is a must. The most useful and efficient system will be the one that
receives the most complete and the most accurate bits of information
for its files.

USES OF RECORDS

Records information provides the basis for interchange of such information among the various units of the department, and between
the department and numerous other individuals and agencies with
whom it communicates. Officers working together during the same
hours of the day are in a relatively good position to keep each other
informed because of their rather frequent contact with each other.
Personal contacts provide the major means of communication. But
what about these officers and the rest of the department? They have

no direct line of communication beyond their own sphere of contacts. Their written reports and related documents serve as their major means of communications.

Other members of the department, or some other agency, who must take follow-up action, such as continuing an investigation, or returning to a specific address to verify that a dog which has bitten a child has been correctly placed under quarantine by its owner, must act upon the report on the assumption that all of the information has been recorded accurately in its entirety. The information in the initial report provides the base for the follow-up work.

Because all officers are required to complete their reports during the same working day or within a very short time afterward, it is possible for one officer to assume an investigation inaugurated by another in the event that the original officer does not continue for some reason. The reports filed to date, together with their accompanying data from related files, are available for review. They allow the investigation to continue without interruption.

Records of filed reports provide a factual record of work performance: work that has been done and work to be done. The officer who not only performs well in the field, but also prepares complete and factual reports accurately reflecting his good work, is a double threat in the competitive service. In addition to serving as a tool by which the quality of his work may be evaluated, his reports provide a means to ascertain the quantity and the nature of the work he has performed.

BASIC RECORDS FILES AND THEIR USES

Every police agency has a different structure for its records system. Special needs and interests of the many individuals involved in the evolution and development of the systems have made them as distinctive and original as a set of fingerprints. There are several basic files that are more or less standard, with minor variations of course. They include the master—or alphabetical—index of all named persons, places, and things listed in reports; the report files in which the original reports are maintained; stolen and pawned object files; and several other files.

The Master Index

This is usually found in the form as a massive collection of three-by-five index cards used for an alphabetical listing of all named persons, places, and objects that will be found elsewhere in the system. The cards serve strictly as an index, although some agencies will actually carry in the "alpha file," as it is sometimes called, some original and complete records, such as field interview cards. By search-

ing through the master index, it is possible to find a wealth of information in the various other files for which it serves as the index.

Some of the many bits of information that will be found on the
cards in the master index will be names of victims, witnesses, suspects,
wanted felons, and persons who died under circumstances when the
police were notified of the death, such as suicides; individuals who
have made purchases of concealable firearms from local dealers, and
others who have licenses or permits to carry concealed weapons. Some
"alpha files" contain nicknames of persons who are known to the majority of their friends and neighbors only by those partial names, or
"monickers." The index also includes the names of persons who repossess vehicles and the purchasers from whom they are repossessed,
and the names of individuals who have been interviewed under a
variety of circumstances in the field. This is only a partial description
of the contents of the master index. The only limitations to the extent
of the master index in the police department are space and the imagination of the people using it.

Report Files

The originals of all reports are filed for a period of time. In some
cases they are microfilmed and permanently stored in compact form;
the filmed copies become the originals, and the bulky letter-sized
originals are destroyed. The reports may be filed under a single numbering system, in chronological sequence as the incidents were reported to—or came to the attention of—the department, or they may
be separated under several different categories with different numbering systems and stored in various places.

The Crime File

Each reported offense is classified according to the Uniform Crime
Reports classification system. Since 1930, the Federal Bureau of Investigation has served as the central clearing house for crime statistics
in the United States. With very few isolated exceptions, virtually every
police agency in the country contributes information concerning their
statistics to the system. The information is cataloged in a variety of
ways and published annually in booklet form. Each contributing
agency maintains its own collection of bits of information to satisfy
the reporting requirements of the system, usually in the form of a
three-by-five card file, or computer cards if the agency utilizes electronic data processing (EDP).

The crime file is an excellent source of leads for an investigation,
providing that the modus operandi portion of the original report has
been accurately filled out by the reporting officer. The file is separated
by crime classification, and then divided into "cleared" and "un-

cleared" categories. Although the primary purpose of this file in most agencies is statistics, it doubles quite efficiently for a "modus operandi" file.

Crime file information cards contain the case number of each offense, the type of crime, date and time of occurrence, description of the property stolen and its market value, the location of the crime and the type of real estate attacked (market, parking lot, city street, or private residence). The card also gives the name, address, and occupation of the victim, and any "trademark" or unusual circumstance about the case that may serve to identify the culprit. If the name or description of the suspect is known, or if a person has been arrested, that information will also be indicated on the card.

Serial Number File

Serial number files are maintained by local departments and by some state agencies that have centralized clearing houses for criminal information. Whenever the serial number of a stolen item is known, the number is included in this file. The method of filing may vary, but it is usually in numerical sequence according to the last three digits of the number. For example, an item bearing serial number 7Z09253 would be filed in the 253 file. Also filed in the same location are serially numbered items that have been pawned or sold to secondhand dealers, who are required to report such transactions to the police department and a state agency.

By placing both stolen and pawned items into the same file according to serial number, the hope is that the two may meet in the files and thus arm the investigators with sufficient data to investigate the circumstances surrounding the sale or pawn transaction, solve the crime, apprehend the thief, and return the stolen property to its owner. In addition to cards on stolen and pawned items, the serial number file might contain cards on new dealer sales of handguns or any other item bearing serial numbers on which the local jurisdiction requires report of transactions.

Stolen Object File

This is another file that is common to many police departments. Any identifiable object that has been stolen is carded and filed according to its classification. There is considerable dependence upon the thoroughness of the reporting officers for this particular file to serve any practical purpose. A stolen radio, for example, would be filed as a transistor, subfiled again by name of manufacturer, and possibly filed again into another subcategory of style or brand name. Watches are subfiled under "man's" or "woman's," calendar, yellow or white metal, manufacturer's name, and popular name. Accuracy in describing the object may be the determinant as to whether it will be recovered and

returned to its owner.

Pawned Object File

As in the case of serially numbered items, the local department or a central clearing house may classify and file stolen objects in one file and pawned objects, plus others that are sold to secondhand dealers, in another with the ultimate objective of matching the items in the file and causing an investigation to be conducted that will eventually end in return of the stolen property to its lawful owner. The clerical personnel in the records division should check cards destined for one file against the other, and vice versa, whenever the opportunity presents itself, as a matter of routine. This check is simplified to a great extent when the information is committed to an electronic data processing system which has an automatic matching procedure built into its program.

Location File

The location file may be designed according to either one of two plans: the street and number system, or the grid system. Cards are prepared for each crime and/or arrest for any of a number of specified offenses, or they may be made for all crimes and arrests, depending on the administrative decision made by the individual department head. For maximum utilization, the information is cross-referred to the object file, serial number file, and the crime file. In the grid system, the police agency's jurisdiction is divided into reporting districts, which consist of square blocks, groups of blocks, specific streets, single locations (frequent incident bars, recreation centers, and other places determined by the operator of the system to require special attention), or the reporting districts may correspond to census tract boundaries. In the street and number system, the file is arranged according to numbered streets and lettered streets in logical numerical and alphabetical sequence. This file can be used quite conveniently in conjunction with spot or pin maps, which show special problems or types of crimes by location.

PUTTING THE FILES TO WORK

The files discussed in this chapter comprise only a small portion of some records systems. Some agencies create separate files for literally dozens of different uses, and they are usually cross-indexed for efficiency. But consider the possibilities of just those files covered in the preceding pages.

In case number one, you respond to a burglary call. While investigating, you discover that the culprit entered through an unlocked back door during daylight hours while the occupants of the house were away. The culprit very carefully ransacked the house, taking care not to destroy any property, and took only money. While in the house, the culprit turned on a different radio station than that ordinarily selected by the owner of the house, indicating that he had a particular desire to listen to a certain type of music while he worked. The investigation reveals no other information. There are no latent fingerprints to be found. Actually, the culprit left behind a trademark although he left very little evidence. There is no known suspect in this crime.

Probably the first place you should go upon arriving at the office to prepare your report on this case, if time and departmental procedure allow, is the record bureau. Check the crime file for daylight residence burglaries, both the solved ones, and those that have yet to be solved. Other crimes with similar circumstances, such as the method of entry and the selection of music on the radio, may indicate the possibility that they have been committed by the same person. Perhaps there is a similar one or two that had been cleared by arrest some time in the past. If the latter situation occurs, you may have at least a possible suspect, because most people—including burglars—are creatures of habit. If there are other cases with similar MO's, you should include this information in the report. The investigator who follows up on the case will attempt to determine whether the burglar follows some sort of pattern, such as always committing his crimes in a specific area, or on a particular day of the week, or at the same time of the day. He will also consider the strong possibility that a firm lead on one crime will result in the eventual solution of all of the similar offenses.

In case number two, you arrest a young man for theft of an eight-track stereo tape deck from a car parked on the parking lot at the football stadium. While questioning him, the subject admits to stealing other items of a similar nature, but he cannot remember when or where. A check of the stolen object file may reveal a series of similar thefts of stereo tape decks. By retrieving the original reports and discussing the cases with the subject, you may be successful in clearing up a series of thefts rather than just the one. Other sources of information to check while conversing with this willing confessor are a map and the location file. By discussing the various locations where he may have committed theft, you may find that he is a parking lot specialist. Check similar crimes that have occurred on parking lots throughout the city, and again you may strike pay dirt.

Case number three may be a little different. During a routine field interview of a person observed under suspicious circumstances, you discover that he is in possession of several objects, such as transistor radios, household appliances, and a television set. He is unable to provide a reasonable explanation for such possession. By searching the stolen object and the serial number files, you discover that one or more of those items had previously been reported stolen.

The greatest limitation on your imaginative use of your records system will be imposed by the time that may be involved. There are occasions when the pressure of other field responsibilities will prevent your maximum utilization of those records, but there are other occasions when the time is available and it should be put to use.

EXERCISES AND STUDY QUESTIONS

1. Of what value are field notes?
2. What type of notebook does your department require?
3. What procedure would you use to be sure that only the part of your notebook that is relevant to the instant case will be admitted during the trial?
4. Recount the format of your field notebook entries on an imaginary robbery call.
5. List three advantages of using an officer's daily log.
6. In what ways do the reports serve as administrative tools for determining department needs for new policies or review of the standing policies?
7. What is your department's attitude toward the use of first person singular when preparing reports?
8. What is a crime report *trademark?*
9. What is the value of a *location* file?
10. What is the "master index"?

SUGGESTED SEMESTER OR TERM PROJECTS

1. Make a sample book containing all of the major report forms used by your department and the recommended procedure for filling in the various information requested.
2. Devise a checklist type of report form that will replace the literally dozens of other types of forms and reports that are required for miscellaneous service.
3. Prepare a summary of all of the types of files in your police department and discuss how each type of file may be used in different kinds of investigations.

REFERENCES

CALIFORNIA BUREAU OF CRIMINAL IDENTIFICATION AND INVESTIGATION, *Modus Operandi and Crime Reporting*. Sacramento, Calif.: State Printing Office, 1955.

DIENSTEIN, WILLIAM, *How to Write a Narrative Investigation Report.* Springfield, Ill.: Charles C Thomas, Publisher, 1964.

FEDERAL BUREAU OF INVESTIGATION, *Manual of Police Records.* Washington, D.C.: Government Printing Office, 1963.

———, *Uniform Crime Reporting Handbook.* Washington, D.C.: Government Printing Office, 1966.

INTERNATIONAL CITY MANAGERS' ASSOCIATION, *Municipal Police Administration,* 5th ed. Chicago: International City Managers' Association, 1961.

UNITED STATES ARMY, *Criminal Investigation FM 19-20.* Washington, D.C.: Government Printing Office, 1951.

WILSON, O. W., *Police Administration.* New York: McGraw-Hill Book Company, 1963, Chap. 18.

———, *Police Planning,* 2nd ed. Springfield, Ill.: Charles C Thomas, Publisher, 1957.

———, *Police Records, Their Installation and Use.* New York: Public Administration Service, 1951.

Field Interviews

CHAPTER SIX One of the police officer's basic responsibilities is to do whatever is within the scope of his duty and authority to maintain his assigned district as free from crime and disorder as possible. In fact, one of the principal factors considered in evaluating his efficiency and effectiveness is the *absence* of crime in his district. The intelligent, well-trained officer knows that field interviews are among his most useful "tools of the trade," because it is largely through their use that the officer prevents and represses criminal activity. He is most productive in activities such as arrests and crime clearances when he aggressively makes personal contact with the people he observes during the course of his patrol activities, particularly those who arouse his suspicions, and when he conducts thorough field interviews with those people.

Every officer should know the character and nature of business of as many people in his district as possible. He should also know the identity and character of those who are occasional and frequent visitors **139** to his district. In many instances, it is his responsibility to know what he can about certain "first time" or "one time only" visitors to the district he patrols. The only effective means whereby such identification and character determination can be accomplished is by *observation* and *interrogation*. One of the most immediate ways to get an answer to your question, "I wonder who he is and what he is up to?" is by making contact with that person and asking him. Although this is the most obvious method, too *few* policemen choose to use it as a matter of routine, which it should be.

OBJECTIVES OF FIELD INTERVIEWS

There are three principal objectives of having a department-wide, organized field interview program as opposed to the "catch-as-catch-can" individual operations of just a few individual officers. These objectives are: (1) identification, (2) prevention and repression of crime, and (3) centralized records of field contacts. Let's cover each of those three separately.

1. IDENTIFICATION. As we mentioned earlier in the chapter, the officer is responsible for knowing the people who live, work, and pass through or seek recreation in his district. He should know the identity and places of residence of people with criminal records and criminal tendencies as demonstrated by their past actions, which are a matter of record. The officer should likewise know the identities and any unusual hours or habits of the residents, such as the milkman who leaves home at 3:00 A.M., the man who works in the post office until 2:00 A.M., or the doctor whose business may take him out of the house at all hours of the day and night. The officer should know the businesses in his area and be aware of their irregularities in business practices and hours, such as overnight inventories, restocking the shelves between two and ten in the morning, or deliveries made at nighttime to avoid parking problems. By having made previous personal contact with literally hundreds of people on his "beat," the officer knows who has the criminal records, who are the burglars, or thieves, and who is peddling narcotics. Armed with such information, he is better prepared to take appropriate action, such as a cursory search, surveillance, utilization of an undercover officer, or immediate arrest whenever the circumstances call for his official response.

2. PREVENTION AND REPRESSION OF CRIME. An active and alert police patrol with an objective field interview program creates a continuous awareness of the omnipresence of the police. The law-abiding citizens have the feeling of security in knowing that their safety is assured, and the criminal knows that he has a greater chance of getting caught at his illicit activities, or when he is in possession of contraband. The criminal who knows that the police know him, his record, his

address and method of transportation, his crime specialty, and the names and addresses of his associates, is less likely to commit his crimes under circumstances when he also knows that the officer is aware of his presence in the immediate or general vicinity.

3. RECORDS. Every field interview or field contact (which may include mere observation of known criminals under circumstances which merit a record of time and place but no necessity for a conversation) should be made the subject of a permanent or semipermanent record entry in the department files. A printed card the same size as the standard three-by-five cards used for a master alphabetical file is ideal, because it can be placed directly in that file along with other cards pertaining to the same individual.

The field interview cards provide a ready source of information about physical description, times and locations of contact, vehicle description, associates, employer or school, and circumstances surrounding such contacts. The cards showing records of field interviews are most helpful in locating possible suspects and witnesses. Lovers in the park may later develop into victim and suspect in a rape case. The employee moving inventory from one store to another at 2:00 A.M. may turn out to be someone who was fired for theft two weeks previously who is stealing his former employer's inventory. There are many examples we can use from personal experience, such as the "student" with the stolen portable typewriter, a car thief driving a "borrowed" car, a "witness" to a hit-and-run accident later identified as the suspect, and known burglars observed in the area at about the same time a burglary was reported. Quite often a field interview card in the police file is more current than a telephone directory published ten months earlier. The advantages of maintaining a permanent record of field interview records far outweigh the disadvantages. For the individuals who are interviewed rather frequently, it would probably be advisable to maintain only those cards related to the most recent two or three years.

LEGALITY OF THE FIELD INTERVIEW

For many years, the courts throughout the United States have held that police officers have the duty to protect themselves and the people who live in, and visit, their jurisdictions, and that they may stop and question any subject who arouses the officer's suspicion if the conditions at the time warrant such inquiry. In one of the two early leading cases in California, the California Supreme Court stated:

> The duty of every good citizen is, when called upon, to give all information in his power to the proper officers of the law as to persons connected with crime; and this should be held to require that

all proper information should be given on request of a personal nature, as affecting the one of whom inquiry is made, when the circumstances are such to warrant an officer in making an inquiry. A police officer has a right to make inquiry in the proper manner of everyone upon the public streets at a late hour as to his identity and to the occasion of his presence, if the surroundings are such as to indicate to a reasonable man that the public safety demands such identification. The fact that crimes had recently been committed in that neighborhood; that the plaintiff at a late hour was found in the locality; that he refused to answer proper questions establishing his identity, were circumstances which should lead a reasonable officer to require his presence at the station, where the sergeant in charge might make more minute and careful inquiry.[1]

Recognizing the need for legal justification of the field officer's participation in a program of conducting field interviews in circumstances warranting such inquiry, many states have followed a trend of enacting laws requiring that certain people cooperate with the inquiring officers whenever public safety demands both the inquiry and the cooperation. Some of the laws, such as those in New Hampshire, Delaware, and New York, authorize the police to stop and question persons who they "reasonably suspect" are committing, have committed, or are about to commit a felony or serious misdemeanor. In many of these cases, the detention is not considered an arrest, but if the officer reasonably believes that he is in "danger of life or limb," he may search the subject to insure that he does not possess any weapons or other items which would imperil the officer's safety. Providing that reasonable cause exists for the original stop and inquiry, some cases have indicated that this search may also extend to items under the immediate control of the persons searched, such as a woman's handbag or a man's attaché case. If the officer finds weapons when conducting such a search, he may make an arrest for the violation and conduct a thorough search incidental to the arrest.

Some states, including California, make it a misdemeanor in the disorderly conduct category and declare the person to be in violation of the law if he ". . . loiters or wanders upon the streets, or from place to place, without apparent reason or business and . . . refuses to identify himself and to account for his presence when requested so to do, if the surrounding circumstances are such as to indicate to a reasonable man that the public safety demands such identification." [2]

Although the law quoted above and others like it do not actually give the officer statutory authority to temporarily detain a person for field interviews, the courts have consistently approved of this procedure in their various interpretations and decisions. There is some interference with an individual's freedom of movement during a field

[1] Miller *vs.* Fano, 134 Cal. 106 (1906).
[2] California Penal Code, Section 647(e)

inquiry, but the action is not a statutory arrest. It is merely a legal detention.

WHEN TO CONDUCT A FIELD INTERVIEW

A good policeman is suspicious by nature, always on the alert for anything that appears out of the ordinary. What is ordinary, of course, depends on where he is, the time of day, and the culture and habits of the people where he is. He notices people and events that are incongruous with the "norm." Some of the factors that should be taken into account when establishing reasonable cause for temporary detentions for field interview contacts are: hours of darkness, a place where crimes of a particular nature are frequently and currently taking place, a neighborhood where there has been a recent rash of burglaries, the individual observed has a record of criminal activity that has been occurring in the particular neighborhood where the contact is to be made. Other factors might be cases in which the subject is driving in an erratic manner, two persons are sitting in a parked car at a time and place that does not fit the circumstances, or individuals are overtly violating a traffic law or criminal code. Going back to the laws, consider the individual who—because of circumstances—appears as if he is committing, did commit, or is about to commit, a felony or serious misdemeanor. Consider the following factors as general grounds for a temporary detention for a field interview:

1. There must be a rational suspicion by the officer that some activity out of the ordinary is occurring, or has taken place.
2. Some indication must exist to connect the person under suspicion with the unusual activity.
3. There must be some suggestion that the activity is related to crime.

The circumstances must be sufficiently unique to justify the officer's suspicions, and he should be prepared to explain the circumstances causing him to choose to conduct a field interview. A police officer is an acknowledged specialist as an observer, and the court will expect you as that officer to call upon your expertise, your training, and past experiences with similar circumstances to "lay the foundation" justifying your cause for conducting the field interview.

There need not be sufficient cause to justify an arrest or a search, but there must be sufficient cause to indicate to you that your failure to make inquiry into the matter would amount to a dereliction of duty as a conscientious police officer.

Whenever there is sufficient cause to temporarily detain an individual for a field inquiry, there is also sufficient cause to perform a cursory "pat down" of the individual for any weapons with which he 143

Figure 6.1   Whether it is Hilo, Billings, or your own city,
the field interview is an integral part of police patrol.
Courtesy of the Police Department, Hilo, Hawaii, and
Billings, Montana.

may attempt to inflict violent injury upon you or some other person.
Although there are many occasions when a field interview situation
may not call for a search for weapons, certain factors may indicate
the need for a "pat down." Consider these points when deciding your
course of action:

1. The nature of the suspected criminal activity, and whether a weapon
   would be used.

2. Your situation: Are you alone, or has assistance arrived?

3. The number of subjects and their emotional and physical state (angry, fighting, intoxicated).
4. Time of day and geographical surroundings.
5. Prior knowledge of the subject's reputation and/or any police record he may have.
6. The sex of the subject or subjects encountered.
7. The behavior and apparent agility of the subjects.
8. The circumstances as they present themselves to you at the time, and as you evaluate them.

FIELD INTERVIEW PROCEDURE

Use this procedure as a general guide for making field contacts, but always adjust your procedure to fit the individual contacted and the circumstances involved.

Location to Choose for Field Interview

If you are in a well-lighted business area, or an industrial complex where there are many high fences and buildings with few open driveways, try to make the contact near a streetlight in the middle of the block. If you are in a residential area where there are many driveways and open areas, choose an intersection for the contact. The reason for selecting these contact locations is to make it easier for you to pursue the subject if he should decide to run. It is easier to chase a subject down a street than through back yards and alleys.

The Approach on Foot

If you are walking toward the subject and meeting head-on, let him walk past you, then turn toward the subject facing his right side. If you approach him from the rear, have him turn so that you are initially on his right side. Depending on the circumstances leading to the field contact, you may order the subject to stop and place his hands on the back of his head or some place where you can see them. If you do not wish to alert him to your suspicions, you may merely state that you wish to speak with him. Avoid offensive terminology when directing the subject to submit to a field interview. Do not place your hands on the subject except to frisk, search, or control him.

The Approach by Automobile

Prior to making the stop, communicate by radio your location, the place where the stop will occur, the license number of the vehicle, and any other pertinent information that you have time for. Such other information should include the number of occupants, clothing descriptions of occupants if you believe a pursuit is about to take place when the occupants alight, and a statement to the effect that you have reason to believe they are armed. Also, if you anticipate the need for follow-up units, request them. A follow-up should be automatically assigned, but the dispatcher may be compelled by a personnel shortage to assign units on a priority basis. Yours would be at the top of the list.

When approaching the suspect car, be on the alert for any sudden movements by the people in the car. There may be a sudden panic stop by a timid individual who suddenly realizes that it is he whom you wish to stop. The subject may attempt to ram the police car, or try some evasive action to avoid the contact. If the subject appears to be armed and it looks as though he may shoot at you, back off and follow at a safer distance until follow-up units arrive and you can make the stop with the aid of several additional units. At this time, also watch for any objects that the vehicle's occupants may throw out the window. Narcotics are often disposed of in this manner.

Making the Auto Stop

Pick your location where there is adequate lighting, and where you will not be at too great a disadvantage should the subject or any of his passengers choose to attack you. You should try to maintain visual control of the people at all times. Signal the driver to pull over to the side of the street, and point to the location where you wish him to go. Use the red light and horn—or siren—to attract the driver's attention and to signal other vehicles to make room for you and the vehicle you are stopping. The object of the maneuver is to stop the other car as quickly as possible, then conduct the field interview while attracting the least amount of attention from other people.

Once you have the vehicle stopped and the cars are not parked in a hazardous location, turn off the overhead red lights to avoid setting up a distraction for passers-by. If necessary to divert traffic away from your vehicle and the one that you have stopped, or to alert other police units to your exact whereabouts, do not hesitate to use the lights.

In some cases when you have information or reason to believe that the subjects in the vehicle you are attempting to stop may have committed a felony, you may choose to draw your revolver, pull alongside the other vehicle, and order the driver to stop while pointing your revolver at him. This is a tactic extremely difficult for a lone officer to perform. If time and circumstances permit, it is wiser to refrain from attempting to make contact until a follow-up unit arrives on the scene to cover you while making the stop.

When stopping felony criminals consider the following points: Some felons actually believe they are being stopped for a minor traffic

Figure 6.2 The police car should be parked about three feet farther from the curb to provide a "walking line" for the officer. Courtesy of the Police Department, Scottsdale, Arizona.

violation and they will "play it cool" to receive their citation and avoid the arrest for the felony they had committed, hoping to avoid the detection of the officer. Other felons may consider the gun a challenge that must be met with violence, and they may begin firing at you. Let the circumstances indicate your course of action, but first try the red light and siren, or the horn and hand signal. If the suspect shoots at you, attempt to back off and avoid a gun battle while you are operating your vehicle.

The final stopped position of the cars should be with the suspect car parked legally at the curb, and the police car to the rear and slightly to the left. By placing the police unit to the left, the relative positions of the cars makes a reasonably safe walkway alongside the suspect car caused by the offset obstacle to the rear, the police car. Leave about 15 feet between cars to allow room for movement through —but not a place for anyone to stand in—the space between the cars. Leave the headlights on at night and if you have a fixed spotlight, turn it on and train it into the rear window onto the rearview mirror of the suspect car. This should illuminate the interior of the suspect car.

The Approach

Two Officers. This procedure may be used for a two-man unit, or a lone officer unit with another lone officer unit as a follow-up. The passenger officer or back-up officer approaches the stopped car from the right rear, and stops just short of the rear window at a vantage point where he can see inside. He should flash his light inside to make

Figure 6.3 Safe position for officer when making initial contact. Courtesy of the Police Department, Scottsdale, Arizona.

an inspection of the interior, primarily to ascertain if anyone inside is armed and prepared to attack, and secondarily to alert the driver and any passengers he may have that there is more than one officer present. While he is assuming that position, the driver officer is outside the unit standing behind the door. He stays at that position for several reasons: one is that in the event the suspects attempt to shoot him, the car door serves as a partial shield that may deflect the bullets; another is that the officer standing at the driver's side of the police unit is in position to immediately get into the vehicle and take off in pursuit in the event that the suspects attempt to drive away. Once the follow-up officer has assumed his position alongside the right rear of the suspect vehicle and the officers see that the suspects make no attempt to drive away, the driver officer approaches the suspect vehicle cautiously on the left side and assumes a position just to the rear of the front door.

By standing slightly to the rear of the driver's door of the suspect vehicle, the officer places the driver at a slight disadvantage by causing him to have to partially turn to look at the officer. From this position, it is more difficult to fire a gun without having to signal to the officer by his movement some indication as to his intentions. If the suspect suddenly swings the door open, there is less chance that it will strike the officer.

ONE OFFICER. Alight from the vehicle and pause momentarily to determine if the driver is going to attempt to leave, or if you are going to be attacked. Walk along the left side of the vehicle, stopping first to look inside the back seat and to survey the general interior before approaching the driver. Some officers have developed a technique of sliding across the seat and alighting from the passenger side of the police car, giving the people in the other car the impression that the

Figure 6.4   Approaching the suspect's vehicle. Look into rear seat area then stand to the rear of the front door. Courtesy of the Police Department, Scottsdale, Arizona.

driver is still in the car. If it is possible for the officer to slide across the front seat, this technique may be effective until the time that he reaches the right rear side of the suspect car. From that point, he must either approach the suspects along the right side of their vehicle, or he must cross in front of his own unit to approach the suspect vehicle. Whichever method of approach you use, keep your suspects in plain view at all times and watch them continuously. Very few of the people you contact in field interview situations are any actual threat to your physical safety. The danger is that you will probably never know which ones are dangerous until the moment arrives when something out of the ordinary occurs.

Figure 6.5   Position of interrogation. Courtesy of the Police Department, Scottsdale, Arizona.

Stand slightly forward and to the right of the subject at slightly more than arm's length away. If he appears to be left-handed, stand to the side of his left hand. Look for the wrist watch, which most people would wear on the weaker hand. Stand at about a 90-degree angle from the subject. From this position, it is possible to grab the subject's arm and ward off a blow that he may intend to wield. Some weaponless defense instructors recommend that the officer assume a head-on position slightly out of range for the suspect's hands or feet to be used as offensive weapons against the officer.

If there is more than one subject, attempt to separate them as soon as practicable before questioning them in order to prevent them from preparing a standardized list of answers to your questions. Until assistance arrives, stand in the position of interrogation next to the leading subject and have the others stand on the other side, all in plain view.

If there are two officers and one subject, the officer who will conduct the interview should stand at the position of interrogation, while the second officer stands to the rear and the opposite side. If there are two officers and more than two subjects, use the same basic posture with the subjects between the officers. Once you have searched them, if necessary, separate them and question them separately.

The Interview

Maintain a friendly, yet not overly familiar, attitude. The attitude of the subject of the interview may be a reflection of that of the officer.

Identify the subject. One of the first questions to ask him is where he lives. He may be anticipating your asking him for a name and he may be prepared with a fabricated one, but he is less likely to have thought of a false address.

Take out your field interview card or notebook only after you have identified the individual. Some people tend to become uncooperative when confronted with something that indicates the imminence of a permanent written record.

Determine the nature of the subject's business at the location where you contact him.

Ask the subject where he is going and where he has been. The story should logically relate to his explanation for being where he is when you contact him.

Determine how familiar the subject is with the neighborhood if he claims to be a frequent visitor.

Ask questions to satisfy your curiosity and your suspicions. Ask positive questions to secure positive responses, such as "Where is your car?" or "When was the last time a police officer questioned you?" Do not make the mistake of providing the subject's negative answers for him by asking questions such as "You don't have a car, do you?" or "You have never been questioned by the police before, or have you?"

When you do not wish to alert the subject to the fact that you may suspect he is a wanted felon or that he matches the description of a person observed at a crime scene, it is advisable to use subterfuge while making the initial contact. The purpose of the deception is to avoid alerting him to your suspicions until you are at a position of advantage. It may appear natural for you to ask the subject if he has seen a car you are looking for or if he is the person who called to report an abandoned car.

If the subject's answers and his behavior continue to pique your curiosity and suspicions, you may change your line of questioning as soon as you have a position of advantage.

If the subject's answers, attitude, or other behavior indicate that there is no further cause for action or detention, complete the form or notebook entry required by your department and conclude the interview. If the circumstances indicate the need for further inquiry, continue the interview. Never lower your guard and "assume" that the subject presents no danger to you. He probably does not, but you do not know that.

1. If there are two or more subjects, separate them as soon as practicable prior to questioning.
2. Check for identification. Be sure that the documents describe the subject. Indicate on your field interview card or notebook the types of documents used and any numbers the documents bear.
3. Ask the subject to repeat the nature of his business in the area.
4. Secure a statement as to where the subject is going and where he has been.
5. Check out the story when possible. If two persons are providing separate information, compare notes.
6. Fill out a complete description of the subject, including:
   a. Visible scars, marks, tattoos.
   b. Deformities, unusual characteristics.
   c. Membership data as indicated by cards presented for identification, car club jackets, lapel pins, car plaques, and business cards.
   d. Design of heel and shoe prints, and shoe size (particularly of those subjects you identify as having burglary records).
   e. Subject's statement regarding past criminal record and/or prior contacts with the police.

Use the radio or a telephone—if available—to check records on the subject for a prior record and to ascertain if he is wanted.

Arrest or release the subject, depending on the circumstances as indicated by your investigation to this point.

Conduct a pat-down, or cursory search. If circumstances warrant your field contact with the subject, the same conditions justify the pat-down for any offensive weapons with which the subject may attack you. The timing depends on the circumstances of the individual case, but should occur early unless a brief interview indicates to you that you do not wish to further restrict the subject's movement. If you do pat down the subject, do it early to avoid later regrets.

Complete filling out the field interview card or the notebook entry. When writing your reason for the field interview, indicate *what it was about the subject and/or the circumstances that caused you to first decide to proceed with the field interview.* Be specific, as this justification should be considered *reasonable cause* for the interview, the detention, and any other action you should take. Without this information, it is conceivable that you might lose an otherwise good case.

Conclude the field interview promptly.

1. To the "legitimate" subject, a word of caution about recent crimes in the area, a brief explanation of the field interview program and its necessity, and a "thank you" for his cooperation.
2. To the "suspicious" subject, a word of advice pertaining to the process of the field interview and its possible significance to him, depending on the circumstances of the contact and the character of the subject.
3. If the interview and accompanying circumstances lead to the need for more intensive investigation and discussion of the matter at hand

Figure 6.6 Interrogation is an art. One of the most important factors is to establish rapport and maintain a friendly atmosphere. Courtesy of the Police Department, Aberdeen, South Dakota.

with the subject, you may have "focused" on him as a suspect in a specific offense and a custodial interrogation may follow.

INTERVIEWING THE SUSPECT OF A CRIME

Constitutional Guidelines

Before you may begin a custodial police interrogation in which you intend to question an individual about his involvement—or suspected involvement—in any criminal act, you must advise him as follows:

> You have the absolute right to remain silent. Anything you say can, and will, be used against you in court. You have the right to consult with an attorney, to be represented by an attorney, and to have one present before I ask you any questions. If you cannot afford an attorney, one will be appointed to represent you before you are questioned, if you desire.

The suspect must understand and communicate to you his understanding of the wording of the admonishment and its significance as it relates to him in his present predicament. If he does not understand any of the words, or their meanings, they must be explained to him. Once you have an agreement with him that he understands the words and their meanings, the Supreme Court has ruled: "the defendant may waive effectuation of these rights, provided the waiver is made voluntarily, knowingly, and intelligently." You may proceed with the questions only if the suspect understands the admonishment and you gain an affirmative response to this question:

> With these rights in mind, are you ready to talk with me about the charges against you?

The suspect must give his oral waiver and consent to continue with the interrogation. A mere lack of response in the form of silence does not constitute a waiver. Once the suspect exercises his right to remain silent and indicates that he does not wish to answer any of your questions, the interrogation must cease if you are to have any of his statements pass the test of admissibility in court. Do not attempt to persuade him to change his mind or engage him in any "games" in an effort to trick him into changing his mind or giving you information inadvertently.

The preceding admonition and the accompanying procedure evolved out of several years of court decisions and was finally crystallized in its present form by the U. S. Supreme Court in its decision now known as the Miranda Decision. On June 13, 1966 the U. S. Supreme Court delivered a decision dealing with the "admissibility of statements obtained from an individual who is subjected to *custodial police interrogation* [italics added] and the necessity for procedures which assure that the individual is accorded his privilege under the Fifth Amendment to the Constitution not be compelled to incriminate himself." The cases referred to in this decision included: Miranda v. Arizona, Vignera v. New York, Westover v. United States, and California v. Stewart.[3] The guidelines in this chapter are based upon this and subsequent decisions.

A "custodial interrogation" is one that is conducted under circumstances when the subject of the questioning process is "significantly deprived of his freedom" in the words of the court, and under circumstances when the investigation is focused upon the subject at an accusatory stage of the investigation. Victims and witnesses are not in custody and not in an accusatory stage, meaning that they are not suspected of a crime. There are many occasions when an officer questions people in field interview situations to ascertain their identity and the nature of their business in a particular location at an unusual time or under suspicious circumstances, or to determine ownership of certain unexplained property in their possession. In most of these cases, the questions are asked and satisfactory answers received without incident and the interview never reaches an *accusatory* stage when the officer would focus on the subject as a suspect in a specific crime. Under most of these investigatory situations, it would be a personal affront to the subject of the questioning to advise him of his constitutional right to remain silent and to have an attorney with him, because to do so would be insinuating that he is suspected of having committed some sort of criminal act. In some situations, of course, the field interviews do lead to accusatory circumstances and at those times it is necessary to lead into the "Miranda admonition," as described earlier.

Once advised of these rights, the subject may exercise them and say nothing, requesting the presence of an attorney. He may waive the rights by stating that he does fully understand them but that he still wishes to talk and answer your questions. Once he waives the rights he may reconsider at any time. In the words of the Miranda Decision:

> If, however, he indicates in any manner and at any state of the process that he wishes to consult with an attorney before speaking there can be no questioning. Likewise, if the individual is alone and indicates in any manner that he does not wish to be interrogated, the police may not question him. The mere fact that he may have answered some questions or volunteered some statements on

---

[3] All cases listed in this instance are covered in Miranda *vs.* Arizona 384 U.S. 436 (1966).

his own does not deprive him of the right to refrain from answering any further inquiries until he has consulted with an attorney and thereafter consents to be questioned.

If an individual is not actually the subject of a custodial interrogation, as when you are on the scene conducting the preliminary investigation (including most field interviews), and he makes any spontaneous declarations of any type—including what may amount to admissions or a confession—his statements are admissible in court regardless of whether you advised him of his rights to remain silent and to an attorney. There is no way of predicting circumstances under which a person will make such spontaneous declarations, and there can be no insinuation that you obtained statements of this nature under "custodial conditions."

If an individual is arrested and there is to be no questioning, there is no need to admonish him regarding his constitutional rights at the time. In some situations it is the wiser course of action to wait until after the heat of the situation has cooled down to the point where it is possible to rely on a rational discussion. Consider the following as an example of a time when it would hardly seem suitable to perform the advisement rites:

An officer is parked on a side street near one of the city's main boulevards when he hears from a radio broadcast that a car containing two occupants in a green, two-door sedan, has just left the scene of an armed robbery. The victim attempted to thwart the robbery by shooting at one of the suspects, but he was disarmed and beaten. The lone officer is only about three blocks from the scene of the crime, and suddenly a car matching the description of the wanted one looms into sight. The officer negotiates a turn onto the street in medium traffic, and is about five cars behind the suspect car. He radios in for a cover unit and decides to follow the suspects until they are out of the way of other cars and his follow-up unit is near to cover him. Suddenly, the driver spots him and begins a high-speed attempt to escape. The officer radios in this new information, then turns on his red light and siren and takes up the chase.

The chase involves high speeds through medium to heavy traffic, including going against several signals and signs, barely avoiding some serious accidents. Finally, after about two miles of pursuit, the officer edges the suspect car to the curb. They stop, and he jumps out and approaches the suspect car in an effort to get to them before they gather their wits and use any weapons that they might have.

The officer knows that this is not the academy-recommended procedure, but he believes it is better under the circumstances because there are so many other cars and pedestrians around that he believes he can avoid gunfire. He grabs the door handle, opens the door and tells the suspects to get out. Shocked by the fast action of the officer, the suspects get out of their car with no struggle. As he quickly searches the suspects for weapons, one of them tries to attack him. The officer subdues the one suspect and is met by some resistance from the other. He regains control of the suspects just as the follow-up unit arrives. He takes both suspects back to the other police car, thoroughly searches them this time, and places them in the back seat of the car.

At that particular moment when the action has calmed down at the scene, would you advise the suspects of their right to remain silent and to have an attorney present when they are being questioned? Are you prepared to begin an interrogation at that time and under those conditions? It is not difficult to imagine what the response would be from the suspects at that moment if you were to ask them, "Do you want to talk with me?" If you believe that an on-the-scene interrogation is essential to clear up some vital facts of the case, or that it would be tactically wise to question the suspects at the time, then it is imperative that you proceed with the Miranda admonishment.

If you have sufficient evidence to lead to an arrest based on reasonable cause, and the tactical decision is to wait before any questioning, then do not advise the subject of those rights at that moment. When you make an arrest solely on a warrant, make the following determinations prior to admonishing the subject or questioning him: Are the officers who investigated the case and who should conduct the interrogation available? If so, contact them and follow their instructions. If the warrant is from another jurisdiction, do not admonish the arrestees or attempt to conduct any interrogation, as you have no information to prepare you for an intelligent interview.

The warning regarding the individual's constitutional rights and his exercise of those rights, or waiver of such rights, only affects the admissibility of the subject's statements when later used against him in court. One exception to this provision is that in some states laws have been enacted which require that any minor who is arrested must be admonished regarding certain rights, including those to an attorney and against self-incrimination, whether the subject is to be questioned or not. A child may waive those rights in the same manner as an adult, but when he does, the question arises as to whether he could actually comprehend the true meaning of the admonishment to make a value judgment, and then, whether he could make an intelligent waiver with his limited knowledge. This is a matter for the interviewing officer to decide at the time and the courts to rule on later.

Miranda warnings need not be given in cases when the suspect is required by "implied consent" laws involving driving a vehicle while under influence of alcohol to submit to a blood or breath or urine analysis for the purpose of determining blood-alcohol percentage. The suspect need not be admonished prior to giving handwriting examplars, before having his fingerprints or photograph taken for identification purposes, or before standing in a lineup. An individual may require his attorney to be present for the purpose of observing the lineup to assure his client that it is being handled correctly, but he need not be advised of his rights as provided in the Miranda Rule for that purpose. He may be asked to speak during a lineup for identification purposes, and that is not a violation of the court's rule. The Miranda Rule applies strictly to the admissibility of an individual's statements in court when used against him in his trial, and those statements that were elicited from the individual during a custodial interrogation.

In certain cases when an individual has exercised his rights against self-incrimination, he later indicates of his own volition that he wishes to resume the interview and that he wishes to voluntarily make statements or a confession. Under these circumstances such statements will be held admissible. The subject must initiate the action, however, and there can be no attempt on the part of the officer to take the initiative to gain the statements under conditions when it would appear that the subject was coerced or enticed to subsequently waive those rights.

Preparation for the Interrogation

Prior to the interrogation of the suspect, be sure that you have all the information concerning the suspect and the case at your disposal. Be sure to provide for his safety and comfort, and proceed with the same preparation as for any other interview. Give the Miranda admonishment and advise the suspect why he is being questioned. There are two basic approaches to most interrogations: the sympathetic approach, and the direct or logical approach. Keeping in mind the fact that the subject has the right to discontinue the interrogation at any time he chooses, and the fact that you must discontinue the interrogation at that time, consider the guidelines presented in the following section in securing statements from the people who do waive their rights and indicate a desire to talk with you.

THE "ART" OF INTERVIEWING

Of the many police activities the officer must perform, interviewing truly approaches the category of "art." It takes talent, a natural inclination to perform the task well, study and practice to develop the basic skills, and continual self-analysis and cultivation of the talents and skills involved in the questioning process. The real artist studies himself, then adapts his own personality to the various situations and the individual personalities of the many people he questions. He develops a style that is distinctive, and he improves with studied experience. No one is a "born interrogator" any more than he is a "born marksman." The officer must have an intense interest in human nature, a desire to develop the skill, and the ability to learn from each interview experience.

One of the basic characteristics of the average human seems to be that he is gregarious and likes to talk. He must talk about his successes, his failures, his good and bad luck, his ambitions, himself, others, and—quite significantly—he feels a compulsion to talk about his crimes when he commits them. Many experts theorize that it is the intense desire to share experiences with others that causes the criminal law violator to confess his crimes. Theodor Reik, a student of criminal psychiatry and a protégé of Freud, advanced his theory that an individual who commits a crime is haunted by the guilt feelings caused by violating his own ethical standards, and the terrible truth of the crime begs to be let out through confession. He called this the compulsion to confess. This is congruous with the beliefs of many skilled police interrogators, who have often encountered individuals who demand to be heard, and who freely and voluntarily confess to atrocious crimes that are so repugnant to the confessors that they must purge themselves of the terrible secrets or suffer a lifetime of torture. Once they tell of their crimes, they show distinct signs of relief, and they seem to look forward to whatever punishment society has prescribed for them. The penance of punishment may help cleanse them of their crimes.

A key to the development of the "artistic" interviewer is his ability to see each new person that he interviews as a different individual with his own set of values and a distinctive personality quite unlike that of any other human. The officer who hopes to develop this skill must constantly be mindful of the individuality of the people he questions and should constantly guard against allowing himself to oversimplify a problem by stereotyping individuals into "categories" that may seem to him to be all alike. Once he begins to generalize in this manner, the "artist" fades and the "report-taker" emerges. Your responsibility as a professional police officer is to strive to perform as the "artist" interrogator.

OBJECTIVES OF THE INTERVIEW

There are four basic objectives in the interview or interrogation: (1) ascertain the truth, whatever it is; (2) secure complete information in detail; (3) distinguish fact from fantasy; and (4) have a target (the truth) and proceed according to a plan.

Sympathetic Approach

The sympathetic approach is usually more effective than the direct approach, because the individual who has committed the crime usually feels remorse and guilt for having done something that he knows is wrong. To call him a thief or a liar will surely end the interrogation before it begins. Accidental offenders, or first-time criminals respond to this approach most readily. Others who will usually respond to sympathy are sex offenders, persons who have committed crimes of passion involving intense emotional feelings, and people who have sensitive personalities.

The technique in the sympathetic approach is to indicate an interest in the person as an individual. Show him that you can understand why he would have done whatever it is that he did. Be kind and considerate to the individual, who is entitled to your respect. His crime may have been indicative of animalistic tendencies, but if you are to gain his confidence and respect, and his confession, it is imperative that you appeal to his human qualities in a rational and understanding manner. Be friendly, yet not "phony," in a professional way. Your role as the interrogator is not to scold or punish the criminal violator.

Logical Approach

The direct approach is most likely to work with pre-adolescents, recidivists, and those types of criminal law violators who commit crimes against property, which indicate their cunning and disregard for the property of others. There are some people who commit their crimes in spite of law, either in defiance of it or because they do not agree with it and see no reason why they should obey the law. White-collar crimes, vice operations, and organized crime offenses are hardly likely to be committed by amateurs, and whenever a violator of one of these types of crimes is questioned, the best results will probably be obtained by telling the individual what he is being questioned for, presenting him with the facts, then soliciting from him any statements he wishes to make. Although I doubt that there is any individual who is totally without emotional feelings, except perhaps the sociopath, the people who respond to the logical approach seem to be those whose crimes involve intelligence or cunning, rather than emotional involvement as in the crimes of passion and sex offense.

Techniques for the logical approach generally consist of keeping the interrogation simple and to the point. State why the subject is being questioned and give him sufficient information to show him that you have reasonable cause for the arrest, while avoiding the **159** mistake of giving him more information than you hope to receive. You may give him some of the details of the case, then simply state that you believe he has a "side" to tell, and that you want to hear it to determine the true facts of the case. Occasionally, this technique proves so effective that the suspect cooperates fully and when he does give his "side" of the story, it becomes apparent that there has been no crime. If his story consists of lies and discrepancies, point them out to him and ask for an explanation. While using this technique, never assume that the suspect is lying and the victim or witnesses are entirely correct. Many times the suspect will speak the truth, and that truth may bear no resemblance to the account of the crime as presented by the accusers.

Operational Suggestions

If in doubt as to which approach to use, try the sympathetic technique first, then direct questioning. Once the suspect indicates that the interrogation is over, it is. Beware of the confession that is too easy to obtain. As long as the suspect is willing to speak about his crime freely, have him prove his points by describing all the elements of the crime, plus whatever additional information may be necessary to prove his actual guilt. Finally, never underestimate the suspect or overestimate yourself.

CONCLUSION

Implementation of an active and objective field interview program is essential to the successful and effective operation of the modern law enforcement agency. The program not only gives the officers an opportunity to prevent and repress crime by meeting and counseling the actual or potential criminal law violators, but also provides the officer an additional vehicle for contacts with the law-abiding people in his district.

Indiscriminate field interviews and accompanying searches for weapons are not warranted. They must be based on *reasonable cause* factors and the officer must be able to articulate them. An officer must check into any individuals or circumstances that appear at the time to be deleterious to the good order and the peace of the community. The officer's diplomacy may ease the strain in situations that appear to him at first to be quite suspicious, but after the contact turn out to be strictly legitimate and aboveboard. If the officer handles it correctly, the field interview will result in a favorable contact with someone who will appreciate the officer's diligence and efficiency in looking after his safety by making such field inquiries, particularly at times and places where suspicious circumstances warrant it. The law-abiding

resident will gain confidence in the knowledge that while he is enjoying the privacy of his own home in relative safety, the policemen
outside are looking after his peace and safety.

EXERCISES AND STUDY QUESTIONS

1. What justification does the author give for calling interrogation an art?
2. What is Reik's theory on the individual's attitude toward confession?
3. What must the interrogator know about the case before he engages in an interrogation?
4. What courses of action would you recommend if you are working on an important case and find that you have an incurable personality clash with the subject you had intended to question concerning a criminal matter?
5. What are the four basic objectives of an interview?
6. What are some of the "indicators" of deception that may manifest themselves when you question a suspect?
7. Recount the exact wording of the Miranda admonition.
8. Discuss the value of the field interview process.
9. List and discuss at least five subjects or situations that you believe would demand a field interview.
10. Describe how you would establish rapport with a male college student, a middle-aged housewife, and a cross-country truck driver.

SUGGESTED SEMESTER OR TERM PROJECTS

1. Starting with the McNabb and Mallory cases, write a history of the significant court cases on confessions and admissions in your own state's courts and in the U. S. Supreme Court.
2. If your department does not have a field interview program, prepare a justification for one. Design the "F I" card and outline the department's policies and procedures for successful implementation of the program.

REFERENCES

COLEMAN, JAMES C., *Abnormal Psychology and Modern Life,* 2nd ed. Chicago: Scott, Foresman & Company, 1956, pp. 60–105, 172–217, 244–490.

FREUD, SIGMUND, *Psychopathology of Everyday Life.* New York: Mentor Books, 1951, pp. 102–118.

INBAU, FRED E., and JOHN E. REID, *Criminal Interrogation and Confessions.* Baltimore: The Williams & Wilkins Co., 1962.

162

REIK, THEODOR, *The Compulsion to Confess—On the Analysis of Crime and Punishment.* New York: Farrar, Straus & Giroux, Inc., 1959, pp. 179–356.

STUCKEY, GILBERT B., *Evidence for the Law Enforcement Officer.* New York: McGraw-Hill Book Company, 1968, Chap. 7.

Crimes in Progress

CHAPTER SEVEN   There are few calls for police service that more directly involve the field policeman than the "crime in progress" call. The response must be immediate and with the precision of fine machinery. Time is precious. Response time is often the determinant of whether the victim will suffer death or serious injury, and the element of time also determines whether the culprit will be apprehended at the scene or elsewhere, if at all.

When possible, there should be some preparation and planning for the inevitable crime in progress to assure a fine degree of precision in handling the call and apprehending the suspect. During the planning process, locate those places within the city or county area of your jurisdiction that are potential crime hazards, such as banks and liquor stores for robberies, drugstores and restaurants for burglaries, and as many other places likely to fall prey to the criminal as can be anticipated.

Map out the surrounding areas, such as streets, alleys, and dead-end   **163** streets, or cul-de-sacs. List and indicate the locations and numbers of entrances into the buildings. What are the most logical places where a burglar might enter? Exit? Are there any low-hanging obstructions that will either provide the culprit an additional means of escape by access to the roof, or that an officer may run into in the dark? Who are the informants in the neighborhood, and how will they act under stress? Ask yourself virtually every question about the crime that may occur at each location, the suspected criminals you may encounter, and the victims and what their reactions may be under various in-progress crime situations. In every way possible, work out the police coverage of the crime that may someday occur, although it may be only once. If not this location, there is little doubt that it will be another place with similar characteristics. Consider all possibilities of escape, including time of day and various related traffic factors. Planning should be a regular part of your routine while you are on patrol and there are momentary lags in the demands on your time and energy.

"IN-PROGRESS" COMMUNICATIONS PROCEDURE

When receiving the call that a crime is in progress, the communications operator should immediately alert the various units and divisions that will be involved in the action, preferably by use of a "hot line," as described in Chapter 3. Impress upon the informant the importance of staying on the telephone, or at least keeping the line open, if it is at all practicable. When you begin the conversation with the calling party, state, "Don't hang up. Stay on the telephone!" Ascertain as quickly as possible the exact nature of the crime, whether it is a robbery, a burglary, or a theft that occurred three days ago. To some people, every crime is a robbery, and their emotions may be so involved that it is a "right now" situation even though the suddenly discovered crime may have occurred several days earlier.

Secure the precise address and location within the building or place where the crime is occurring. Get as much descriptive data as possible about the suspect(s), including the number of suspects, distinctive clothing, the description of any hostages who might be taken away, any weapons, and the vehicle used, if any. Determine the location of the calling party and whether he is in any danger of being observed by the suspect or in danger of sustaining injuries if he should remain at the place. Broadcast the information and handle the essential preliminary assignments while keeping the caller on the open phone line, then secure from him any additional information that he may have to give about the initial event or any continuing sequence of events.

When first receiving the call concerning an "in-progress" situation, alert all units in the area of the nature of the event. Once the alert is broadcast, the units in the immediate vicinity should acknowledge receipt of the call and give their respective locations. The unit closest to the scene should be assigned to handle the call. This may not be the unit assigned to that particular district, but the urgency of the situa- tion may call for a deviation from normal procedure. If there is a department policy that requires the district unit to be assigned the call, a reassignment may be made after the initial response has been taken care of. At this moment the most important need is to have a police officer at the crime scene as quickly as possible. After assigning the unit that will handle the call, designate follow-up units, and instruct all other units to proceed to key locations around the crime scene. These locations should not be so close to the scene of the crime that their effectiveness will be reduced. Although the call is "in-prog-ress," there is a strong possibility that the suspects will soon be leaving —or may have been gone for some time—and too many units in the immediate vicinity will be a waste of time and effort for the officers responding.

FIELD UNIT RESPONSE

If there is a possibility that the suspect is still at the crime scene and that he is unaware that the police have been alerted, the object in your arrival is to get there as quickly as possible without signaling your arrival. Use red light and siren only if the dispatcher instructs you to do so. The factors that should be taken into consideration for a "code three" assignment are the urgency of the situation, the safety of any victim who may be under attack, the time of day, and traffic conditions for the responding units. Get to the scene of the crime as quickly as possible, but do not sacrifice your own safety or that of other people on the way. Know your streets and as much about your district as possible. There is usually some uniformity, some system in num-bering the lots, all even numbers on one side, odd numbers on the other. The lapse between numbers may be in multiples of two, four, or ten, but whatever the configuration it is probably uniform through-out the city. The naming and numbering system may also be accord-ing to some master plan.

En route to the scene of the crime, be on the alert for virtually anything or anybody that appears to be in the area. It is possible that certain individuals may not fit the given descriptions of the sus-pects; there is a strong possibility that the descriptions were not accurate. Most of the people whom you will encounter will have per-fectly legitimate reasons for being where they are, and some of those persons may have information concerning minor items surrounding the crime that may help you further identify the suspect and his auto-mobile and possibly lead to other valuable evidence. Call for a fol-low-up unit to check these people out and take down their names, addresses, and telephone numbers and any other information about them that you may refer to later should you have reason to question them further. The field interview card is an appropriate device to use for this purpose. Your role as the responding unit is to go directly to the scene.

Except when you wish to announce your arrival at the scene as a strategic move to distract the perpetrator of the crime in an effort to prevent serious injury to his victim, make your arrival as quiet as practicable. Make your approach to the location by way of parallel streets in order to avoid letting any lookout who may be in the area see your unit until about the moment you arrive. Avoid squealing tires if possible, and the sudden braking sounds of your unit sliding into "home plate." The arrival of your unit should sound and appear the same as any other vehicle approaching and stopping in the neighborhood.

Once you are in position and observe the exact location where the crime is believed to be taking place, determine whether it is in fact occurring. Upon your arrival, radio in your "arrived on the scene" transmission, and any other information that is of immediate significance. If it is evident that there is no need for the follow-up units that are on the way, advise communications to call them off. If you are immediately made aware of needed assistance, such as an ambulance or rescue equipment, broadcast that information as well.

Keep communications informed as to what is going on at the scene. The 10- to 15-minute delay that sometimes occurs between the original "there now" call and the next transmission from any of the units at the scene of the "crime in progress" call may seem an eternity to the concerned patrol commanders and the dispatcher personnel, not to mention the many other units on the same radio frequency who are following the events with considerable anxiety.

If the circumstances at the scene allow you to do so, attempt as soon as possible to establish a telephone connection with the communications center. Hopefully, the dispatcher or desk officer who received the original phone call was successful in getting across to the calling party that the line should be kept open so that the caller would continue to feed information concerning the on-going crime—if possible—and to hand the telephone instrument to the first officer to arrive on the scene.

Once the officer on the scene establishes telephone or radio contact with the headquarters personnel, he may report on the current status and progress on the case. He continues passing on his instructions for follow-up units, requests whatever assistance he needs from other police units and other emergency services. While he is questioning the victim and/or witnesses about the crime, the officer may relay by telephone such pertinent information as descriptions of suspects, the suspect vehicle, his direction of travel, and any other information that will aid in the location and capture of the suspect if he has left the scene by the time the officer arrived at that location. While this is all going on, the dispatcher personnel will continue broadcasting the necessary information.

The follow-up unit should proceed directly to the scene and determine whether his presence is required at that location. He will assist in the initial response to ascertain if the crime is still in progress and to take whatever immediate action is warranted. He will then assist in locating and interviewing the victims and witnesses, searching for the suspect and taking him into custody, and generally work as the partner to the officer originally assigned the call. He remains at the crime scene until his presence is no longer necessary, and then takes part in the area search for the suspect.

TACTICS BY TYPES OF CRIMES

Robbery in Progress

First determine that the crime is actually a robbery and that it is still in progress. A robbery involves the taking of another person's property from that person or from his presence by means of force or fear. If the robbery is still in progress upon your arrival, make an immediate assessment and detemine your course of action. Take a position out of the line of fire and as much as possible out of the suspect's line of sight as well. Use the police unit or part of the building as a shield against any impending attack by the suspect. Determine if there is any immediate danger to the victim, such as an on-going attack, or obvious immediate need for medical aid.

If the circumstances require your immediate confrontation with the suspect, approach him with extreme caution. It is at this point that many policemen lose their lives either through carelessness or indecisiveness. Consider the possibility that your immediate approach may startle the suspect and lead him to take a hostage or to physically abuse his victim more than he may have already done. Under these circumstances, he may also attempt to kill or injure you as well as his other victim. If you must enter, do so quickly, moving to your right to make yourself a less conspicuous target and to compensate for any flinching the suspect may do if he fires a weapon at you. Attempt to assume visual and physical control of the suspect as quickly as possible.

If you ascertain upon your arrival that there is no immediate additional danger to the victim, and if the suspect is not yet aware of your presence, remain outside at a vantage point and wait for help to arrive. There is no need to be foolhardy, and actions that are too hasty may cause serious injury or death to both yourself as well as the victim. If possible, wait for the subject to come outside so that the advantage will be yours.

There are several excellent reasons that it is better to wait for the suspect to come outside. If the suspect is not aware of your presence, he may see no need to take a hostage. There may be less provocation to cause the suspect to inflict further injuries on his victim if the suspect's efforts to escape from the crime scene do not seem to him to be frustrated. While you are waiting for the suspect to come outside, your follow-up units may have additional time to arrive. When the suspect does come out you have the advantage of cover provided by your vehicle, trees and shrubbery, walls of the building, and various other hiding places.

If you know that the suspect is gone when you arrive, immediately determine as best you can the condition of the victim. If there is no apparent urgency for rendering first aid, stop for just a moment and plan your action, trying under the circumstances not to destroy certain items of evidence that might be instrumental in securing a prosecution. Think of where the suspect might have walked and his possible point and method of entry, then do what you can under the circumstances to preserve the evidence.

Proceed with as much deliberation and calmness of bearing as possible. The people you contact during the investigation of a robbery are inclined to be under severe emotional stress. Your charisma may be the necessary steadying influence that will make it possible for the victim and the various witnesses to remain calm. Consequently, they are likely to be far more effective in aiding the investigation.

Burglary in Progress

A burglar alarm is activated, an open door is found, or someone may actually be observed inside a building. Any one of these situations may prove to be a burglary in progress. Or they may not turn out to be any more than a faulty alarm system, a door left open by a careless employee, or the owner of the store taking an all-night inventory. Each must be handled by the patrol officer as if it were a possible burglary in progress.

The statutes defining burglary vary somewhat among the various states. In some jurisdictions, burglary may be the term used to define the crime of breaking into a building for the purpose of committing theft. In other states, including California, the crime of burglary involves any entry (whether a breaking into the building occurs or not) with the specific intent at the time of the entry to commit the act of theft or some other felony.

The burglar is a felon. He must be apprehended and prosecuted. Every means possible should be utilized to take the burglar into custody with the least amount of force or destruction. When it is apparent, or when all appearances lead you to believe that a burglary is in progress, you should anticipate that at least one burglar is inside and immediately plan your strategy to block his escape and capture him.

Arrange for adequate assistance before entering a building that may be occupied by a burglar. Unless there is someone inside who may be in danger of attack from the culprit, you are at a tactical advantage by remaining on the outside with the suspect inside. Time is on your side. If a silent alarm system is utilized by the establishment, there is a possibility that the suspect inside is not yet aware of your presence. If possible, do not enter until your back-up officers are in position and you have the entire building covered.

Do not overlook the possibility of calling for assistance from adjoining jurisdiction to cover the building and to attempt capturing the suspect should he attempt to exit from the building. It is better to have too much help, if available, than too little.

While you are waiting for back-up officers, place yourself in a position of advantage from which you may observe as much of the building as possible near the area where the suspect is most likely to exit. Look up at the roof, which is a popular hiding place for some burglars who believe that police officers do not look up. When the assisting officers arrive, place the first two officers at opposite corners of the building. In the event the building is oddly shaped and difficult to cover from the opposite corners, consider placing the officers at opposite corners of the block. From these positions, they may not be in a position to apprehend the suspect, but they will see anyone who enters or leaves the area under their surveillance, which is important in this type of operation. Place additional officers at the places through which the suspect may exit.

Check for anyone in the vicinity who is either on foot or in a vehicle. It is not likely that a lookout will linger for long after your arrival, but some people serving in that capacity have remained throughout the entire series of events. They were successful in not being detected because of the plausibility of their "cover" role and explanations for being where they were located. Lookouts may pose as deliverymen, workmen, utility meter inspectors, a stranded motorist working on his automobile, a pair of "lovers" sitting in an automobile, or a man walking his dog in the neighborhood. Do not overlook the most obvious, the person who appears as if he is trying to get out of the area without your detection of his presence.

If there are no readily visible signs of entry at any of the doors or windows, consider the roof. Many roofs are accessible by climbing on boxes, adjacent utility poles, drain pipes, fences, or other nearby roofs. Some merchants lock their ground floors and windows quite securely, but leave upstairs windows or skylights unlocked because of their seeming inaccessibility. There are many other methods of entry, such as a tunnel from another side of a fence and up through the floor, or a hole broken through the wall from an adjoining suite in the same building.

Approach the place where you intend to enter very carefully and deliberately. It is preferable to have the burglar come out rather than to go in after him. Keeping this in mind, pause and give him the opportunity to come out at your invitation. If the suspect comes out with the merchandise he has stolen, it is easier to prove his intention to steal those items he is carrying, which is one advantage of waiting for the suspect to come out. The most important advantage in waiting is that there is less likelihood that someone will be injured in the ensuing action when you begin to make your entry into the building.

Determine in advance exactly who is going to enter the building. Never have officers at opposite sides of the building enter. The officers who enter should do so as a single team, and they should work close together while constantly keeping an eye on each other. Either work back-to-back or side-to-side, or alternately take the lead with one officer behind the other in a leapfrog pattern. The purpose of this method of coverage is to assure each man that his partner knows exactly who and where he is in the darkened and deserted interior of the building. Without such a system it is not unlikely that one officer could walk into the pointed barrel of another officer's revolver.

If the point of entry is a door, look at the ground or floor at the entrance for footprints or any other evidence the culprit may have left while entering. Consider the possibility that he may have left fingerprints on the door or doorknobs. It may be necessary to give first priority to apprehending the culprit, while obliterating some of the evidence you might have otherwise been able to collect. Preservation of life and property includes your own as well as that of the other people you serve and protect.

When you use a flashlight, hold it away from your body, preferably with your weak hand. Most inexperienced shooters have a tendency to flinch to their left while shooting directly at the light source. When entering the building try to avoid making a silhouette of yourself by standing in the center of the doorway and, at the moment you enter, consider turning off your flashlight. When you open the door, stand to one side out of the line of fire if the suspect should choose to attack you. Open the door by slamming it against the stop to make sure no one is hiding behind the door. Step in quickly and immediately to the side out of the doorway. Wait until your partner follows suit. Then stand and listen for a few moments to get accustomed to the new lighting conditions and the sounds inside the building. There are some noises characteristic to the building that can be quite disquieting if you are not accustomed to them. Refrigerators, freezers, electronics equipment, animals left inside for security, clocks, heaters, and air conditioning devices all sound differently in a strange building.

Once you are inside and have determined that the suspect is not in the room where you are, make liberal use of the flashlight, then turn on the electric lights in the room. When you use the electric lights as you go through the rooms, consider the advisability of turning them back off before walking into the next room. Otherwise, there is a possibility that you will silhouette yourself and jeopardize your life. Each time you enter another room, slam the door to the stopper or the wall to make sure there is no one standing behind the door.

Make a thorough and methodical check of the entire building to determine whether a crime has been committed and whether the suspect may still be inside. When people are hiding, they discover that they can literally shrink into spaces they never realized they would fit into. Look up! Burglars sometimes hide on closet shelves or in attics above closets where they sometimes go undetected. Attics, large drawers, incinerators, storage cabinets, behind doors, under desks, and practically any place in the building is a potential hiding place. Once you have searched a particular room, or portion of the building, "clear" that searched area by closing the door and placing articles of furniture in strategic locations so that they would have to be moved for someone to pass through that area. If sufficient manpower is available, and if the area to be checked is large, an officer placed at a strategic location can guard closed and cleared areas.

As you proceed in the building search, make spot rechecks to compensate for the possibility that you may have a clever burglar who escaped detection, or who sneaked past the searching officers. One morning a team of my fellow officers who were checking out a building did a very thorough job of searching but apparently overlooked one obvious place. After the officers left the building, the burglar broke out and activated the alarm again. After some time, they were able to catch the burglar in a nearby orange grove. When he was questioned about his ability to avoid detection by the searching officers, he stated that he had hidden under a desk in the office in the light manufacturing building. One officer had searched that room, discovered the phone, called the police station and conversed with the telephone operator for a few minutes, then had left the office and resumed the search with his fellow officers. The suspect stated that he had had a great temptation to untie the officer's shoelaces but decided not to.

If you find the suspect inside the building, search him immediately and use appropriate restraining devices. Never assume that he is working alone. Look for an accomplice either inside the building or nearby outside. This is one type of police activity for which the use of trained dogs is exceptionally valuable.

If it is determined that a crime was committed, proceed with the initial crime scene search and the preliminary investigation. If it turns out that the building had not been burglarized, but just left open, secure the building. In any event, contact the owner and advise him of your presence while requesting that he make an appearance. You may do this by phoning him direct from the office in his building if you can ascertain who he is, or you may have your communications personnel contact him. One method for determining the name of the owner is to check through records for a recent crime, such as a check case in which that business was listed as the victim. The report should reflect the names, addresses, and phone numbers of key company personnel.

Questioning the Suspect

If you are going to question the suspect at that time and expect to use his statements in court at his trial, be sure to admonish him of his right against self-incrimination, and of his right to counsel and to have counsel with him when he is questioned. However, consider the fact that the burglar may be making statements during the actual commission of the crime prior to your admonishment that will be admissible under most circumstances because they are part of the "res gestae." The "res gestae" encompasses the crime and the surrounding circumstances that all constitute the crime. Spontaneous declarations made by the suspect may also be totally admissible.

What to Do with the Weapon

What should an officer do with his service revolver while inspecting the interior of a building searching for the suspect? Ask yourself, "Where would be the best place to carry the revolver so that it would serve its purpose most efficiently?" In the holster. By keeping your revolver in its holster, you have it in a very accessible location, and your gun hand is free to handle doorknobs, to push aside obstacles that are in the way, to push the doors back to their stops, and to perform a variety of tasks while the other hand is holding the flashlight. If you practice regularly, you have no doubt found that it takes virtually no more time to draw your weapon from your holster and fire it than it does to fire a revolver that is already in your hand. The time factor involves your reaction to the incident calling for your response.

If an officer holds a gun in his hand, there is also a tendency to cock it unconsciously. On one occasion an officer did just that: he cocked his revolver while checking out a burglary scene, then replaced the revolver in his holster. He had not been aware that he had cocked the revolver and did not check it when he replaced it. Several hours later, that same officer was working a traffic control problem when he placed his hand on his gun in a resting position. He pushed the hammer when he placed his hand on the gun and shot himself in the foot.

A shotgun is completely impractical to use for checking out a building, except when there is a known felon inside, and one officer takes care of the door-opening and searching procedure, while the officer with the heavy armament stands back and "covers" the searching officer.

Prowlers

If you are familiar with the neighborhood where a prowler is reported, you have a tremendous advantage when responding to the prowler call. With such knowledge, it is possible to stop one or two houses short of the exact location of the prowler, and approach silently on foot without warning the suspect of your arrival. It is also to your advantage to know how the numbers on parallel streets appear, so that you or the follow-up officer may park and wait on the next block in case the suspect chooses to hurdle fences, or to run down alleys.

Approach the prowler's location quietly, driving the police car in the same manner as any local resident would drive home when returning from an evening out. Although your approach should not be too secretive, which in itself would arouse the suspect's suspicions, it should not be as though the occupation army had arrived. It may be to your advantage to stop some distance down the street, turn off the lights, then drive along the curb with the lights out for the last few hundred feet of your approach. Use the emergency brake to avoid activating the brake lights, which would broadcast your arrival. Locate the calling party's address by shining a light on the curb or some other place across the street from the calling party's address.

While approaching the scene, observe all the people who are in the area, whether or not they are making furtive movements, or signaling by suspicious conduct that they are involved in some sort of criminal activity. Someone who is running or sneaking around a place where a prowler had been spotted will automatically be suspect, but do not overlook the possibility that the "cool" individual walking normally along the street may be the real culprit. At the initial stage of the investigation of a "prowler there now" call, question everyone you encounter for possible leads as to the identity and location of the suspect.

Once you have arrived silently without your presence being detected and have made the initial attempt to locate the prowler, it will be apparent to him that you are there. Use plenty of light and conduct a very thorough and systematic search for the prowler. Avoid disturbing the residents in the area. Keep your radio on low volume, close the doors quietly, and keep the noise level of your activity down. While searching, do not assume that any place is too small to hide.

Once you have searched a particular area, post someone at that location to assure yourself that the suspect will not move to a place already searched to avoid apprehension. When using the flashlight, use it in the same manner as when you are checking out a building: out and away from your body. When you shine the light on a suspect, keep the light trained on his face to keep him at a disadvantage if he has intentions to attack you. Watch his hands for any movement that may signal anticipated actions by the suspect, such as an attempt to escape.

When you are searching for a prowler, you are looking for a misdemeanant. Use of a firearm is not justified unless the suspect would attempt to commit some felony, or unless it were necessary under the "reasonable force" decision that you would make when meeting with his resistance to arrest. Keep your revolver in its holster and keep the shotgun in the car. Although there are exceptions, most prowlers are not dangerous.

When working in a team with other officers, be sure to use a rehearsed technique so that each officer will understand what his part in the search for the prowler will be and will have an idea as to the location and activities of his fellow officers. Discuss and rehearse your tactics and the various signals that you will use.

Interview the occupants of the homes on whose property the prowler was observed and ascertain whether the prowler might be a person who has any permission or lawful business on the property. Look for any evidence that the suspect may have left at the scene, such as footprints or semen on the ground beneath a window into which he may have been looking, articles that may have fallen from his pocket when reaching for an object in his pocket, or any other evidence that may have been left there. Look into nearby vehicles in an effort to determine the presence of anyone important to the case who may be hiding. Stand or park for a few minutes at various places while conducting the search to listen for any sounds and watch for any movements that are foreign to the surroundings and may indicate the presence of the prowler. Sometimes the culprit may gain confidence and believe that he may leave his place of hiding without detection and apprehension, and it is then that you may effect the arrest.

The calling party may have decided to have a friend or husband search the neighborhood for the prowler, and the searcher may have armed himself with a shotgun or a souvenir rifle. If at all possible, the telephone operator or dispatcher who receives the original call for police service should ascertain whether anyone is already involved in a search, and if anyone is armed. If someone is armed, advise the calling party to invite the armed searcher back inside the house. When the officers search the premises and the general neighborhood, they will be less likely to encounter an armed individual, who may appear to be an armed suspect rather than a searcher. Under stress conditions, it is sometimes impossible to tell the prowlers from the searchers, and someone could be seriously injured when people carry deadly weapons.

Some prowler calls involve nothing more than outside noises that may sound eerie and frightening to the lone occupant of a house or apartment. Once you find the source of the sound-producing object, point it out to the calling party and recommend steps to eliminate the sound, for example, the trimming or removal of a bush or tree with long branches.

The prowler may be a burglar looking for a place to enter for the purpose of stealing. He may be a jealous separated husband or boy friend who is intent upon doing some spying on his wife or girl friend, or he may be a sex psychopath seeking out another unsuspecting victim so that he may satisfy his prurient desires. In most cases he will be a curious adolescent or young adult with voyeuristic tendencies. The average prowler is not actually dangerous, but he is a potential serious hazard. There is no way to determine in advance whether he is one of those "harmless" persons who wants only to look into other people's bedrooms, or a burglar who intends to commit his crime in spite of any obstacles he may encounter.

Usually when a person inside a house being "visited" by a prowler discovers the presence of that prowler his (or her) actions alert the prowler that he has been discovered. By the time the calling party goes to the telephone and notifies the police that the prowler is in the area, chances of apprehending him are slight. If a young lady were to become aware of the admiring eyes of a prowler looking in from some point of vantage, there would be a greater probability that he would be arrested if the object of his attentions would continue with whatever she was doing, then casually go to the telephone and notify the police department, and resume the same activity until the arrival of the officers.

The prowler might continue to watch the young lady practicing her exercises or combing her hair while the police officers proceed to the scene and attempt to catch the suspect in the act of peeking into the window. If they are successful in making their arrival quickly and silently, they may succeed as well in effecting the arrest. To ask a woman caller to cooperate in this manner to apprehend a prowler is "beyond the call of duty" for her and is too much to ask, but if she insists on helping, this is one method by which we have met with some success in apprehending prowlers.

Whenever there is a chronic situation with a voyeur who continually visits the same places to watch what is going on inside, there should be some preparation for surveillance of those places. Planning to apprehend the prowler should be no less elaborate than when planning for any other major crime. If the prowler turns out to be a youthful offender who is seeking to enhance his sex education in such a perverted manner, his early discovery may lead to psychiatric treatment and counseling, and possibly the redirection of his personality development.

GENERAL COORDINATION AND SEARCH

At the initial stage of an "in-progress" call, there is a tendency on the part of many officers to follow other police units in a "caravan," and to proceed directly to the scene, probably because of the intense desire to apprehend the culprit and to be on hand to "cover" a fellow officer. Both of these procedures must be avoided. The radio dispatcher should be responsible for assigning the units to proceed directly to the scene, and coordinating all the other units by directing them to locations other than the immediate vicinity of the crime scene to take part in the search, if a search is necessary.

The assigned officer is in charge of the response, the investigation, and the search. He continues to be in charge until the arrival of a supervisor, who will assume supervisory control. The supervisor will probably establish a command post at or near the crime scene and he will coordinate the field activities from that location. At the time the field command post is established, the dispatcher at the communications center will discontinue his coordination activities and will provide subsidiary service to the field command post.

Units not assigned to the call will remain in their respective districts unless assigned elsewhere, but should move in the direction of the crime scene or to points of vantage through which the fleeing suspect is likely to pass when attempting to leave the area. Units in the outer fringes of the perimeter of the search should cover the logical avenues of escape from the city. Be sure that if you are maintaining surveillance over a particular street or freeway that you have access to that route yourself or that you are spotting for another unit that does have such access. Ask yourself, "If I were attempting to flee, where would I go and what would I do?" Consider the possibility that the suspect may run or drive very quickly away from the crime scene for a short distance, discard his distinctive clothing or other items he may have worn to confuse the witnesses, and abandon the vehicle. It is not uncommon for professional robbery suspects to have two or three alternate vehicles parked within a few blocks of the location of their crime, and switch to whichever of those vehicles they are able to escape to during the first few minutes before the arrival of the first police units. Once they switch vehicles and discard the incriminating clothing, they find little need to hurry from the scene.

Some robbers have been brazen enough to drive past the scene of the crime, then park and walk up to mingle with the small crowd of onlookers, and inquire of the officers the nature of the trouble and whether they have had any success in locating the robber. For that reason, you should not overlook the possibility that the robber may still be in the immediate vicinity and that he may not be running or speeding away from the scene.

METHODS OF COVER AND SEARCH

There are several methods of searching for suspects who may be at the crime scene or its proximity, or who may have fled the scene and be some considerable distance away. The methods that we will discuss here are the foot, spot, leapfrog, and quadrant methods.

Foot Search

Park your unit some distance—possibly a block or two—from the crime scene or the place where you intend to search. Walk in, using natural cover provided by buildings, trees and shrubbery, or any other objects that will conceal your approach and protect you against missiles that might be aimed in your direction. Stop frequently to look and listen quietly for anyone who may arouse your suspicions. Once you have established the fact that the suspect is not immediately observable, begin contacting anyone whom you see, and secure from them as much information as you can as to what or whom they may have seen. Perhaps a lookout was loitering on the street corner for some time prior to the crime. One of the residents or workers in the neighborhood may be able to point out a car that is strange to the neighborhood and this may be one that the robber "planted" as a possible alternate escape vehicle. Perhaps a witness has seen the transfer from one car to another.

The foot seach is very effective when searching for witnesses as well as evidence in the vicinity of the crime, and sometimes it pays off in the search for the suspect. The robber is usually busy looking for police vehicles and may be caught off guard if you carefully and methodically cover the area on foot.

Spot Cover

This is usually a fixed post, usually at an intersection or some other vantage point overlooking one or more possible avenues of escape. When you are assigned to this type of detail, place your unit in a location that allows constant communications with the dispatcher and with other units, and access to the means by which you will pursue the suspect.

The term "leapfrog" describes the method of search, just as other terms called "zig-zag," "clover-leaf," or "criss-cross." In the leapfrog method, you and your partner alternately take the lead in the search and cover each other as you progressively move on. You may find many variations of this type of search very effective.

Quadrant

Using the scene of the crime as the center of the quadrant grid, divide the area to be searched into four equal "pie-shaped" quarters generating from the center. Assign at least one unit to each quadrant. Each unit begins the search of its assigned quadrant at the outer perimeter, then moves in toward the center—the crime scene—in a zig-zag pattern. The units should overlap each other's quadrant areas and work back outward to the perimeters of their assigned areas again. They continue this until the culprit is located or the search is abandoned.

PLAINCLOTHES ASSISTANCE

Whenever "plainclothes" officers assist in a police incident such as a crime in progress, a pursuit, or a similar incident involving high levels of emotional involvement, they must work in a capacity in which they may be immediately identified as police officers. They should affix their badges to the outside of their chests to aid in the identification. Some agencies now provide their officers with "jump suits" that they may put on over their street clothing, and which have the word *police* and the name of the agency inscribed in large letters across the back.

If someone is required to operate as a communicator or coordinator at a command post, it would be wise to assign a non-uniformed officer to the task. Another method of using the plainclothes officer is to assign him to work in a team with a uniformed officer, or to assign him as the driver of a police vehicle.

One example of how a plainclothes officer may be mistaken for a suspect occurred some time ago, but it could occur again unless the proper precautions are taken for its prevention. One afternoon an armed robbery occurred, and the chase began. As the chase progressed, several police units took part and it soon developed into a caravan. As the suspect vehicle approached each city in succession, a police unit or two from that city moved into place in the caravan and assumed the lead in the chase. In this case, as the robbers entered about the fourth or fifth city, a plainclothes officer in his unmarked unit fell in behind the suspect vehicle. The other police vehicles had fallen some distance behind. The detective unit was successful in making the stop, and the lone officer in that unit approached the suspect with his revolver in his hand. He opened the suspect vehicle door on the driver's side and, with his left hand, grabbed hold of the suspect's arm. The officer was turned in such a way, with his gun in his right hand, and with the left hand holding the suspect, that when the first "uniformed" car from another city arrived, it appeared to him as if the suspect were armed and getting out of the car. However, the officer in that first "uniformed" unit to arrive had seen the plain-clothes officer pull into the caravan and recognized the armed man as an officer.

A second, third, and fourth car from various agencies rolled up to the scene, and several of the officers in those cars were not aware of the armed man's role in the action. To one of them, it must have appeared as if he were one of the suspects. As the plainclothes officer made a sudden move, a shot rang out. The bullet missed the officer, but it struck a wind wing on the car and shattered the glass. It was fortunate that the shot was not fatal. Unfortunately, however, the officer sustained a permanent eye injury from the flying glass particles.

EXERCISES AND STUDY QUESTIONS

1. What is the value of establishing plans for "crime in-progress" tactics?
2. When responding to a robbery reported as in progress, what are the considerations for assigning a unit to respond with red light and siren?
3. What are the reasons for waiting and attempting to arrest the burglar as he leaves the building rather than going in after him?
4. What is a "quadrant cover" and how is it executed?
5. Outline your method of approach into a building in which you believe a burglar may be hiding.
6. What is a "res gestae?"
7. How does the author suggest you hold the police revolver when checking the interior of a building? Do you agree with this? Why? (or) Why not?
8. What is the best method for holding a flashlight when checking a building for a burglar?
9. Where would you position yourself upon approaching a market and observing an armed robbery in progress inside?
10. What is the purpose for a field command post?

SUGGESTED SEMESTER OR TERM PROJECTS

1. Make contingency plans for robberies of three banks in your city, showing how you would go about attempting to apprehend the suspects.

2. Draw up a set of grid maps for your city, identifying the most logical avenues of escape and pinpointing the locations where you would place your officers for spot cover.

REFERENCES

The material for this chapter was devised for academy lectures in patrol procedures. Sources were numerous training bulletins and unpublished information memos from the police departments of Los Angeles, Santa Ana, Riverside, Glendale, and Oakland, California.

Preliminary Investigations

by

Patrol

CHAPTER EIGHT The patrol officer performs various types of investigations, ranging from "investigate the woman screaming," to complicated multiple homicides and series of daylight residence burglaries. In some departments, particularly the larger metropolitan agencies, it has been customary for the field officer assigned to the district where the crime occurs to respond to every call, then to call in specialists for all but the "routine" nontraffic and noncriminal activities. Limits were set on the officer's responsibilities primarily because of the tremendous amount of his time required just to keep up with responding to the calls. Once at the scene, the patrol officer would determine the nature of the problem, stand by to protect the scene, to administer aid and comfort to the victims, arrest the culprit and wait until the specialists arrived. In the large department, this procedure continues to exist, but it is not practicable in the small or medium-sized department. Even in the large departments, the problem of overspecialization will have a tendency to render a department ineffective unless the specialization is kept to a minimum.

Whenever a crime occurs, or its earlier commission is discovered and reported to the police department, the first officer to arrive on the scene is usually the patrol officer in whose district the incident has occurred. Because of his proximity to the scene, his high mobility, and the fact that he is first on the scene, it is most logical that he should be charged with the responsibility for the initial phases of the crime investigation. This chapter covers some of the guidelines for this *preliminary investigation* process, which is normally handled by the patrol officer.

Figure 8.1 The preliminary investigation frequently involves a careful search for latent prints. Courtesy Police Department, Aberdeen, South Dakota.

PRELUDE TO THE INVESTIGATION

Investigations usually begin with personal interviews of people who are either witnesses or victims of the criminal acts of others. Sometimes the suspect is still on the scene, as is common in assault cases, and it is difficult to distinguish the respective roles of the participants in the action in an emotion-packed situation. In one case, two officers responded to the scene of what appeared to be a knife fight between two Mexican Nationals. When the officers arrived, they immediately assessed the situation as one in which two people had been badly injured. One had a deeply slashed throat and the other had a cut wrist that was bleeding from what appeared to be an arterial wound. They had to act.

Neither of the two officers in this situation knew how to speak Spanish, and they could find no one at the scene who would admit to knowledge of English. The officers believed that the nature of the

1. NAME

2. SEX

3. RACE

4. AGE

5. HEIGHT

6. WEIGHT

7. HAIR

8. EYES

9. COMPLEXION

10. PHYSICAL MARKS,
    SCARS, OTHER
    IDENTIFYING
    CHARACTERISTICS

11. CLOTHING
    A. HAT OR CAP
    B. SHIRT AND TIE
    C. JACKET OR COAT
    D. DRESS OR TROUSERS
    E. SHOES
    F. JEWELRY
       (1) RING
       (2) WATCH

wounds were serious enough that they could not wait for an ambulance. They placed both victims in the back seat of the police car and sped them to the hospital for emergency surgery. It was not until about two hours later that the officers discovered that the two people they had placed together in the police unit were actually the suspect in an aggravated felony assault and his victim. It was learned later that during the fight that was started by the suspect, the victim was successful in averting a second slashing swing at his throat by struggling with his attacker, causing the suspect to sustain a cut wrist by the blade of his own knife.

One of the first and most important items on the agenda of the investigation is to quickly assess the situation and attempt to determine exactly what happened. Many questions must be answered. Determine what crime, if any, occurred, and respond accordingly. While making that determination, identify the principals. Who is the victim? Who and where is the suspect? If there is an immediate and imminent threat to the life of anyone at the scene, take steps to apprehend the suspect and reduce or eliminate the threat.

The victim of any type of personal attack should be the first object of concern. Is there any danger of further attack? What is the victim's condition? Is there someone present who can call for medical aid? If first aid is necessary, look after that need, and instruct anyone who is present to assist you.

Quick apprehension of the suspect is high on the list of priorities, particularly if the crime is a personal attack and there is a likelihood that the suspect will repeat the attack unless he is taken into custody. Exactly which order of action you will follow will be determined by the precise facts as they present themselves to you. Regardless of the nature of the situation, use as much care as possible to preserve the evidence that will serve to establish the elements of the crime and the guilt of the accused. Sometimes the destruction of evidence is inevitable when you are administering first aid or performing rescue services, or when taking the suspect into custody. If that is the case, do not overlook the possibility that some of the evidence may be salvaged even though partially destroyed.

Try to make mental notes of the scene and various related factors during these initial stages, although you may have other important responsibilities for the moment. Try to remember if there were any articles of furniture moved, doors opened or unlocked, lights turned on or off, or any footprints or traces of evidence visible. Some evidence is very short-lived and will disappear unless it is quickly collected or recorded.

As soon as possible, attempt to process the short-lived evidence. It will possibly consist of a footprint outside a building in the rain, which may be saved by covering it with a box or a piece of some type of weatherproof material. Sometimes during the night or early morning hours when the grass is wet, the suspect may leave wet impressions on a dry linoleum floor. This wet impression should be sketched and photographed as early in the investigation as practicable, because it will be forever lost once it dries.

Once you have looked after the welfare of the victim, ascertained whether the suspect was present and accomplished the arrest if he was present, and taken the necessary steps to preserve and protect the short-lived evidence, the next step is to protect the entire scene against any further contamination. Define the perimeter and close it to the entry of anyone but those people who are actually essential to the investigation. Call for whatever special assistance you may have available to you, and proceed with the investigation.

THE INVESTIGATION

After all of the immediate demands of the situation have been met, interview the people who are most likely to give you a preliminary description of the suspect and any contraband that the suspect may have with him. Broadcast the information by radio or telephone for immediate general rebroadcast. Pause momentarily and briefly plan your course of action. Consider the type of case. Ask yourself what most likely happened. Where did the suspect go? What did he do with the evidence? Generally attempt to reconstruct the crime scene. This momentary pause may give you time to look at the case more objectively. Proceed according to some logical plan that you have formulated during this pause.

Interview Witnesses

Separate the victims and witnesses. Interview them one at a time to secure as many individual viewpoints as possible. Sometimes a group interview will produce a *jury* description, one which is a composite resulting from a series of compromises between witnesses, and one which will probably be incorrect. Remember that eyewitnesses are not always reliable, but they may be all that you have. Ask questions that compel the witnesses to give you their own information, rather than a feedback of what you believe happened and their agreement that you are right, or nearly so.

Note First Impressions

Right from the start, you should be making written notes of information and evidence as the case develops. In these notes, include information on items that may be of incidental importance as well as of direct evidential value. List items such as your observation that the lights were on although the crime supposedly occurred in the day-time, a cigarette or cigar is still smoldering in an ashtray, a glass window appears to have been broken from the inside when it should have been broken from the outside. Note odors that may be foreign to the place, such as pipe or cigar smoke in a lady's apartment, or the pungent smell of a particular aftershave lotion that you can identify. List your observations about any contradictions of witnesses or victims, and various items of evidence or information that you collect. For example, the victim's statement that a shelf was full of merchandise may be refuted by the obvious presence of a quantity of undisturbed dust on the shelf, indicating that nothing had been on that shelf which could have been removed. The loss may be an exaggeration or an outright lie for insurance purposes.

Figure 8.2 The videotape recorder (VTR) is an excellent aid to the patrol officer who must conduct his own pre-liminary investigation. Courtesy of the Police Department, Huntington Beach, California.

Collection and Preservation of Evidence

There is not a single case that I know of when an officer collected too much evidence. In your initial investigation, consider the pos-sibility that virtually everything you encounter is potential evidence. Touch only those items that you must touch and touch them very carefully. Systematically collect every item that is—or might be—evidence. Sometimes the most seemingly inconsequential items turn out to be the most significant pieces of evidence when the case goes to trial. Consider what some investigators call the *theory of transfer.* In nearly every criminal case, the culprit leaves something of himself at the scene and takes something from the scene. There are exceptions, but never discount the possibility of this occurring.

According to the transfer theory, the suspect may leave behind his fingerprints, footprints, semen, blood, saliva, perspiration, hair, fibers, lipstick, stains, odors, sounds, or his physical description. He may take with him such items as dust or dirt; broken glass in his clothing; the victim's hair, blood, body fluids, tissue; stolen merchandise, contraband, or the victim himself.

During the entire investigation process, record accurate notes and field sketches, preserve and transport the evidence in accordance with recommended procedures, and take every precaution to substantiate your allegation that a crime was committed by proving the elements of the corpus delicti of each offense. Have sufficient evidence to establish the guilt of the suspect.

Whenever taking clothing from the suspect that you intend to search for items of evidence, such as narcotics or broken glass embedded in the material, pack each item in a separate container. The laboratory expert may then testify as to which article of clothing yielded which item of evidence. Whenever taking items of evidence from the custody of presence of anyone, it is a good practice to prepare an itemized list of the articles taken and to leave a receipt with whoever is in charge of the premises.

Consider the following as a recommended policy regarding property and evidence:

> All property, regardless of value, the character or condition of the person from whom it is taken, or the circumstances under which it is acquired by the evidence section of the department, must be labeled and appropriately recorded. In all cases a receipt must be made for property taken or received. Whenever possible, this receipt should be made in duplicate, the original processed along with the evidence or property and the copy given to the person from whom the property is received. No member of the department shall assume a personal interest in, or possession of, any property that comes to him in his official capacity as a police officer. (Rules and Regulations, Police Department, Santa Ana, California. Sec. 10.105.)

TYPES OF EVIDENCE

When conducting the search for evidence, an appreciation of the various types of evidence and knowledge of the methods for collecting the evidence is necessary. This phase of the investigation may be conducted by the officer assigned the initial investigation, or by a specially trained patrol officer designated "crime scene investigator." Regardless of whether you are the officer assigned to collect and preserve the evidence, consider the following information concerning the techniques involved in the process.

Fingerprints

There are three types of fingerprints that may be found at the crime scene: latents, visible prints, and plastic, or molded, prints. The plastic prints are those usually found in soft, pliable substances, such as putty, wax, soap, butter, or grease. Visible prints are those that need no development to be completely visible to the viewer. They may be found in items such as dust, blood, or any smooth and flat surface the suspect may have touched with the ridged parts of his hands or feet when they contained ink or some other substance that might serve as a "printing" medium when coming in contact with the surface. Latents are invisible impressions that must be developed by dusting with a special fingerprint dusting powder, by chemical treatment, by "fuming" with the fumes from burning iodine crystals, or by any other means of drawing out the prints and making them visible for collection by photographing or by transfer to a transparent tape or similar substance.

Fingerprints that have the greatest value in a criminal investigation are those found in places where only authorized persons are allowed, such as in a cash box, the interior of a cash drawer, or inside some other container. Prints found on counters or desk tops, on the outside of a vending machine, or on an object that anyone could have handled during the normal hours of business may be of some value if the suspect claims that he was never inside or near the place where the prints appear. To help in locating these, turn off any glaring overhead lights and use a flashlight at an oblique angle. Consider items the culprit may have touched during the commission of his crime, then dust with fingerprint powder. Searching for latent prints on materials other than smooth surfaces, such as paper, or porous wood, should be left to the expertise of the fingerprint specialist.

Before dusting the surface where you anticipate finding latents, attempt to determine the direction that the ridges are most likely to run. Using a moderate amount of powder, brush with the grain, or the lines of the pattern. Use powder that contrasts with the surface. Once you have developed the latent, or have discovered one of the other types of prints—plastic and visible—take photographs before attempting to transfer the prints to a tape or other lifting material, or before removing them in any manner for preservation.

Following is one method for lifting latents with fingerprint tape.
Select tape that is free of bubbles, then pull a length of the tape free
from the roll in one continuous movement in order to avoid creating
a ridge at any point in the strip. Fold the tape back about ¼ inch on
the end that is free of the roll. Place that end of the tape on the surface
about 1 inch from the print that you intend to lift. Slowly press the
tape down and move toward the print, keeping the free tape from
touching the surface until you press it down. Continue pushing the
tape smoothly until it is about 1 inch beyond the print. Cut the tape
from the roll and rub across the entire surface to assure adhesion. Lift
the tape slowly and place it smoothly on a card of contrasting color,
or on a piece of transparent plastic. There are many excellent materials
available for this process.

Footprints and Tireprints

In dust, dirt, mud, or plastic-type materials, you may find identifiable impressions of shoes or tire treads. They are often as distinctive as
fingerprints, and the law of averages may be applied to show that the
impression found at the scene of the crime was probably made by the
shoes found in the possession of the suspect, or by the suspect's automobile. In one case, at the scene of a safe burglary, there were
prints from two different shoes that indicated that they belonged to
the people who removed the safe from the premises. Some distance
from the scene of the crime, two men were questioned in a field interview situation, and the officer had the presence of mind to look
at the bottoms of their shoes. The comparisons proved that the shoes
worn by those two men matched the impressions left at the crime
scene, and the additional factor of the combination of shoe designs
narrowed down the averages in favor of the prosecution. The combination of designs at the scene of the crime as well as at the field interview, when the two men were interviewed together, was attributed
to more than mere coincidence.

Tool Marks

Simple scratches, striations, and impressions are the most commonly
encountered marks found at the scene of a crime, usually at the point
of a forced entry. Simple scratches with no identifiable characteristics
may occur on the inside of locks that have been picked with the aid
of lock-picking devices. Striations and impressions are made by a
variety of tools, and it is sometimes possible to match the marks
and the tools. Whenever a tool is manufactured it carries with it
certain imperfections that are characteristic to only that tool. The

tool-making tools are imperfect themselves and transfer their own imperfections to each new tool. Each time any tool is used, it undergoes an almost imperceptible change, but its distinctive markings can be identified by microscopic examination. It is impossible to classify and file in any organized manner tools and tool marks, but if the laboratory specialist has the tool and the mark it made he may succeed in "making" the case on the basis of a single item of evidence.

Impressions are indentations made on a surface that is softer then the tool used to make them. They are usually found at the point of entry, or at the hiding place of some object of theft. The most commonly used burglar tool is the screwdriver, and some sort of pry tool is in second place. Hammers or any tool used to strike a surface will make impressions. Measure the impressions and allow for stretching of the material which will actually make the impressions larger than the tools that made them. Take photographs and casts with material especially designed for this use, and take the actual impression whenever possible. This may necessitate taking out part of a door frame or window sill for a courtroom presentation, but it is worth the trouble and expense if you are to successfully prosecute the case.

Keep the tool and the impression separate and make the comparisons by measuring the tool and the impression, rather than contaminating the evidence by placing the tool in the impression possibly made by that tool. The laboratory specialist will make his comparisons by making casts of the impressions and the suspected tool and matching them by microscopic examination and the comparison of photographs.

Striations are parallel scratch marks cut into the surface of some material that is softer than the tool or device that makes them. Any imperfections on the scratching surface of the tool making the mark, such as a slight nick or a blunted portion, will be transferred to the object scratched. Striations are made by a scraping, cutting, or glancing blow across the surface. Tools that may make striations are hammers, pry bars or screwdrivers used in a scratching motion, a chisel driven into metal, a bolt cutter cutting a padlock, a wire cutter, or a brace and bit.

Another common type of striation in criminal investigation is that made by the rifling and interior of a revolver, or other rifled firearm, on the bullet that travels through the barrel. Each time it is fired, the firearm changes, and it is imperative that the bullet and suspected gun be compared before it has been fired many times. Otherwise, the comparison will be worthless because of the change that has taken place.

The procedure for handling striations and the tools that are suspected of having made them is the same as that for handling impressions. They are usually compared by photograph and by microscopic examinations.

At the crime scene, virtually any item may be evidence. Collect and itemize every article that in any way indicates that it may be used to aid the success of the investigation. Bullets or other projectiles are common to crimes against persons. Account for every shot fired and locate every projectile. If a bullet is lodged in a piece of wood or plaster surface, dig out the material surrounding the bullet and let the bullet fall out. Do not alter the markings made by the gun by prying directly on the bullet when trying to collect it for evidence.

Glass particles left at the scene of the crime may match those found on the suspect's clothing as a result of a search with a vacuum cleaner with a special filter. A button found at the scene may have been torn off the shirt of the suspect, and by matching thread or torn material, it may be possible to make an identification of the culprit. Tools and weapons are occasionally left behind. They may be examined for fingerprints as well as impressions or striations that they may have made. Sometimes the suspect will leave behind personal items without knowing it. At one armed robbery of a liquor store at night, two suspects walked in and selected some beer under the pretense of preparing to buy it. The clerk asked the men for their identification because of their youthful appearance. One of the suspects handed the clerk his driver's license, then took out a gun and told the clerk to give him all of the money in the cash drawer. The suspects fled, the one forgetting to take back his driver's license. Imagine his dismay when he remembered. At about the same time, the clerk was on the telephone telling the police that he had just been robbed by the individual named and described on the license. Needless to say, he probably will never make that mistake again after he finishes "serving his time."

Stains, such as those made by blood or seminal fluid, may be classified by blood type and be subjected to other types of laboratory analysis if collected and handled correctly. They may assume many colors by reacting to chemicals that may be on the surface where they are found, and often blood is found that does not resemble the reddish-brown color that one usually associates with dried blood. Seminal stains are usually found on articles of clothing in sex offenses. Collect this type of stain by handling the clothing as little as possible. If wet, allow the stain to dry without folding the clothing or covering it with any other article. Blood is found in various places, and should be stored wet in a closed container if possible, or be allowed to dry on clothing in the same manner as semen.

Bloodstains may be found in the cracks of a freshly washed knife, in cracks in wood or tile floors, in carpeting, in towels or washcloths, in a clothes hamper or wastebasket, or in the drains of sinks or tubs. When collecting bloodstains, photograph and sketch them first,

Figure 8.3 Laboratory analysis of evidence is extremely critical in all crimes, but more so in cases where the evidence is the only witness. Courtesy of the Police Department, Santa Ana, California.

showing their shapes and size, and the direction of the splash. Also indicate on the sketch whether they are dry, moist, or wet.

Collect wet stains by placing the substance in a sealed container with a mild saline solution of 2 teaspoons of salt to 1 quart of water. About 10 cc. of blood is a desired minimum if it is possible to collect that much. If the blood is in soil, remove any insects before storing. Wet stains may be collected by use of a blotter, which is allowed to dry and stored in the dry state. Collect dry stains by scraping them onto a piece of clean white paper and folding up the paper securely or by scraping them into a small glass or plastic container designed for the collection of evidence.

MARKING EVIDENCE

Mark, or in some other way identify, every item of evidence at the time you collect it. Make the mark distinctive enough so that you will later be able to examine the item and positively state on the witness stand that you made that exact mark and, therefore, it is the same item that you collected at the time of the investigation. Some items are of such a nature that it is impossible to mark the items themselves. In those cases, seal the items inside a container and place your mark on the outside of the container. If you use a sealing material, it will be possible for you to testify that you sealed the container and that it does not appear to have been broken.

Items that have serial numbers may not need marking because you may record the number. If in doubt whether to mark, do it. Make the marks very distinguishable, but small and in places where they will not destroy the value of the item you mark. Clothing may be marked with no damage to the material if you make the marks in places such as inside the waistband of trousers, on the manufacturer's label, or on the tail of a shirt. If you have several pieces of glass, sketch the outlines of the various pieces on a sheet of paper, and designate a number to each piece.

CHAIN OF EVIDENCE CUSTODY

When introducing an item of evidence at a trial, you must describe the location where you collected it and the manner in which you collected it. It is then necessary for you and the other people in your department to show the precise route of travel of that item of evidence, to assure the court that it has not undergone any change or other contamination between the time it was collected and the time it was presented in court. To be able to guarantee the most careful handling of evidence and its chain of custody, follow these guidelines when processing evidence.

1. Limit the number of individuals who handle the evidence from the time it is found, to the time it is presented to the court.
2. Each time you handle the evidence, check its condition to assure yourself that it has not been damaged or altered.
3. If the evidence leaves your possession:
   a. record the name of the person to whom it is given.
   b. log the date and time the transfer of custody is made.
   c. log the reason for the transfer of evidence, such as "to evidence man for analysis," or "for lab analysis."
   d. log when and by whom it is returned, if at all.
4. Each person who handles an item of evidence should affix his identifying mark to the article so that he, too, may testify to the fact that it is the same item he handled earlier.
5. Obtain a signed receipt from the person accepting the evidence, or have some procedure for recording the transfer each time it is made.
6. When evidence is returned to your custody, assure yourself that it is the same evidence.

PHOTOGRAPHS

The purpose of photographs is to provide visual aids to the case for the investigators, the prosecuting attorney, and, above all, the judge and the jury. A photograph must be an accurate representation of the scene as it appeared to someone who was present at the time the photograph was taken. If possible, photographs should be taken before anything at all is disturbed. This will make it easier to explain the scene, because if anything has been moved, it will be necessary to explain why. If you must move evidence prior to the photograph, mark the location where it was located so that the photograph will show the mark where something had been removed. For example, in a homicide case, the victim may have been removed to the hospital because it may have appeared that he was still living. The body's location should be marked with a high contrast material, such as a yellow marking crayon.

For close-up photographs, use a ruler or other marker of known size. When the print is made, it will be possible for the darkroom technician to use a ruler and reproduce the exact size of the item in the enlargement. When photographing flat surfaces, be sure to have the film exactly parallel with the surface. Any enlargement will be free of distortion that occurs when the photograph is taken from an angle. With each enlargement, the distortion is exaggerated.

Take background, or condition, photographs to show general conditions at the scene. Orientation may include photographs of the exterior of the building, the hallway leading to the exact location where the crime occurred, and the exact location. These pictures take the viewer on a pictorial journey to the place of the crime. Consider the use of Polaroid pictures for immediate review and evaluation, and other pictures if the earlier ones do not come out. The Polaroid camera is designed for snapshot quality, and it should not be used exclusively.

Color transparency slides are excellent investigative and evidential devices. They may be projected in a fully lighted room on a rear projection screen, or they may be projected in extremely large magnifications on a screen in a darkened room. The possibilities for using slides are excellent, particularly in the examination of minute bits of evidence.

For courtroom admissibility of photographs, the photographs must represent the scene as observed by the person who testifies to that fact. They must be material or relevant to the case, and they must be free of distortion. Photographs also cannot be of such a nature that would prejudice the jury against the defendant. Each photograph used should be one that adds to, rather than detracts from, the case. There must be some meaning to the picture, and it must depict what the accompanying testimony purports that it will depict.

EXERCISES AND STUDY QUESTIONS

1. When you arrive on the crime scene, what is the first thing that you should do? Second? Third?

2. What is *short-lived* evidence? Give an example of at least three types of evidence that would fall into this category.
3. List five types of evidence a suspect might leave behind at the scene of a burglary.
4. List two items that a suspect might take with him from a forcible rape.
5. Where would you be most likely to find latent fingerprints at the scene of a theft of a stereo tape deck from a private automobile?
6. What is a striation? What type of tool would make a striation?
7. How does an impression differ from a striation?
8. How would you collect a wet blood stain?
9. Outline a procedure for a police department to assure the proper chain of evidence custody.
10. Can an evidence photograph be introduced in court by someone other than a photographer?
11. Describe the *transfer theory*.

SUGGESTED SEMESTER OR TERM PROJECTS

1. Develop a set of guidelines for a special crime scene investigation unit in the patrol division. List what training the officer will need and what equipment he will have to put into his unit to function effectively.
2. Make a set of sample evidential items, such as a striation on some surface, an impression, and several samples of items of evidence likely to be found at the scene of a crime.
3. List the elements of all the crimes in your state that are most likely to be encountered by the field officer.

REFERENCES

O'Hara, Charles E., *Fundamentals of Criminal Investigation*, 2nd ed. Springfield, Ill.: Charles C Thomas, Publisher, 1970.

Soderman, Harry, and John J. O'Connell, *Modern Criminal Investigation*, 4th ed. New York: Funk & Wagnalls, 1952.

Vanderbosch, Charles G., *Criminal Investigation*. Washington, D.C.: International Association of Chiefs of Police, Inc., 1968.

Wilson, O. W., *Police Administration*, 2nd ed. New York: McGraw-Hill Book Company, 1963, Chap. 14.

————, *Police Planning*, 2nd ed. Springfield, Ill.: Charles C Thomas, Publisher, 1958. Emphasis on reprinted article in the Appendix by Don J. Finney, laboratory technician for the Wichita, Kansas Police Department, entitled "Police Duties at Crime Scenes," from *American Journal of Police Science*, XXVII, Nos. 2 and 3 (1936).

Tactics

and

Techniques

CHAPTER NINE An ideal arrangement for a patrol officer is to have an operational plan for every anticipated type of event and activity that would call for his attention and his services. A set of guidelines for every conceivable contingency would give the officer a base of information based upon the experiences of others and upon recommended department policies, from which he could work out his own techniques in handling the cases that confront him. Among the most important situations are those that occur with the least frequency, such as aircraft crashes and bomb threats. The priority for events seems to be in reverse of the order of their frequency. The reason for this reverse order is that for frequently occurring events, there are greater opportunities to develop operational guidelines during the normal course of duties, as the events occur. Some incidents occur so seldom that formulation of contingency plans for those incidents will require scheduled planning sessions, during which new guidelines should be formulated and old ones updated.

Plans for special events are developed in the conference room, the field, during actual policing of the special events in question, and in roll call training sessions. Brainstorming sessions, if conducted in such a way that there is no dampening effect on the enthusiasm of the participants, may prove most productive as vehicles for the development of plans. Every available technique should be used to develop the plans, and they shold then be rehearsed in simulated situations if the problems do not present themselves in reality with regularity. As soon as possible following actual or simulated field problems, consider holding a critique session to analyze the strong and weak points, and to firm up the plans where necessary.

When you are planning guidelines for field problems, also plan for the unexpected. Consider the people who will be assigned, who will probably be the same as those currently working the particular hours when the problem is most likely to occur. It is impossible to predict which officers will be on duty. For that reason, the plans should be adaptable to the talents and skills of different officers. The training should involve all officers who are likely to participate in the action. In addition to training, consider the advisability of working out some system for locating department members who have special talents, such as sketching ability or language proficiency. Other officers may be particularly skilled in bomb disposal, locksmithing, medical aid, or operation of special weapons or other equipment. In addition to the officer personnel, there are vast resources throughout the community that are available just for the asking whenever the need arises. A small card file maintained in the office of the patrol commander may prove quite valuable on more than a "sometime" basis.

The following guidelines in this chapter should be studied carefully and modified where necessary to meet the particular needs of your own department. They are tried and proven techniques developed by numerous police officers under actual field situations, and they have been adapted for this text with a view to meeting the needs of most police departments with a minimum utilization of personnel.

AIRCRAFT CRASHES

An aircraft crash involves police response similar to that response that would follow any disaster of the same proportions. The disaster control aspects of the situation are covered in detail in Chapter Ten. Panic or riotous situations, which could possibly develop in the event of a crash of major proportions, are treated in detail in Chapter Eleven. There are several other aspects of an aircraft accident that should be covered separately because of its nature. Injuries and damage are usually of great magnitude because of the large number of passengers involved and the size of the airplane falling from great heights. Aviation is increasing in importance as a mode of commercial and personal travel as well as an integral part of our military defenses. Aircraft crashes—as with railroad and motor vehicle crashes—are inevitably going to happen. Certain procedures should be followed when they do occur.

Military aircraft accidents are the primary concern of the military service concerned. Civilian aircraft accidents are the concern of the National Transportation Safety Board and are covered by the Federal Aviation Regulations for pilots. Methods for responding to an accident involving either type of aircraft—military or civilian—are the same as for medical aid and rescue operations, but there are important differences. Once the immediate emergency needs are met, yet while they are still underway, certain critical factors must be borne in mind. Victims and debris may be dispersed over a wide area surrounding the accident scene, and the danger of fire may be great. Approach the scene with extreme caution. As quickly as you can, take immediate steps to close the area to everyone except those whose presence is absolutely essential.

When approaching military aircraft, stay clear of the front and rear of any tanks or pods that are carried externally on the wings or fuselage. They may contain missiles or rockets. Establish a *no smoking* rule to help reduce the possibility of fire. The following information has been taken from a Department of Defense booklet *What to Do and How to Report Military Aircraft Accidents.*[1]

How to use access hatches, rescue point, exits.

Location of escape hatches, doors, and exits from all military aircraft are indicated by orange-yellow markings on the outside of the aircraft. On jet aircraft a red rescue arrow will indicate the rescue points. Instructions are stenciled at this arrow for the jettisoning of canopies or hatches. Use care in jettisoning these cartridge-actuated devices as they are displaced violently. When operating jettisoning controls always position yourself well to the side.

(The booklet depicts an inverted triangle inscribed *warning*, which gives instructions for jet aircraft equipped with ejection seats. The marking is placed on the side of the aircraft.)

1. Push button to open door.
2. Pull "T" handle out (distance will be specified for various aircraft) to jettison canopy.

Do not raise, move, or tamper with arm rests of crewmembers'

---

[1] U.S. Department of Defense, *What to Do and How to Report Military Aircraft Accidents, Joint Service Booklet #1* (Washington, D.C.: U.S. Navy, 1968). Available from U.S. Naval Aviation Center, Naval Air Station, Norfolk, Va.

seats, or any controls painted yellow and black, as these activate
the ejection seats and are extremely dangerous. Never move any
handle, lever, or device inside the cockpit if you are not thoroughly
familiar with the canopy jettison and seat ejection mechanism for
that particular aircraft.

Before removing survivors, always unfasten the seat belt, shoulder
and/or parachute harness, and oxygen mask as well as radio cords
and oxygen lead.

CHECKLIST: How To Report

Tell the operator (or radio dispatcher) that you wish to report
a military aircraft crash, collect, to the nearest military installation.

When the call is answered, state that you are reporting an aircraft crash, and include at least the following basic information in
your conversation:

1. Give your name and location where calling from.
2. Report that a military aircraft crashed at (time) and that there
   (is) (is not) a fire.
3. Give accurate geographical location, road net, distances and/or
   compass directions on how to reach the crash site. (Prominent
   ground and air landmarks can be useful to both military
   ground vehicles and rescue and fire fighting helicopters.)
4. Crew parachuted (or landed with airplane).
5. Medical help needed.
6. Crew believed to be all dead (give number).
7. Report damage to private property or civilian injuries.
8. Report any of the following:
   a. Number on tail of aircraft.
   b. Type or model of aircraft.
   c. Where someone will meet the rescue team.
   d. Nearest suitable helicopter landing area (flat open field,
      free of poles and wires).
9. Make sure the report is understood.
10. Any other information of possible immediate value.
11. Please wait for any questions before hanging up.
12. Leave number for possible callback, if possible.

The press may be represented and such personnel may be collecting data for their media. The military team that will be dispatched
to the scene will have a press relations officer who will handle all information releases. Except for injured persons, leave everything as
you find it and wait for the military to assume control of the site.
If there is some distance to the nearest military installation, certain
rescue operations may continue, including the extinguishing of a fire
or prevention of further damage, but nothing else should be disturbed
for any reason.

In the event of a civilian aircraft crash, perform whatever rescue

200

ALCOHOLIC
BEVERAGE
CONTROL
INVESTIGATION
AND
ENFORCEMENT

operations are necessary and evacuate the immediate vicinity as a precautionary measure. Notify the nearest office of the National Transportation Safety Board: Anchorage, Alaska; Chicago, Illinois; Denver, Colorado; Fort Worth, Texas; Kansas City, Missouri; Los Angeles, California; Miami, Florida; New York, New York; Oakland, California; Seattle, Washington; and Washington, D.C. If the field office is some distance away, notify the nearest airport that has a control tower and request that the crash be reported to the Federal Aviation Administration. The actual reporting of any aircraft accident is the responsibility of the pilot of the involved aircraft, but notification should be prompt. If the pilot had filed a flight plan while flying under Visual Flight Rules or was flying under Instrument Flight Rules, his failure to report in within a prescribed period of time will cause a search for his whereabouts to be instituted.

When reporting a civilian aircraft accident, be sure to provide the airplane identification number and its exact location. As with the military aircraft, close the area to spectators and allow only authorized personnel. The National Transportation Safety Board or Federal Aviation Administration investigator will assume responsibility for any of the wreckage, cargo, records, or any other items they deem necessary for their investigation. They are the only persons who may release any of those items. According to Section 430.10 (b) of the National Transportation Safety Board regulations, wreckage, mail, or cargo may be moved prior to the time the Board or an authorized representative takes custody of such articles only to:

(1) . . . remove persons injured or trapped.
(2) . . . protect the wreckage from further damage.
(3) . . . protect the public from injury.

Whenever it is necessary to move any items, if possible, arrange to have photographs taken of the scene, prepare a sketch, and make sufficient notes so that you may be able to reconstruct as accurately as possible the scene as you found it.

ALCOHOLIC BEVERAGE CONTROL INVESTIGATION AND ENFORCEMENT

Among the states there is considerable variety in the laws and their application. Laws generally prescribe the conditions under which alcoholic beverages are dispensed and distributed, the people who may serve and be served the beverages, and numerous license regulations. Licensed premises must abide by certain rules of decorum to assure against their becoming "disorderly houses," and the hours of sale are also regulated.

Rather than address the specific laws, which might not apply in the same manner from one state to another, or from one jurisdiction to another, this section deals with the general investigative techniques of alcoholic beverage control violations. The following outline is an excerpt from the California Department of Alcoholic Beverage Con- trol *Enforcement Manual:* [2]

Title: GENERAL INVESTIGATIVE TECHNIQUES IN CONNECTION WITH ABC VIOLATIONS

I. *Identification, preservation and examination of evidence:*

A. Adequate evidence must be obtained by officers in order to establish proof of a violation.
1. Retain alcoholic beverage for evidence. Where necessary, put in evidence bottle.
2. Mark bottles or containers of seized beverage for identification.
3. Seal in presence of person from whom seized if possible.
4. Give the receipt for seized evidence if container is unopened.
5. Handle carefully.
6. If a mixed drink, remove ice immediately. Place mixed drink in sample bottle.
7. Sample the alcoholic beverage by taste and smell.
8. Obtain chemical analysis to substantiate alcoholic content if deemed necessary.

II. *Establishing age and/or identity:*

A. Licensee or employee:
1. Obtain name, address, telephone number, length of association with the premises, length of experience in the liquor business.
2. Establish hours of duty (shift schedule).
3. Observe and record physical condition as to vision, hearing, sobriety, etc.
4. Observe and record physical description and clothing of persons involved.

B. Minors:
1. Determine what documents shown—if any:
   (a) Examine and, if false, seize as evidence.
   (b) Check carefully for alterations.
2. Question minor on age and establish if minor was questioned on age prior to service.
3. Verify age with parent, guardian, or relative.

[2] State of California, Department of Alcoholic Beverage Control, *Enforcement Manual* (Sacramento, Calif.: State Printing Office, 1968), pp. 11, 12.

202

ALCOHOLIC
BEVERAGE
CONTROL
INVESTIGATION
AND
ENFORCEMENT

4. In accepting a birth certificate, bear in mind that this document is proof of age only, and that proof of identity is necessary.
5. All information documents should be thoroughly scrutinized to compare with bearer.
6. ABC Act covers, as minors, all persons under the age of 21, regardless of marital status.
7. A licensee is authorized to demand documentary evidence of the age and identity of any person in his premises.
8. Proof that a licensee obtained satisfactory documentary evidence of age and identity establishes a defense.
9. Note carefully the appearance and dress of the minor.
10. Make a thorough search of minors for false identification even though there may be no claim that ID was shown.

C. Witnesses:
   1. Obtain name, address, telephone number, occupation, business address, etc.

III. *General facts to be noted:*

A. Condition of premises, i.e., lighting, length of bar, size of crowd, demeanor of customers, general description.
B. Number of employees present.
C. Appearance and outward manifestation of buyer.
D. The order for alcoholic beverages.
E. Type of beverage: highball, mixed drink, etc. Identify by name.
F. How served or sold, i.e., placed in bag, box, served in glass, etc.
G. Time order took place.
H. Where beverage came from, i.e., refrigerator, back bar, speed rack, shelf, etc.
I. Cost of merchandise—cash register slip, invoice:
   1. Amount requested by seller.
   2. Type and amount of money presented to seller by buyer.
   3. Amount of change, if any, received by buyer.
J. In case involving "On Sale" premises the officer should observe the consumption, whenever possible.
K. Citation or apprehension of suspect or suspects:
   1. Cite or arrest at scene.
   2. Have witness identify suspects.
L. Search and inspect premises thoroughly.
M. Secure signed statements whenever possible.
N. Secure pertinent information from posted license, i.e., licensee, address, dba, type of license.
O. Accurate time:
   1. Check own time with Western Union or telephone company.
   2. Check time shown on premises and note.
   3. Check time on watch owned by licensee or employee.
P. Note whether or not the licensee was on the premises if he was not directly involved in the violation.

Q. Note whether licensee or his agent(s) were in a position to observe the violation(s).

BOMBS AND BOMB THREATS

Anarchists have been known to use bombs quite effectively to destroy lives and property, and to cause a demoralizing effect on people. Sometimes as devastating as the actual detonation of a bomb is a telephoned threat that there will be a bombing. Although you may be reasonably sure that a bomb will not go off as announced, you are probably in no position to decide to "call the bluff" by telling the caller to go ahead and blow up the building he names in his threat. The call must be handled as though you expect to find a bomb, and your search must be so exhaustive that you are reasonably sure you have not overlooked a single possibility.

There are two reasons why it is of tremendous importance to identify the party who telephones someone to notify them that a bomb has been planted in a particular location. One is that the mere threatening call itself is a crime whether an actual bomb was planted or not. The second is that in the event that there has actually been a bomb planted somewhere, the caller is a key person to locate and question. He may be the individual who planted it, or he may have participated in the crime, or he may have information concerning the crime and want to do what he can to preserve lives without having to identify himself. In the event the telephone receiver who receives the bomb threat call has a tape recorder attachment, now is the time to activate the recorder. It may be possible to match voices later when a suspect is located.

Upon arriving on the scene where the bomb is purported to be, contact the calling party—if he is at the scene—and locate the device reported to be a bomb, if its location is known. Immediately report to the dispatcher that you have arrived, and report also the progress of your investigation to date. Keep in continuous communication with the dispatcher if possible so that any progress reports may be made as the need arises. If the bomb has not been located, take immediate steps to institute a search and protect the people who may be injured from any blast.

Establish a perimeter within which you believe the bomb may be found. Request additional assistance to help keep the area closed, if any need exists. Decide whether to evacuate the premises or to conduct your search without the knowledge of the people who occupy the premises. If the bomb threat involves a school or some other building where infrequent and unannounced fire drills are held, consider having a fire drill to evacuate the building without fanfare. If you must evacuate, do so quickly but in an orderly manner. Your

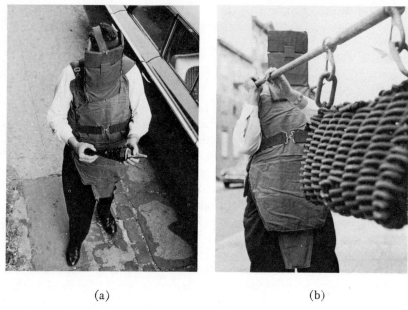

(a)

(b)

(c)

(d)

Figure 9.1 Handling and disposing of bombs is a task for specialists.
Courtesy of the Police Department, New York City, New York.

own calm manner under situations such as this may be the deciding factor in whether or not other people at the scene will panic. Keep cool at all costs.

Search the premises for the device, with one officer in charge of the search. Be sure to search every available part of the premises, including those where you believe no bomb would be planted. A bomb may be any size or shape, and be placed inside any kind of container. When you find any object that looks as though it may be the object of your search, evacuate that portion of the building and isolate the device. Allow no one to enter the area or to handle the object. At this point you should have someone contact the nearest military installation or one of the larger neighboring police departments—unless your department is that one—and request the services of an explosive ordnance disposal team. If such a team is at your service, protect the area and wait for their arrival, then continue the call as with any other incident.

If there is no bomb disposal team available, and the task of removing the suspected bomb from the premises falls into your lap, proceed carefully with the operation yourself. Have gas and electric utilities shut off if possible. Set up a *no smoking* policy immediately. Remove any flammable or explosive substances from the vicinity of the suspected object to avoid a more serious problem than would occur if only a suspected bomb would go off. Do not attempt to open any container or twist any mechanism. If you must remove the device from the premises, do so with extreme caution. Some explosives may detonate quite readily, while others require another explosive to cause a chain series which results in the final explosion of the more powerful material. Move the device to an open area, place it under guard, then contact a bomb expert by radio or telephone and follow his instructions.

CIVIL AND DOMESTIC DISPUTES

Other than prisoner transportation and arrest situations, the most dangerous situation to which a patrol officer responds is the disturbance call involving some civil or domestic dispute. He is usually called to the scene by one or more of the participants. Once he arrives, his primary purpose is to prevent any of the participants from committing any criminal act in his presence. He determines whether anyone had committed a crime prior to his arrival and if the suspect is on the premises to be arrested. Following his preliminary inquiries, the officer's role then takes on the characteristics of an invited arbiter. He is asked for advice and assistance, and is expected by the inquirers to provide such advice and assistance.

Diplomacy and tact are put into play almost constantly during these "referee" sessions. Occasionally the officer is reminded by the calling party that it was he who called and that the officer should enforce his side of the argument, regardless of all other considerations. The police officer is not—nor should he be—the "big, bad man who is going to get you if you are naughty," or "the man who is going to take you into a dark room and beat you up with his stick," or any other type of bogeyman used as a device by adults to frighten children.

During my own experiences as a field police officer, I have encountered certain individuals who complain loudly and bitterly to the press, or to some demagogue opportunist, or sometimes even directly to the police chief, about police abuses of arrestees and other persons. These complainers are exactly the same individuals who make unusual demands of those same police officers during neighborhood or family disturbances. One lady, for example, who was in the forefront when it came to "committee reports" of alleged police abuses, had a husband whom she found extremely difficult to handle. One time when she called the police, she demanded that the officer "beat him up to teach him a lesson like I know you do with others." On another occasion that lady demanded that the officer take her husband down "to the station and lock him up to teach him a lesson." Whatever the action a police officer takes, it should be appropriate for the circumstances as a matter of his considered judgment, and not in response to the emotional demands of angry persons.

The telephone operator or dispatcher who receives the original call for police presence at the scene of a civil dispute sets the tone for the officer's initial response. From the details of the situation provided by the calling party, and from the tone of voice and sense of urgency transmitted through the telephone to the dispatcher, the dispatcher makes the determination as to how many units will respond and with what speed. When determining if police service is actually being requested and if an officer should be sent (rather than an immediate referral to another agency), the dispatcher or telephone operator who takes the call should do the following:

1. Find out exactly what is happening, or as nearly as possible. Listen to the background noises as well as to the voice of the calling party.
2. Determine if someone has been injured and is in need of immediate medical attention.
3. Determine if there is an immediate and imminent danger confronting someone who is on the scene.
4. If there is such a danger, who or what is it?
5. If someone is armed with some sort of weapon, find out what type of weapon, the present whereabouts of the armed subject, and the individual's state of emotionalism and/or sobriety.

6. Find out from the calling party—if possible—and by checking the
records files if this is a recurrence of some similar activity that has
occurred in the past. What happened that time? (Check records, if
time permits, that is.)

7. Keep the caller on the telephone as long as necessary.

8. As any new developments arise while you are still talking with the
calling party and the assigned officer has been dispatched, keep that
officer updated on any information that will assist him in responding
to the call.

9. Dispatch only those officers that are necessary to effectively handle
the situation.

10. If the situation calls for response from another police agency, such
as in a contiguous jurisdiction, or from an organization or agency
that is specifically geared for this particular problem, advise the
calling party that another agency should handle the matter. Instead
of instructing an emotionally involved caller to dial another telephone number, either help him transfer the call or take what information you need, then instruct him that you will call the other
agency and handle the matter. Do not add to the caller's frustration
and/or anger by stating: "Sorry, ma'am, that's not our jurisdiction.
Try the sheriff's office. . . . No, I don't know what their number is,
but I'm sure they are in the book."

11. Send cover cars, if necessary. Consider the specific location of the
call, the individuals involved, experience with the nature of the call
and the principals, the neighborhood characteristics—which may be
hostility toward the police in general—and the information you receive by telephone.

12. Call off the units that are no longer needed if there is a change in
the circumstances at the scene as reported by the first officer to
arrive and other officers.

As the officer assigned to handle the call, your responsibility is
to handle the case as well as possible under the circumstances. Any
advice that you give should be kept to a minimum. Your role is to
restore order, to protect the combatants from themselves and each
other, to arrest for violations of the law when necessary, and to give
instructions or take whatever action the circumstances dictate to settle
the matter during your first visit. Whatever advice you give should be
presented in such a manner that they will accept it and act upon it.
Any warning you give concerning future arrests should the situation
recur must be soundly covered by the law, because if it does continue
and you do return, you are committed to make the arrest you promised.
It is virtually impossible to make everyone at the scene happy, but
they must be placated sufficiently to heed your advice and discontinue
the disturbance. Following are some of the more commonly encountered civil dispute situations and a few basic guidelines to use when
taking effective police action.

Arguments and fights among family members have probably been going on for some time and have been building in intensity prior to anyone's call for police intervention. There may be deep-seated emotional problems and irreconcilable differences with the outward manifestations in the form of verbal or physical violence serving only as symptoms of the problem. Under these circumstances all you can hope to do is to control the symptoms.

Avoid as much as possible what might appear to be prying into other people's personal affairs. Do not give legal advice. Instead, suggest that the people contact a lawyer they trust and in whom they have confidence. They should then seek his legal advice and agree to follow whatever advice he provides. There are qualified, licensed marriage counselors available for family advice. Once you temporarily take care of the symptoms, the people should consult expert advice to work on the real underlying problems. Do not take sides or become embroiled in the argument that may be taking place. This is the time to protect life and property against injury or destruction, not a time for gallantry to defend the unknown degree of honor of a woman whom you do not know over an issue that is none of your personal concern. Neither is it the time to agree that the husband is correct because you, too, are a husband and you would take a similar course of action.

In a domestic dispute situation, you may find that you will become the object of attack. Love and hate are strong emotions, and they do not seem to be entirely unrelated. One spouse may be verbally and physically abusing the other spouse until a third party comes along and attempts to defend the person under attack. Suddenly the third party —in this case a police officer—becomes a mutual threat, and both spouses join together to overcome that threat. This is a phenomenon that occurs with alarming regularity.

Children may develop antipolice attitudes out of some domestic quarrel in which the police officer becomes involved because he has been called upon for help. This antagonism probably occurs through a transference process. The father may come home drunk and beat the mother. The children become emotionally involved because their security is threatened, or their father may find some reason to punish them in an unusually cruel manner. Eventually the mother calls the police because she cannot defend herself or the children.

The officers arrive and assess the situation. The mother consents to the arrest of the father, may even demand it under these conditions, because she fears for the safety of the children and herself. The man goes to jail, sometimes after a violent struggle with the arresting officers. Unfortunately, this often occurs in the presence of the children. Through this twist of fate, the police officers—not the father—

become the hate objects of the children, because the officers further
threatened their security by taking their father out of the home. The
financial difficulties relative to posting bail or losing salary for the
time in jail—possibly the loss of a job—are sometimes also blamed on
the police officers.

Whenever possible during family fight situations, attempt to have
the children removed from the scene. Whatever action that ensues is
then less likely to involve them so emotionally. A violent arrest scene
is not savored by anyone and will hopefully be avoided altogether.
During your assessment of the situation on your arrival, you may
determine that a crime such as felonious wife or child beating had
taken place or was occurring during your arrival. Or you may observe
that the environment is detrimental to the health and safety of the
children, which may call for the arrest of one or both parents for
maintaining an unfit home, for being intoxicated, or for performing
lewd acts in the children's presence. In most situations, arrests will
not be made, but many times such action is imperative.

In an emotion-packed domestic quarrel, it is not unusual for one or
both of the principals to demand the immediate arrest and incarcera-
tion of the other party. At this point, the officer's discretionary powers
come into play. Analyze the situation. What is the present physical
and emotional state of the participants? What signs are there of physical injury? What evidence is there that the purported action took
place? What do the witnesses—if any—say? What is likely to happen
after you leave? Is a crime being committed in your presence? Do you
have reasonable cause to arrest for a felony that did not occur in your
presence? If you believe that an arrest is warranted and can be effected
in a legal and ethical manner, then by all means make the arrest. If
you believe that the arrest is not the answer to the problem, you may
refuse to accept an arrest by a private person if you do not believe
there is legal justification for the arrest.

Another frequently used alternative is to advise the parties to come
into the office of the police department or the prosecuting attorney
(depending on your own department practices) during the next business day and to discuss the matter at that time. Then, if it is determined that an arrest should be made, steps will be taken to secure a
warrant and effect the arrest. This latter proceduce gives the principals
some time to reflect on the matter and to unemotionally make a decision that will have long-lasting effects. If you choose to use this alternative and so advise the principals, you may still need to warn
them that if you should have to return you will be compelled to
reassess and some arrests will have to be made after all. Remember,
though, do not make a promise that you cannot keep. Once you have
made such a statement, you may be committed to take action or lose
your effectiveness. Idle threats are more devastating than taking no
action at all.

The police officer is not a bill collector. He does not have the authority to evict tenants from other person's homes or apartments, unless he is the civil division deputy from the sheriff's department, who does so by court order. The patrol officer acts as an agent of the jurisdiction for which he serves in his official capacity, not as a personal representative of any landlord or his tenant. As with any other incident requiring his attendance, the officer's role is that of police officer.

When responding to a dispute involving property rights and eviction notices or similar disturbances, approach both adversaries and advise them that your presence is to keep the peace and to prevent the commission of a crime. If they ask for legal advice other than an explanation of the criminal laws they may be contemplating violating, refer them to an attorney of their choice. Legal services are generally available to indigent persons at nominal costs, and small claims court actions for lawsuits involving amounts of money that would probably include the cost of rent may be instituted at a cost of just a few dollars.

In some disputes in which tempers are flaring and the participants appear to be at an impasse, it may be necessary to order an end to the argument to avoid more serious problems that would inevitably lead to an arrest of one or both of them. The landlord may seek assistance through the courts, with eviction proceedings, and secure the services of the sheriff. Either party may seek legal advice. Both must be advised to discontinue their argument.

Mechanics' and Innkeepers' Liens

An auto mechanic or service station operator may retain custody of an automobile until the cost of repairs are either paid for or some arrangement agreeable to mechanic and owner is worked out for payment. Operators of hotels and rooming houses may hold certain belongings of the tenants to enforce collection of rent. All merchants, businessmen, and others who provide goods and services are entitled to just payment for those goods and services.

When you are called to the scene at which the matter appears to involve nonpayment of charges for merchandise or repairs, or some other type or service, question all participants and witnesses carefully. Although a police officer may not act as a bill collector in a civil matter, many nonpayment situations are nothing more than flagrant acts of theft or "defrauding an innkeeper" violations. If there is some dispute regarding charges, they usually involve an amount that the party refusing to pay claims is too high. Whatever their statements, advise them that certain property may be held to enforce payment of debts. Also advise them of the laws concerning theft. If the matter cannot be amicably settled by the participants in your presence, advise them to seek legal advice. In the meantime, they should usually pay the bill to gain possession of the property being held and to avoid a charge of theft. If the charges are too high, a judge or jury would have to decide that point.

Repossession Disputes

Modern contracts are carefully prepared. They have been modified and clarified so many times that many of them are quite standard and free of "loopholes" that might render them invalid. About the only method that can be used to nullify the average contract is to show that some type of fraud was involved to induce an individual to enter the agreement.

The title of the property covered in most sales contracts rests with the seller until the total debt is paid. Any default in payment is generally covered in the contract, which provides for repossession. There arc only three persons who may legally repossess: (1) the seller and his full-time employees, or (2) a successor in interest (buyer of the contract from the original seller) and his full-time employees, or (3) licensed collection agencies acting in behalf of their clients who are either sellers or successors in interest.

Repossessions must be made in a peaceful and a lawful manner according to the various laws that involve such acts. When your presence is requested at the scene of a repossession dispute, as with all other situations, your role is that of a disinterested third party who is not personally involved. You may inquire of the repossessor his legal relationship to the act that he is performing. If he cannot show proof of his identity as one of the three persons listed in the preceding paragraph and cannot show evidence of the existence of such a contract, you may have reasonable cause to arrest him for theft or attempted theft should he continue to repossess the items in question. If the buyer acknowledges that the contract does exist and he accepts the identity of the repossessor, but adamantly refuses to relinquish control of the property, advise him that the repossession is probably legal but cannot be carried out unless it is a peaceable one. If the participants cannot work out the problem in your presence, advise the repossessor to discontinue his efforts to avoid causing someone's arrest. He can go to the courts and seek assistance of the sheriff, who may enforce the repossession.

DEAD BODY CALLS

When responding to a reported death scene, your first responsibility is to determine if death has, in fact, occurred. If there is any possibility whatsoever that there may be life in the victim, take immediate steps to attempt to preserve the life. This is unquestionably your first responsibility. Some bodies indicate by their appearance that death has unquestionably occurred, and you may proceed accordingly. Look for the presumptive and positive signs of death when examining the body, and note the observations you make.

The presumptive signs, which indicate that death has possibly occurred, but not conclusively, involve body temperature, heart beat, and respiration. To determine if the person is breathing, look for any movement in the area of the lower border of the rib cage. Absence of any respiration indicates death or a condition that may be produced in drowning, electrocution, or narcotic overdose cases in which the respiratory process is arrested. For the heart beat, feel the pulse or gently feel for heart beat by placing a hand on the left chest below and to the right of the nipple. Body temperature decreases at a steady rate that varies with the individual. When death occurs, there may be a perceptible change in temperature. When examining the body for temperature, note any differences in temperature at the various parts of the body. If death has occurred not too many hours before your arrival, the differences in body temperature may help the medical examiner to determine the approximate time of death.

There are three basic manifestations that are considered positive signs of death: absence of muscle tone in the eyes, rigor mortis, and post-mortem lividity. The third, post-mortem lividity, appears on the portions of the body that are closer to the surface on which it rests. It is a discoloration and appears something like a light purple bruise with no obvious outer bruise on the skin surface. Lividity is actually a settling of all the body fluids by the pull of gravity to the lower parts of the body, and it begins about one-half hour to three hours after death. If it appears at some part of the body other than where it would be normally as a result of gravity flow, it may indicate that the body has been moved after death. Because of its resemblance to a bruise, do not overlook the possibility that it is actually a bruise.

Rigor mortis is a hardening, or calcifying, condition of the muscles throughout the body, usually beginning with smaller muscles and progressively developing in the larger muscles. For this reason, it appears to start at the face and head and work down to the feet. Actually, it is working in all parts of the body at the same time. Depending on the physical condition of the victim at the time of death, rigor mortis usually begins about three to five hours after death, is complete in eight to twelve hours, then begins to disappear after about 48 hours. Sometimes a condition occurs which resembles rigor mortis and is misleading to the observer. This condition is known as a cadaveric spasm, which is an immediate rigidity of the entire body caused by an intense emotional situation that occurs at the moment of death. It is known to happen in crimes when the death occurs in a violent struggle or at an emotional peak. When examining the body,

check various parts of the body to ascertain the presence of the rigor,

check various parts of the body to ascertain the presence of the rigor, but do not attempt to disturb the condition. Once the condition is "broken" by movement, it does not return.

The third positive sign of death is the total absence of muscle tone in the pupils of the eyes, the eye muscles, and the eyelids. This is also one of the first places that the decaying process in the human body begins. When checking for muscle tone, also look for a film that forms over the eyes, caused by the drying of the fluids that once were produced by the tear ducts.

Only a doctor or a coroner may legally declare death, and until the arrival of such a person, it is your responsibility to make every effort to sustain what life may exist, except when there are such conditions as to positively establish the existence of death. The coroner takes charge of the remains and his possessions, and in cooperation with the office of the coroner, the police department investigates deaths as to their cause to determine what criminal law violations were committed, if any.

If there is a possibilty that the death is anything other than "natural," by disease, or by accidental means, the investigation continues immediately. Except in departments that assign specialists to take over the investigation immediately, your role as patrol officer is to assume the responsibility for the initial investigation. Specialists should be called in as early in the investigation as possible to handle laboratory and identification work, and the follow-up investigator may begin his follow-up at the same time you are conducting the initial investigation. Following is a list of guidelines that should be followed for the investigation of any suspected death:

EXAMINATION OF THE VICTIM. Look for signs of life, or death. Make mental notes (write them later as soon as practicable) about the differences in body temperature, state of rigor mortis, and other presumptive and positive signs of death that you observe. Consider the possibility of securing a dying declaration from the victim if he is still alive and coherent.

IDENTIFY THE VICTIM. Identification may be made during the victim's dying declaration, or by examining personal effects. The property of the deceased is the responsibility of the coroner, but an officer may examine certain property to make an identification and to pursue the investigation. Sometimes the identity of the deceased will lead to the person who caused his present condition, or to friends or relatives who should be notified of the death and may be of possible assistance in the investigation.

DETERMINE THE CAUSE OF DEATH. The cause may be obvious, but do not overlook the not-so-obvious. For example, a known heart patient was found dead under what appeared to be "natural" conditions. The officer handled the case as he would handle any other heart patient until the ambulance had taken the victim to the morgue, and it was discovered that two bullet holes were in the victim's chest. Sometimes the coroner or medical examiner has to investigate extensively to ascertain the cause of death.

PROTECT THE SCENE. The scene includes the place of the death and the immediate surrounding area. Every death that occurs under unusual circumstances must be considered a possible homicide until the investigation establishes that it is not.

QUESTION WITNESSES. Separate the witnesses and question them about the identity of the victim, and any other matters that seem pertinent to the investigation.

REMOVE THE BODY. Prior to the body's removal, arrange to have photographs taken, and prepare a field sketch. Note the exact location of the body, its position, and any relevant information. If there was an immediate removal of the body because of a belief that life may have existed, make notes of your recollections of the scene at your arrival.

SEARCH. Search the immediate and general area for any evidence that may lead to the eventual solution of any crime that may have occurred, or that may aid the investigation in any appreciable manner.

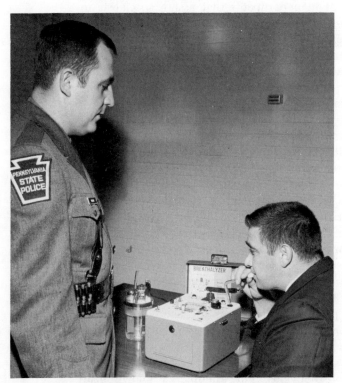

Figure 9.2 The breathalyzer is one of the more effective and least expensive means of determining blood-alcohol percentages. Courtesy of the Pennsylvania State Police.

RECONSTRUCT THE OCCURRENCE. By organizing the statements, the facts, evidence, and whatever else is available, attempt to determine the cause of death and the circumstances surrounding it. Establish a motive for the homicide, if one is aparent. The motive is not necessary to prove guilt of the accused, but it often leads to the identification of the guilty party.

REPORT. Prepare whatever reports are required by department policy and be sure that they adequately reflect all of the facts as they presented themselves to you during the investigation.

INTOXICATION CASES

Traditional police responsibility for arresting and incarcerating the drunks, alcoholics, and other persons whose actions in public indicate their apparent lack of ability to care for their own welfare, rests with the patrol officer. The primary reasons for taking such a person into custody are to protect him from himself and from the dangers of the elements, from traffic, and any other hazards that he may be exposed to while in his intoxicated state.

Intoxication is relative, and the officer's discretionary powers are great in this area. The laws vary, but those concerning intoxication in public cover persons who are intoxicated to the degree that they are unable to care for their own welfare, and are in that state as a result of overindulgence in alcohol, drugs, or other intoxicating or stupefying substances. One of your first considerations is to determine that the subject's condition is not caused by some type of illness, poisoning, injury, or other condition, brought about by some situation other than voluntary ingestion by the subject, knowing that the substance used had intoxicating or stupefying effects. Look for the identification bracelet that many diabetics wear to warn anyone finding the victim of diabetic shock that the subject needs immediate medical attention. Question the subject about any illness he may be suffering from, and look for evidence of the intoxicating substance.

If there are any signs of injury or illness, take the subject to the hospital. If you determine that the subject is in the state of voluntary intoxication that labels him as an intoxicated person, and you decide to lodge him in jail, handle him as you would any other arrestee, but show extra consideration for his safety because, by law, he is unable to care for his own safety.

LOST CHILD

This is one of the most important of all police activities and should involve maximum personnel assignment at the earliest opportunity

Figure 9.3 Searching for a lost child is one of a police department's most responsible functions. Dogs are excellent aids in this type of activity. Courtesy of the Police Department, Lexington, Kentucky.

after the parent reports the child as missing. There has usually been some lapse of time prior to the parent's report. Therefore, time is more of essence because of the distances the child may have traveled or the length of time the child may have been exposed to the many hazards he might encounter and possibly not be able to cope with.

Consider the possibility that the child may have been taught to fear the police uniform, and may hide from the searching officers without realizing that they are trying to reunite him with his parents. Some children who are the object of a search may hide and play games with their searchers. It is not uncommon for the child to be uncooperative because of the many vagaries of the innocent child's mind and his unfortunate lack of understanding of the role of the police officers and other searchers.

Secure any information you can regarding any earlier case in which the child ran away. The parents can sometimes provide valuable information, although they may be somewhat reluctant to do so because of embarrassment. If the child has run away or wandered away before, ascertain where he was discovered on the earlier occasion.

Consider the age of the child. Where would you go if you were that age? What type of entertainment or adventure would you pursue if you were on your own away from the sometimes prohibitive control of parents who may disagree with a five-year-old boy's concept of fun and excitement?

Search the immediate premises, including any container that could hold the child or any smaller object. The child may have gone into hiding to avoid some form of punishment, yet he might not want to stray too far from the security of home. The child may have left the home and the premises earlier, but he may have returned and may now be in hiding under a bed, in a closet, in a refrigerator or freezer, or possibly in a tree hideaway.

Establish the exact time and location at which the child was last seen. Set up a grid pattern on the jurisdiction map, and divide the search area into well-defined areas with specific assignments to assure complete coverage. Consider the maximum distance the child may have traversed during that period of time, then add more distance for additional coverage. Each assigned officer should then start at the outermost point and search the assigned area in a zig-zag or clover-leaf manner, working in toward the center, or the location where the child was last seen, then working back out to the perimeter.

Use the loudspeaker on a police unit and consider having the parents, a relative, or a close friend of the child, broadcast the appeal to the child to come out of hiding. Their voices may have a greater value than that of the searching officer.

Never overlook the possibility of a kidnaping, and begin an early search for any evidence of such an event. Check the files for any known or suspected individual who may live or be suspected of performing his crimes in the area. Locate and question him, if available. Rather than harassment, this procedure is actually an assurance to him. It gives him an opportunity to completely exonerate himself early in the investigation.

Continue a relentless search until you find the child.

MENTALLY AND EMOTIONALLY DISTURBED INDIVIDUALS

Civil laws usually provide for temporary custody of an individual who appears to be in need of immediate emergency observation because of some emotional or mental breakdown. He is called to the attention of the patrol officer usually through some erratic behavior or act of violence that the subject's friends or relatives cannot handle without assistance.

In some states, the patrol officer is empowered to take a person whom he suspects of being in need of emergency care to a psychiatric clinic, and to have him subjected to a period of observation by psychiatrists, if the officer believes such action is necessary to the health and safety of the subject or other persons.

When responding to a call involving an individual who appears mentally or emotionally disturbed, be extremely careful to handle him with understanding, diplomacy, and tact. Symptoms may include such things as dramatic and sudden changes in behavior, a loss of memory, and intense feeling that people are plotting against him. He may talk to himself or claim to hear voices, or he may be displaying dangerous behavior. The mentally or emotionally disturbed individual may be in a very docile mood for a while, then become extremely violent without any apparent cause. For that reason, whenever you believe you have such a person in custody, use ample restraining equipment as a precautionary measure for his protection as well as your own.

Some felons may feign mental illness when arrested in an attempt to avoid punishment for their crime, using the pretended condition of disorientation as a defense against the claim that they formed specific intent to commit their crimes. To place a suspect with this motive in a psychiatric ward might put you in a position in which your suspicions and subsequent action in handling the suspect as a mentally ill person may provide the subject his defense. He can show that you were obviously impressed with his lack of mental or emotional control because you placed him in a psychiatric ward for mental observation. If there are obvious manifestations of such mental or emotional upset, you have no choice but to act accordingly and place him under mental observation. But if there is some doubt and the case is an extremely important one, it might be sounder judgment to place him in an isolated cell by himself and immediately consult with the prosecuting attorney. The attorney may decide to have a psychiatrist conduct an immediate examination and make his evaluation, to assure proper care and treatment for the suspect if he is truly in need of psychiatric care. Some jurisdictions have a standing procedure that requires an immediate psychiatric evaluation at any time a criminal homicide suspect is arrested. This policy allows the officer to obtain a determination as to the suspect's mental state as soon after the commission of the crime as possible. At the same time, the act of causing the psychiatric evaluation carries with it no reflection of any opinions the arresting officer may or may not have had.

As an aid in understanding the mentally and emotionally disturbed, the following descriptions and definitions are presented from a layman's point of view. They are merely items of information, and in no way should they ever be used as a guide for making any type of diagnosis.

A *psychosis* is a gross and persistent falsification of conventional reality which leaves the person unable to manage that conventional reality with any degree of effectiveness. The major components of psychosis are delusions and hallucinations. A *delusion* is a faulty belief that is motivated primarily by the individual's needs or wishes and has no basis in fact. An *hallucination,* conversely, is usually manifested in a visual image that is quite vivid and real to the individual who experiences it. The hallucination does not actually exist, but there is probably some correspondence between the hallucination and some actual sensory input, and the individual is willing to take some action based upon that perceptual experience. Many people have hallucinations under unusual situations and are not necessarily suffering from psychosis, but the hallucinations do not recur once the situations have passed. Hallucinations include those visions that appear in the middle of a desert highway as puddles of water or an oasis in the middle of sand dunes. Another hallucination might be something that looks like a prowler, which is actually a hibiscus shrub brushing against the screen.

Paranoia is a set of fixed delusional beliefs that are accompanied by clear and orderly thinking outside the delusion system. The true paranoid, or "classical paranoid," as some psychologists may refer to him, may be highly intelligent and so persuasive that he will successfully recruit other persons to help him in his war against his enemies. He may not be as easily identified as the individual with a *paranoid reaction*, who does not handle the problem with as much logic or intelligence as the true paranoid. Paranoia manifests itself in inferences and beliefs that the subject is "being talked about," "being made fun of," "is the object of a hate campaign," or that someone is trying to get rid of him. The paranoid has been described as "vigilant, suspicious, distrustful, insecure, and chronically anxious." According to some theorists, the paranoid may justify his intense hatred of some object, such as Hitler's hatred for the Jews in Germany, by stating, "I hate you so intensely because you hate me and you are trying to get rid of me."

Schizophrenia is a thinking disorder. According to some experts, approximately 80 percent of the mentally ill population is schizophrenic. There are several subcategories of schizophrenia, such as the catatonic state, demonstrated by the patient's rigidly held position for sometimes interminable periods of time; and the hebephrenic state, in which the subject continually acts childlike and silly. Indications of the schizophrenic condition appear in three different ways: One, the subject's language may be rambling or tangential, he may make up meaningless rhymes, or echo everything he hears. Two, the subject may show his split personality by an incongruence between his expressed ideas and his emotional responses, which indicate two thought processes operating simultaneously. Three, the subject may isolate or alienate himself from the rest of society and pull himself into his personal shell.

As a patrol officer, you are likely to encounter the mentally or emotionally disturbed individual under almost any type of circumstance. Many people are emotionally upset for the moment because of the nature of the situation, such as an intense family fight or a repossession confrontation, but their emotionalism leaves and they return to a state of relative normality. Whenever you encounter any person who appears to you to exhibit symptoms that indicate problems of a mental or emotional problem more deep-seated than just the immediate circumstance, these few guidelines may assist you in dealing with that person:

1. Make no attempt to physically or orally threaten the subject. He will probably respond more favorably to kindness and understanding.
2. Maintain an outward appearance of complete self-control. Make your conversation and your actions as calm and toned-down as possible, yet be firm and direct.
3. Make use of friends or relatives who know how to talk with the subject and who will tend to cause him to have more confidence in you if he sees that those persons have trust and confidence in you.
4. If you must take him into custody for some purpose, do so with calmness and deliberation, and use ample restraining devices to avoid further complications.

MISSING PERSONS

Many times friends and members of the family report someone missing. Most of the time when such a situation occurs, that person has isolated himself for a purpose. Relatively few of the reported missing persons are actually the victims of amnesia, or become confused and lost. They are missing by choice. If the missing person is a juvenile, the matter will be handled as a juvenile case, with the child referred to his parents and possibly—in serious cases—to the juvenile court. In the case of missing adults, there is a somewhat different procedure.

Whenever a person is reported missing within a few hours beyond the time when he should have arrived home from work, or is overdue on some sort of trip, it is good practice to take whatever information the reporting party wishes to provide, and to advise that person how to go about checking with hospitals where unidentified injured persons may have been taken. In addition, it is advisable to attempt to reassure the reporting party with what information you have about the lack of serious freeway accidents or aircraft crashes, or with the information that your department has no unidentified victims of any crimes of violence reported during the time that the person has been missing. Beyond that first phase of taking the report and assisting the reporting party, the next step is to wait a reasonable time for the "missing party" to return.

If there is some evidence or strong reason to believe that the missing person has met with some type of forced absence or violence, an immediate investigation should begin. In other missing person cases, after a reasonable time has elapsed and the party has not yet returned to his expected destination, a concerted effort should be made to locate him. Once the individual is located, if he or she is an adult, and indicates a desire not to have his whereabouts made known, your own department policy may require that you notify the reporting party that you found the missing person in good health and that he does not wish his whereabouts made known. In the event of a missing husband, consider the possibility of an impending nonsupport situation with the husband absenting himself. If this is the case, the matter will be a criminal one. Every missing person case should be given adequate attention, but it must be carefully handled within the framework of department policy.

NUISANCES

There are two general types of nuisances that require the attention of the police department: the public nuisance, and the attractive nuisance. Both may involve criminal code violations—and they often do—but they also involve civil, nonpolice, matters.

The public nuisance often involves misdemeanor crime violations such as disturbance of the peace, boisterous conduct, loud and unusual noises during prohibited hours, drunkenness, assaults, delinquency of minors, vagrancy, and vice violations. It encompasses a multitude of encroachments on the peace and dignity of the community at large as well as the many individuals who are disturbed.

General public nuisances involve law violations such as offensive advertising signs that are too large or placed in locations where ordinances prohibit them, disagreeable odors caused by abandoned refuse in a vacant lot, automobiles that are either abandoned or placed on blocks in the street for repairs that never seem to get done, and the maintenance of an excessive number of animals for the size of the house or lot. An abandoned building that becomes the residence of drunkards and vagrants may soon present itself as a public nuisance.

One type of public nuisance that presents a special problem is the "party house." It is usually occupied by two or more young people who legitimately pay the rent and then have parties involving more people than the place can accommodate. These often become too raucous and noisy. The place might become a gathering place for young people to violate the liquor laws ostensibly under the cover of "private property asylum," or a place for numerous narcotics and dangerous drug law violations. In some jurisdictions, it is possible to cause the owners and occupants of the homes or apartments involved to discontinue the nuisance or to vacate the premises. This action is possible if it can be shown to the court that the "party house" threatens and generally disturbs the "public" in the persons of the surrounding residents and others who are disturbed.

An attractive nuisance is usually given that designation because it is a condition or place that attracts children and which poses an imminent threat to their health and safety. The nuisance may in itself be entirely legal or innocent, but by its own nature it attracts young people who cannot understand the significance of the threatened danger. A legal definition of "attractive nuisance" has been presented as "an unnatural condition that attracts infants who do not understand the danger, and injury results because of the condition." Here is a list of what might be considered attractive nuisances under certain conditions:

1. Building under construction.
2. Abandoned or unoccupied buildings that have not been adequately secured to prevent entry.
3. Swimming pools without adequate fencing, gate locks, and reasonable means of prohibiting swimming without responsible persons in attendance.
4. Accumulations of water of unknown, or excessive, depth.
5. Piles of dirt, sand, or gravel.
6. Excavations.
7. Ladders and scaffolding.
8. Dead trees and accumulations of dead foliage.
9. Telephone and power poles with cleats close to the ground, making it possible for easy climbing.
10. Unattended construction machinery or farm implements that can be started without an ignition key.

Figure 9.4 Officers frequently inspect this canal which runs through Billings, where several children have drowned. Courtesy of the Police Department, Billings, Montana.

Some attractive nuisances are prohibited by specific criminal laws, such as an abandoned refrigerator with the locking mechanism left intact, or an unattended motor vehicle with the motor running. They should be diligently investigated and the laws enforced. Most of them are prosecutable under civil law, in tort actions. There are three types of conduct that may be considered cause for action: (a) intentional, (b) negligence, and (c) acts at peril. The third type involves certain situations when the defendant may be considered liable without fault, or culpability. Nevertheless, the loss of the lawsuit means two things: someone—probably a child—suffered the loss of life or some form of injury, and the defendant suffers the loss of money.

The patrol officer's role in this matter is twofold. He should attempt to protect children by frequently checking the locations of such attractive nuisances, and he should remind the owners or other persons in charge of the nuisances of their existence and the possibility that they may suffer losses in tort actions. Whenever children or other persons are found at those locations, they should be told to leave, and the parents of the children should be notified of your action so that they may attempt to exercise appropriate controls to prevent tragedies from occurring. When notifying the owners or other responsible persons of the existence of nuisance conditions, prepare reports to permanently record the fact that you fulfilled your responsibility at that point. If the hazardous condition continues to exist, more formal action may be taken in the form of registered letters directed to the offenders, or, possibly, civil action filed by the city attorney on behalf of the people to protect the lives and limbs of their children. Of course, private individuals will probably also take action on their own in aggravated situations.

PARADES AND SPECIAL EVENTS

The primary police responsibility at any special event, such as a parade, festival, or other occasion involving a greater than usual number of people, is to expedite vehicular and pedestrian traffic, and to keep the traffic lanes open for emergency vehicles. Spectator safety is paramount, particularly the safety of young children who may not be capable of looking after their own safety. Direct your full attention on the people, utilizing crowd and traffic control procedures.

ROUTINE POLICE SERVICES

The matter of responding to routine calls for service and assistance involves a series of policy decisions by the chief of police and his staff. It is a physical impossibility for the police department to provide all of the services that would be requested once the service is started. The policy decisions should be made decisively, they should be communicated to all members of the department, and they must be uniformly applied by all of the officers. Personalized service for certain individuals merely opens the door for a long series of "modifications" in policy and procedure for certain individuals on a favoritism basis.

Merely having police officers on duty and on constant patrol throughout the various parts of the city encourages some people to believe that the policemen are there to serve their whims. Such people do not consider any of the myriad other responsibilities with which they are charged. "They are on duty already, so why not have them do it?" may be asked by a councilman who has no idea of the full extent of the burden already carried by the police department. A simple reply to that question is "Why not, indeed?" Using that over-simplified logic, why not assign certain of those services to the fire department, recreation leaders, license and building inspectors, or any-one else who is ". . . on duty already"? The duties of the police de-partment are defined, and they must be limited if the department is to be held responsible for the safety of the people in the community and their property. Escort service, messenger service, and a wide variety of other services are regularly provided by private enterprise for profit—or loss. Taxicabs are in the business of transporting persons for hire. Is it equitable for the police department to compete with private enterprise by providing free services to some people, while most others utilize the facilities of private businesses? Many of these services are not police responsibilities, and their perpetuation should not be tolerated. Tradition may be a safe answer to the question "Why are these services performed?" However, tradition does not necessarily offer the correct answer. Consider the advisability of performing the courtesy services listed in the next section, then respond to them in accordance with the policies of your own department.

Fire Scenes

A fire scene is the responsibility of the fire department commanders and their personnel. They handle the rescue operations and extinguish the blaze. The police responsibility is the same as at any other location where crowds of people congregate: vehicle and pedestrian traffic and crowd control. Divert traffic away from the scene to prevent any further damage or injuries than might already have occurred. Keep the streets open to allow for the ingress and egress of fire vehicles, ambulances, and any other vehicles and equipment required by the fire department.

Passers-by and casual spectators must be instructed to leave the immediate area of the fire to prevent any major disaster. Once you have handled the matters required of you in your police officer ca-pacity, it is a matter of good practice to contact the ranking fire de-partment officer and determine if there is any need for your assistance in rescue operations, or any security matters involving the fire equip-ment or valuable property at the scene. If the situation warrants it,

you may find it necessary to declare the area of the fire a disaster area,
then to diligently enforce the area control as long as the emergency
exists.

Rescue and First Aid

A police officer is authorized and—in some states—legally required
to administer first aid and to perform rescue operations whenever the
need arises. One of the prime considerations to bear in mind relative
to that statement is that first aid does not mean to practice medicine,
or in any way to exceed the limitations of "first aid" treatment. Once
you assume such treatment, you are liable for exercising reasonable
care, which has clearly been defined and described in your training.
Any rescue operations are subject to the same requirements.

Courtesy Services

Many courtesy services are performed by the patrol officer as a
matter of routine, most of them because it has "always been done."
Whichever of these services your department performs should be
executed with tact, diplomacy, and courtesy. They are free services
and there should be no expectation of anything in return. A few of
these services are described in this section.

a. Check a house to see if the vacationer, who is calling from about
a hundred miles away, did remember to turn off the gas furnace and
lock all the doors.

b. Deliver a message to someone who has no telephone, but who
is needed in the office because of some company emergency that cannot wait.

c. Deliver a death message to the wife of a laborer who has been
buried alive in a landslide. In such situations, consider stopping along
the way to pick up the family minister, rabbi, or priest for spiritual
guidance to the survivors. Neighbors may lessen the strain. Sometimes
it may be wise to notify the fire department rescue team that you are
going to deliver a message in the event that that unit is needed for
an emergency in case of a cardiac arrest or other side effect from the
shock. If the person to receive the message is known to be gravely ill,
it may be advisable to call the family doctor and have him accompany
you when you deliver the message or have him make the delivery.

d. Help a bedridden invalid who needs immediate assistance in
securing an emergency delivery of medicine, or in being lifted back
into bed after falling out. One serious problem that could result from
giving such assistance is the creation of a dependence by the invalid
on the service provided on a few occasions by the district policeman.
If such a dependence becomes a habit and is allowed by the department, the invalid might someday call for emergency service that the

department cannot provide because all of the officers are busy, and because of such failure to respond, the invalid's condition may worsen or he may die. The question may be asked in court: "Why was the police department negligent in not responding to that man's call for help?"

e. Escort a frightened or cautious lady, or child, down a darkened alley to her apartment in a high crime area when a sex killer is at large.

f. Give directions or provide other informational services for guests or tourists in town. In many cases, the policeman on the street represents the entire community to the inquirer, and that officer's attitude is interpreted as the attitude of the entire community.

g. Help someone who has locked himself out of his home or automobile to break in. Some burglars and thieves have actually been assisted by unsuspecting police officers who have been entirely innocent of any criminal involvement. Some persons have sought the assistance of the police in gaining entry, then complained about the method used by the officer who assisted them. This type of service should be strictly on an emergency basis. Occasions when there is clearly an indicated need for your assistance would be when a person's life may be endangered, which might be the case when a child is locked inside a car with the motor running, or when an individual who has locked himself inside a house has indicated his intention to commit suicide.

Whenever you assist a person in gaining entry in a routine problem situation, be sure to get satisfactory proof of identification and ownership of the property, and limit your participation to advice except in unusual cases, as with elderly persons or invalids. When you actually assist in such matters, consider the advisability of having the persons assisted sign a waiver relieving you from liability. This procedure may help to avoid a later complaint.

FAMILY AND MARRIAGE COUNSELING

Many times during the course of his duty the officer is asked to give advice to children who are on the verge of delinquency, to wayward husbands, and to just about anyone on virtually every question ranging from love to money to philosophy. The officer demonstrates his real mettle when he can assist the people while avoiding giving any advice that he is not legally or ethically qualified to give.

MONEY ESCORTS

Certain businessmen request an escort to the night depository of the bank. If there are escort service companies available, any services of this nature by the police department should be on an emergency basis only.

Following are guidelines for responding to utility or other public service problems:

1. Street lights out or damaged. The lighting is to provide people with sufficient illumination to assure them of safety on the streets. The lights should be replaced as quickly as possible. Look for malicious damage, which may indicate some purpose to use the darkness as a cover for illicit activities.

2. Electricity out and electric wires down. The line that is out may be providing electricity for a kidney machine or an emergency surgery, as well as for hundreds of homes and apartments. Locate the wire that is down or the place where the cable has been cut and notify the power company immediately. While waiting for the arrival of the repair crews, keep curious onlookers away and take whatever precautions that are necessary to protect the area. At your convenience, contact your local power company and ask for their instructions on what they would prefer that you do to keep the wires under control and to prevent serious injury to yourself as well as to others.

3. Damaged water mains or fire hydrants. When water mains or fire hydrants are broken, there are two dangerous effects that should be overcome as soon as possible. One is an almost sudden drop in water pressure in that area, and the second is extensive soil erosion, particularly on a hillside. Either could be disastrous if not handled as an emergency situation.

4. Telephone lines down. Telephone repair crews should be notified as soon as the broken line or cable is discovered. Many emergency services depend on the telephone as their only means of communication, and cannot function effectively without it.

5. Broken gas pipes. Domestic natural gas has odor-producing gas added and it is easy to detect if present in any quantity. The natural gas itself is odorless and may not be detected as easily, but lines extending within populated areas usually have the easily detected odor.

If possible, locate the source and extent of the leak. Immediately notify the gas company and ask for any special instructions they may wish to give you pending the arrival of their repair crews. Immediately evacuate persons from the vicinity of the broken line. Instruct the people to turn off all fires or flames, to refrain from smoking, and to avoid doing anything that might cause a spark, including turning electric switches off or on. If the gas leak seems to be inside a building or confined space, do whatever you can to allow maximum ventilation.

6. Defective streets and sidewalks. Holes and broken places in cement or asphalt may not be readily visible to the pedestrians who use the sidewalk or the drivers who use the street. Any defects in either of these surfaces should be reported as quickly as possible to

the street department so that they may be repaired. If they are allowed to go unrepaired or with no warning barricades or lights of some type, the city might be held civilly liable in the event a lawsuit is initiated.

7. Traffic signs, signals, other controls. There is obviously a purpose for these various traffic control implements. Allowing any one to go for any length of time in a state of disrepair, or to be missing altogether, could result in traffic congestion or a serious traffic accident. Some signs lose their painted surface or their reflective quality, or they become illegible because of overhanging tree branches or shrubbery. If there is a need for them where they are, the traffic control devices should be functioning fully as intended.

TOWING VEHICLES FROM PRIVATE PROPERTY

The most important advice that could be given on this topic is to check with your own local laws and procedures. There is considerable variation from one jurisdiction to another. If the vehicle has been stolen and abandoned, or if it is evidence in some type of criminal case, it should be impounded or stored. If the vehicle has been merely left on someone's private property, the owner may consider charging storage and holding the vehicle to enforce collection of the fee, or he may have the car towed away at his own expense. In most cases, the matter is a civil one, and the property owner must decide what to do.

HANDLING ANIMAL CALLS

How to handle stray animals, if this is a police department function in your jurisdiction at all, varies with local laws and policies. Animals that are suspected of having rabies require special handling and quarantine for a required period of time. If it is necessary to dispose of an animal suspected of having rabies, the head should not be destroyed, since the brain is used for analysis. If you must dispose of an animal, never do it in the presence of children.

STRIKE DUTY

The key to effective police action at the scene of a labor-management conflict is to be completely fair and objective. It is not the role of the officer to assume that either side is right or wrong. The police responsibility is to establish contact with both the company being struck and the leader of the strikers, and to point out the police role to enforce the law and to protect life and property. Ask for the co-operation of all parties on both sides of the dispute. The police concern is compliance with the laws and protection of the people from personal injury or property damage.

When working at the scene of a strike, provide for the free flow of pedestrian and vehicle traffic on the streets, the driveways, and the sidewalks. Whatever you do, handle the matter in such a way that it does not indicate any alliance or sympathy with either side of the dispute. At one strike situation, officers erred by using the company parking lot for their personal vehicles. At another, some of the officers used the company cafeteria to eat their lunch, and at still another, one or two of the assigned officers took advantage of discount prices to buy hams. None of these actions can be condoned any more than an officer can be allowed to carry one of the picket signs for a young lady who may have stopped to rest her feet.

Injunctions are often obtained to keep the pickets to a minimum number. Enforcement of injunctions is handled by bailiffs of the court, such as the sheriff, marshal, or constable. The municipal police officer cannot generally enforce injunctions. Arrests should be made for flagrant violations, but any situations that have personal animosity involved as well should be referred to an office conference on the following day. Take all the necessary information and prepare a complete report. After a night of calm deliberation when the parties can discuss the matter away from the picket line, a more appropriate course of action can be worked out. Of course, this is limited to nonaggravated situations and should not include cases in which it is clearly obvious that an arrest is necessary.

For detailed coverage of strike situations that call for more stringent police action, refer to the next two chapters on matters of civil disturbances and riots.

SUICIDES AND ATTEMPTED SUICIDES

An attempted suicide is a direct responsibility of the police officer in his role to protect life. He must take whatever steps he can to protect the life of a person who may want to end it himself. Sometimes a person with suicidal tendencies may attempt to bait an officer into a situation in which he hopes the officer will shoot and kill him. Sometimes an officer is confronted by such a person and the circumstances may cause the officer to fulfill his wishes. Hopefully, such a situation will be avoided if at all possible.

When responding to an attempted suicide call, make every effort to preserve the individual's life. Although the person may not be "mentally ill" by definition, but experiencing a severe emotional crisis, he should be handled as a possible mental illness case and subjected to an examination by a psychiatrist. Some jurisdictions provide for temporary civil commitment of people who attempt suicide until such time as they may be examined by a medical and psychiatric team, and a determination made as to which treatment is best to prevent a recurrence.

Many fallacies exist concerning suicide, and some of these fallacies have been attacked by a Suicide Prevention Center at the University of California at Los Angeles Medical Center. Consider some of the fallacious views when responding to an attempted suicide call or when taking information concerning an individual's threat to commit suicide either immediately or some time in the future. One fallacy that has prevailed for some time is that a person who threatens suicide will usually not go through with it. It has been generally believed that such threats are bids for sympathy or attention, which they are. But it has also been shown through extensive study that the individual will commit suicide if he does not solve his problem in some meaningful way.

Another fallacy about people who attempt suicide is the belief that they are so intent on killing themselves that they cannot be convinced to change their minds. This has been proven to be an invalid argument. Many people have been talked out of self-destruction, and, given proper treatment, they may permanently change their minds. They do not necessarily have to be suicidal for life.

All people who choose to attempt self-destruction are not necessarily mentally ill. The condition may be the result of complete despair or severe emotional problems caused by failure or unhappiness. Once the crisis is past, the individual may realize how meaningful and full life may be and he may never repeat his attempt to commit suicide.

Some university medical centers and medical associations have established "crisis centers" or similar services that provide psychiatric and psychological counseling by telephone for anyone who experiences an intense emotional or personal problem that he or she cannot cope with and who feels that there is no one else to turn to. There is no doubt that such centers have saved countless hundreds of lives.

EXERCISES AND STUDY QUESTIONS

1. What are the presumptive signs of death?
2. What are the positive signs of death?
3. What is a cadaveric spasm?
4. True or false: People who threaten suicide probably never will.
5. When approaching a crashed military airplane, why must you avoid the externally carried pods on the wings?
6. What is the best method to preserve a cocktail or a mixed drink for evidence?

7. What are the two reasons that it is important to identify the caller of a bomb threat?
8. If you are working the desk and receive a request for a policeman but discover that the caller lives in another agency's jurisdiction, what course of action would you take?
9. Under what circumstances may a service station or garage enforce a mechanic's lien?
10. What is your advice to a repossessor who cannot make his repossession over the objections of the person who is in custody of the property to be taken back because of a delinquent debt?
11. Who may legally declare death in your jurisdiction?
12. What is the legal definition of "intoxicated" in your jurisdiction?
13. What is the difference between a delusion and an hallucination?
14. List five types of "attractive nuisances."

REFERENCES

"FACTS ABOUT SUICIDE, AND SOME WARNING SIGNS," *Today's Health*, (June 1967), p. 33.

FEDERAL AVIATION REGULATIONS.

LOS ANGELES POLICE DEPARTMENT, *Daily Training Bulletins*, Vols. I and II. Springfield, Ill.: Charles C Thomas, Publisher, 1954 and 1958.

MATTHEWS, ROBERT A., and LOYD W. ROWLAND, *How to Recognize AND Handle Abnormal People—A Manual for the Police Officer*. New York: National Association for Mental Health, 1960.

MERKELEY, DONALD K., *The Investigation of Death*. Springfield, Ill.: Charles C Thomas, Publisher, 1957.

STATE OF CALIFORNIA. DEPARTMENT OF ALCOHOLIC BEVERAGE CONTROL, *Enforcement Manual*. Sacramento, Calif.: State Printing Office, 1967.

UNITED STATES DEPARTMENT OF DEFENSE, *What to Do and How to Report Military Aircraft Accidents, Joint Service Booklet #1*. Washington, D.C.: United States Navy, 1968.

Special

Patrol

Problems

INTRODUCTION

CHAPTER TEN In the course of his routine and extraordinary phases of patrol activities, the patrol officer makes many critical decisions. Foremost among those decisions are when to shoot and when to pursue, or when *not* to shoot and when to abandon a pursuit once begun. As discussed in Chapter One, these are discretionary decisions that the policeman must make as a professional police officer frequently operating as an independent agent.

There are certain police activities that the officer must perform with great wisdom and restraint. They include use of firearms, emergency and pursuit driving, arrest and searching techniques, prisoner control, transportation of prisoners, and disaster control. All of these topics are covered in other sources but it is imperative that they also be included in a treatment of police patrol tactics and techniques. This chapter deals with each topic individually.

232

Figure 10.1   Mastery of the skill in using the weapon develops the officer's confidence that he will be prepared to use it when he must. Courtesy of the Missouri Highway Patrol.

USE OF FIREARMS

The carrying and use of the firearm should never be taken lightly. The gun as a police weapon is a defensive weapon, but it is an instrument that can cause death, and death is the potential result of every shot fired. Contrary to the fictional image of the police officer's use of the firearm, the patrol officer is actually called upon to use his weapon very rarely, considering the many thousands of times that he contacts potentially dangerous persons in physical arrest situations. The police officer weighs the use of his weapon with tremendous respect for the human life that he may be compelled to take. In fact, it is probably such a tremendous respect for human life that causes the man to become a policeman in the first place.

An officer is not exempt from the legal and moral responsibilities of using extreme good judgment when resorting to the use of his weapons, and those responsibilities are far more exacting than they are for the average citizen. An officer should never remove his gun from its holster except when he believes that he has cause to use it. It is not intended to be used to frighten people. The officer should never point the gun at anyone except when he fully realizes he may have to shoot it to protect someone's life, or to prevent the escape of a person he knows to have committed a felony, or whom he has reasonable cause to *believe* committed a felony. He should never shoot his gun unless he has a definite target and accepts the fact that the death of someone may result from the shot fired. He should never threaten to shoot unless he has legal and moral justification to do so if it is necessary to carry out the threat.

WHEN TO SHOOT

The use of deadly force by a police officer is justified only when it is necessary to preserve another life that is in imminent danger from an aggressor whose actions clearly indicate the threat that he presents, and when there is no alternative to prevent his escape or stop his attack. The officer may have a legal justification to shoot a person, but not a moral one. A gun is an officer's "tool of the trade," and when he carries one he must make a series of mammoth decisions. He must be committed to the taking of another person's life if such an act will ever be necessary, but he must likewise be committed to doing so only to preserve the life of someone else and there must be no alternative. When the officer fires the gun, there is no cancellation of its imminent effect.

A warning shot is flagrantly inadvisable. If the loud sound is what you want, use a blank pistol or a firecracker. A projectile fired from an officer's gun leaves with such force that it should be aimed directly at the target the projectile is intended to hit. A warning shot fired into the ground will ricochet or travel some distance and eventually strike something, possibly killing an innocent person or destroying valuable property.

An officer may use reasonable force to effect an arrest. What is reasonable depends on the specific set of circumstances that present themselves to him, and he must consider the entire picture when deciding what is reasonable. "As much force as is necessary" depends on the interpretation of the officer at the moment he shoots. The police officer is not an executioner. It is not manly to be *brutal*. It may take more of a man to decide *not* to shoot. Homicide is justifiable only when the person is known for a fact to have committed an atrocious crime, such as murder, aggravated assault, robbery, or forcible rape, and it is necessary to take him into custody and prevent his escape. If there is no alternative but to use deadly force against that individual for fear that all hopes of catching him will be lost, and that he is likely to commit another crime of a similar nature that poses an imminent threat to the life of another innocent victim, shooting the individual is morally justifiable.

Some people ask: "Why not shoot the criminal in the arm or the leg? Why kill him? Why not use a dart gun as they do with animals? In response to the last question, the dart-hypodermic projectiles available at the time of this writing can cause death; just as any other projectile can. The effective dose of the nicotine or other chemicals used to render the object unconscious depends on its size and weight,

the condition of its health, and specific resistance to the particular
drug that is used. A pre-set dose would have to be loaded if the officer
were to fire when necessary, and such a dose may be fatal.

As for shooting a suspect in some nonfatal part of the body, that
is what occurs in most police shootings. The police officer is usually
confronted by a moving target. He must lead the target and aim for
the spot where the target is expected to be when the bullet gets there.
The shooting is under extreme stress conditions, and in most cases at
least one shot has already been fired at the officer, or he is under
attack when he has the first opportunity to fire his weapon. The
recommended procedure is to shoot at the largest part of your target
so that you will hit it, rather than miss and take a chance of killing
some innocent person.

The laws for excusable and justifiable homicide are much broader
than department policies. This is as it should be, I believe, if the
legislature believes that the laws are just, and if the department policy
is equally just, although more stringent. There are always the unusual
situations when the officer's judgment is not functioning as clearly as
it should, particularly under stress conditions. Under such circumstances he may exceed the limits of his department's policy, yet still
be well within the bounds of the law. He has latitude for error while
still being within the law. If the officer is charged with the responsibility for making the awesome decision as to when to shoot, he should
be given the authority to act in accordance with that responsibility.
He must make a decision in three seconds or less, which a body of
learned justices may study for three months and render a five to four
decision.

When establishing guidelines on *when to shoot,* consider the following list of criteria: [1]

1. Deadly force should be restricted to the apprehension of persons who
   in the course of their crime threaten the use of deadly force, or to
   those instances when the officer believes there exists substantial risk
   that the person whose arrest is sought will cause death or serious
   bodily harm to others if his apprehension is delayed.
2. The use of firearms should be flatly prohibited in the apprehension of
   misdemeanants, since the value of human life far outweighs the gravity
   of the crime.
3. Deadly force should never be used in cases when the subject is merely
   suspected of the crime, no matter how serious the crime that he may
   have committed.
4. An officer should either have witnessed the crime, or should have
   sufficient information to know as a *virtual certainty* that the suspect
   committed an offense for which the use of deadly force is permissible.

---

[1] The President's Crime Commission *Task Force Report* (Washington, D.C.:
U.S. Government Printing Office, 1967), pp. 189–190.

5. Officers should not be permitted to fire at felony suspects when lesser force could be used, or when the officer believes the suspect can be apprehended reasonably soon thereafter without the use of deadly force, or when there is any substantial danger to innocent bystanders. Although the requirement of using lesser force when thought possible is a legal rule, the other limitations are based on sound public policy.
6. To risk the life of innocent persons for the purpose of apprehending a felon cannot be justified.
7. Officers should never use warning shots for any purpose. Warning shots endanger the lives of bystanders and, in addition, may prompt a suspect to return the fire.
8. Further, officers should never fire from a moving vehicle. However, officers should be allowed to use any necessary force, including deadly force, to protect themselves or other persons from death or serious injury. In such cases, it is immaterial whether the attacker has committed a serious felony or misdemeanor, or any crime at all.
9. In order to enforce the firearms policies, the department regulations should require detailed written reports on all discharges of firearms. All cases should be thoroughly investigated to determine whether the use of the firearms was justifiable under the circumstances.

PURSUIT AND EMERGENCY DRIVING

Pursuit and emergency driving involve the same driving skills that the field officer should master for normal driving, with an extra emphasis on defensive driving techniques. For this type of driving, you must be at your peak efficiency and extremely alert, a condition that is actually enhanced by the increased activity of the nervous system and other body functions that are stimulated by the excitement of the situation. However, most police vehicle accidents occur during "normal" patrol driving, and it is imperative that you be equally alert at all times to avoid serious injury and property damage.

One of the prime considerations when making the decision to begin a high-speed "code three run" is the nature of the situation. The decision is made by the dispatcher in accordance with established policies when it is in response to a call for service or help, such as a "no detail" accident (injuries, if any, are unknown) or an armed robbery in progress. The situation in the field that arises in the officer's presence requires his individual decision as to whether or not to pursue. He must immediately evaluate the situation and decide whether it is imperative that an apprehension be effected.

Relative locations of the police unit and the vehicle to be pursued play a significant role in the evaluative process. Is it possible to get into position for the chase without causing an accident or jeopardizing the life of pedestrians? What is the estimated speed of the violator, and how fast will the police car be required to go in order to overtake him? Is another police unit in a better position to apprehend the

violator if he is notified by radio of the wanted vehicle approaching
his location? These questions must be repeated throughout the pursuit
in a continuing process of reevaluation.

If it appears that the pursuit is not possible, it is better to use your
time and efforts to alert another unit to the description, the direction
of travel, and any other pertinent information that will enable the
other unit to locate and apprehend the violators. By means of radio,
it is possible to actively pursue the individual in coordination with
other police units.

Once you make the decision to pursue, get into position as quickly
and efficiently as possible. Notify the dispatcher of your pursuit, the
nature of the situation, the direction of travel, your location, and a
description of the pursued vehicle. The information that is most critical at the beginning of the pursuit is the direction of travel. Other
units in the area may be in a position to assist in the pursuit, or they
may clear traffic on side streets to reduce the possibility of traffic
collisions involving the police car or the pursued vehicle. During the
chase, make frequent broadcasts to keep headquarters and the other
police units advised of your changing location and any additional need
for assistance.

If you use the red light and siren as warning devices, *use* them.
Keeping a siren at a growl and turning on the lights only at intersections are unwise and generally illegal (there are exceptions, of
course). An emergency vehicle is authorized to violate the rules of
the road only when functioning in a "code three" situation, which requires red light and siren. Never assume that anyone will see the light
or hear the siren, particularly when you are approaching intersections,
but use them nevertheless. At extremely high speeds and on roads
where there are no side streets, such as a freeway or expressway, the
siren may serve no useful purpose once the driver of the pursued
vehicle clearly understands that it is he that you are chasing and it is
apparent that he has no intention of stopping. When the siren is not
operating but the vehicle is going at high speed, the siren fan may be
spinning at high speed, but in the opposite direction to that when the
siren is on. By turning on the siren at such high speed, you may be
causing more of a drain on the electrical system than the car can
handle. The fan must be stopped then started in the opposite direction,
a process which may actually "short out" the system. If you must turn
on a mechanical siren while going at high speed, first depress the
siren brake button, then activate the siren.

Use your seat belts, safety helmets (if you are so equipped), and
any other safety devices provided by the automobile manufacturer
and your department. Avoid ramming another vehicle during a high-
speed chase. There is too great a chance of loss of human life during
such an operation. Shooting any type of weapon at a fleeing vehicle
is likewise irresponsible folly that should be limited to fiction, except

in extreme cases when there is absolutely no other way to save a human life. In both of these situations, however, it is most logical to assume that the pursued vehicle will be caused to go out of control and someone may die or be seriously injured as a result. Drivers of other vehicles, pedestrians, or occupants of buildings in the area may become the innocent victims of an officer's poor judgment.

While driving under pursuit or emergency conditions, approach each intersection with extreme caution, slowing down to avoid an accident with someone who may not hear or heed the warning siren of the approaching police car. Never pass a vehicle on the right with your red light and siren on. You may encounter another individual who is completely oblivious of your proximity until just the time you start passing him, when he suddenly sees or hears you and does what he is required by law to do: immediately drive to the right side of the road and stop to allow the emergency vehicle to pass.

Caravans of several pursuing vehicles should be avoided. There is no need for more than two or three cars to be directly involved in the chase of even the most dangerous criminal. Consider the driver who pulls over to the side of the street to allow the police unit to pass, then immediately returns to the traffic lane and follows the police car to see where it is going. Such a driver normally returns to the traffic lane at about the same time that the second police car reaches the same spot. The second police car is probably not operating with red light and siren, thereby placing him in a civilly liable position, not to mention the hazards involved at the time.

Roadblocks may be utilized, but they should seldom, if ever, involve the placement of police vehicles directly out into the traffic lane to present a physical, impassable barrier. Barricades, flares, and other objects may serve the purpose without assuming the risks of causing loss of life or destruction of property.

Always consider the possibility that the pursued vehicle will stop suddenly and without warning. The driver may actually not be aware of the chase; he may be under the influence of alcohol or drugs. He may suddenly realize the futility of attempting to lose the police vehicle. Another possibility is that the driver of the pursued vehicle may make the sudden stop to gain a strategic advantage by stopping before the police vehicle, placing the officer in front of him. He could then either attack the officer from this position of advantage, or he could make good his escape by making a quick U-turn, or by alighting from the vehicle and getting away on foot. Keep some distance between your vehicle and that of the subject you are pursuing to avoid the possibility of colliding with him when he stops suddenly, or of placing yourself at a position of disadvantage in front of him.

Whenever pursuing another vehicle, there may be a time when it is strategically sound judgment to abandon the pursuit. During a high-

speed chase when it appears futile to assume that the pursued vehicle
will stop for any of a number of reasons, there is always the danger
that the chase will become a matter of personal pride to the officer
driving the pursuing vehicle. It may be a matter of competition in
driving skill, and the officer may become so intent on winning that
the objective of his chase is no longer clear to him. Under conditions
that develop during such a contest, any subsequent actions during the
chase and eventual capture of the suspect may be quite injudicious.
The intelligent and professional police officer cannot lose control of
his faculties to the extent that he loses his objectivity.

Protection of life and property still applies to the high-speed chase,
and it includes the lives and property of the individual being pursued,
the officer, and any innocent people who might become involved in a
traffic collision as a direct result of the chase. At some time during
the chase, it may be necessary to abandon the chase to uphold this
police responsibility. The decison to abandon the chase involves factors
such as the seriousness of the situation precipitating the chase in the
first place, the possibility of identifying the driver and the vehicle for
a later arrest with a warrant, and the road conditions at the time of
the chase. What is the weather condition? Are there other vehicles,
pedestrians, or school children nearby that might be injured if the
chase continues? Consider also the likelihood that the driver of the
pursued vehicle will slow down to a normal speed once he makes
good his escape. Or will he continue jeopardizing the lives and property of everyone who gets in his way until he either collides with
something, runs out of gas, or is apprehended? There are many times
when circumstances may dictate the abandonment of the chase.

Ramming Vehicles?

"Only in extreme cases and only when the calculated risk indicates
that lives of innocent persons would be saved by such action and that
present danger to the officer driving the ramming vehicle is not imminent": That might be the policy statement of a police department.
Ramming is foolhardy, and there are very few times when such action
is worth the risk of your life or that of another person. A very skillful
driver may succeed in pulling alongside another vehicle, locking the
two together, then edging the other vehicle to the side of the road.
Or he may actually brake both vehicles to a stop, taking advantage
of the other driver's hesitancy to accelerate and his willingness to
allow himself to be stopped in this manner. Ramming has about the
same value as shooting at a car in the hope of puncturing a tire or
rupturing the gas tank. The chance of ricochet is greater than either
of these two hoped for effects.

In an urban community of any size, there is always the possibility that there will be more than one emergency vehicle traveling along the streets in response to different and unrelated emergencies. The possibility of two or more of them colliding always exists, particularly when the emergency vehicles belong to different agencies, which have no idea of what the other is doing. At best the situation is complicated and hazardous, but the danger can be compounded if more than one vehicle is responding to a single emergency. In this case, the vehicles' convergence is imminent. Several agencies may be involved in a single incident, or only one. For example, a routine injury accident involving gas spillage will require code three response by a police unit, at least one fire unit, and an ambulance. Each is a separate and distinct agency and usually on a different radio frequency.

Considering the hazards involved in code three, the following guidelines should be established and followed:

1. Only one police unit will use the red light and siren on any one emergency call.
2. The unit responding to the assignment, or initiating a pursuit, will identify his unit and broadcast by radio the location at which he begins using the red light and siren.
3. The dispatcher should repeat the acknowledgment, and broadcast to other units his location and direction of travel, if known.
4. The assigned unit will broadcast an "arrived on scene" (10–97) transmission to indicate the conclusion of the trip.

Escorts

In traffic that is flowing in the normal fashion for the location and time of day, driving a police vehicle with red light and siren operating is extremely hazardous. To drive a police vehicle with red light and siren for the purpose of clearing the way for a following vehicle being escorted is generally unwise and places too many lives in jeopardy. The officer driving the police vehicle is actually driving both of them, and he is assuming responsibility for the skill and judgment of the other driver as well.

The driver of the escorted vehicle may be emotionally upset or physically incapable of performing under these conditions. It may be that he should not be driving even under normal conditions. He may not be skilled enough to maintain a safe distance behind the police vehicle and may either get lost or follow too closely. Since the escorted vehicle would not be equipped as an emergency vehicle, it would appear to others as just any other car that might be following a police car on an emergency call.

Consider the possibility of the police vehicle's clearing the way for itself and the car following. The drivers of other vehicles must yield to the emergency vehicle, and they pull over to the side of the road and wait until the police car passes. They then immediately pull back into the street and resume driving with the normal stream of traffic. The escorted vehicle speeding along behind the police vehicle may be forced to stop because of congestion that is caused by the resumption of the traffic flow, or because of a traffic control sign or signal.

What of the legal considerations? Under no circumstances does the escorted vehicle become an emergency vehicle. The driver does not become exempt from the traffic laws, and he cannot be exempted from any civil liability in an accident that may occur during the escort operation. In most jurisdictions, state law prohibits any type of escort with the use of red light and siren. Any justification for a breach of the law allowed by a police officer would have to concern an extremely grave situation. The exception would have to be justifiable not only in his own eyes at that moment, but also in the eyes of his superiors, the courts, and the other private persons who enjoy no such immunity and who would expect the escorted vehicle's driver to be held to answer for breaking the law in the same way as they would be held to answer.

In view of these considerations, it would seem that the best method of operation is to decline the request to serve as an escort, and to either call an ambulance or transport an injured person in the police vehicle, which is an emergency vehicle when operating with red light and siren.

Transporting Injured Persons in Police Cars

A police vehicle is not an ambulance. There are times, however, when there is no other feasible means of transportation available under certain emergency conditions. In such cases, use of the police vehicle for this purpose is not improper. Consider these hypothetical situations, and you be the judge as to what course of action the patrol officer should follow.

(1) While parked near an intersection, the officer sees a two-door late model sedan speed through an intersection while the traffic signal for his direction of travel is red. The car narrowly misses another car, which had just started with the green light. The officer pursues the violator and chases him for about two blocks before he is successful in getting the driver to stop. As the officer alights from his patrol car, citation book in hand, he meets an extremely agitated middle-aged man. The man literally shouts at the officer that he must get to a hospital because he has been stung by a bee, and he will suffer serious consequences because he is allergic to bee stings. He hopes to reach the hospital before he loses consciousness, and he asks the officer to

please get out of his way so that he can resume his fateful journey. What would you do?

(2) A young man and woman drive up to the officer, who is parked alongside the street, bringing his activity log up to date. The man says: "My wife is having a baby. Will you escort us to the hospital?" In this case, are you going to perform the requested service?

(3) In response to a call for service in an "unknown trouble, see the woman" call, the patrol officer is met by a woman with a small child in her arms. The child is unconscious and seems to be losing its normal color. The woman hysterically screams that the child had lost consciousness while eating a piece of beef, and she cannot revive him. The officer begins mouth-to-mouth resuscitation and determines that there is a possibility that life still exists in the child, but that he will probably die without immediate medical attention. No ambulance is available because of a major traffic accident on the highway in which several people were killed and others injured. The child is dying and needs attention. What is your decision?

Rather than answer these hypothetical questions, which, due to many unexplained factors, are more for the purpose of rhetoric than a direct answer, formulate a set of standards so that you may make value judgments. Ask yourself the following questions before making your decision: Would transporting the individual increase the severity of the injury? Is the service in direct competition with another agency's service that is available and actually better prepared to handle the matter? Is the need really an emergency? Is it wise to allow a person to drive a vehicle when it is possible that he may lose consciousness at any moment? Is another emergency service available? Is the individual under arrest? What are the alternatives? The decision you make each time a situation arises is actually based upon consideration of the alternatives, and selection of the right one.

Legal Aspects of Emergency Driving

There are four or five basic laws in virtually every jurisdiction that provide for the emergency operation of appropriately equipped and authorized vehicles, including police vehicles. For your consideration, five examples of such laws follow:

1. Whenever an emergency vehicle approaches while displaying legally authorized red lights and sounding a siren, the drivers of other vehicles shall yield the right-of-way and wait for the passage of that vehicle. Although most laws are quite specific about *both* red light *and* siren operating, some case law has been generated because of the impracticability of operating a siren on a freeway at extremely high speeds, and under certain conditions it may be permissible to use red light only. These are exceptional cases, however, and the need rarely manifests itself.

2. Emergency vehicles are exempt from most regulations, such as speeding, right-of-way, stop signs and signals, and other rules of the road when responding to an emergency, engaged in rescue operations, in actual pursuit of a violator, or when responding to a fire *if* the driver is sounding the siren and displaying the red light.

3. Emergency vehicles are generally exempt from civil liability when operating in accordance with the emergency provisions, and when properly using the legally required red light and siren clearly indicating "emergency vehicle" character.

4. The driver of an emergency vehicle under any conditions, including emergency conditions, is not relieved from the duty to drive with due regard for the safety of all persons using the streets and highways. Moreover, the law does not protect the driver-officer from the consequences of an arbitrary and unnecessary exercise of the privileges granted in the exempting sections. The officer is thus limited to real emergency needs, and is prohibited from using the red light and siren to avoid a traffic signal because of impatience rather than actual necessity.

5. Emergency vehicles are forbidden to use the siren or to drive at an illegal speed when serving as an escort *except* for the preservation of life, or when escorting supplies and personnel for the armed forces during a national emergency.

ARREST TECHNIQUES

Use of Force

An officer may use whatever force he deems necessary to make an arrest, to prevent an escape, or to overcome resistance. According to the laws of justifiable homicide, the officer may be justified in taking the life of a felon who may be fleeing or resisting arrest. He may also be justified in using deadly force to overcome resistance to his execution of some lawful process, or to quell a riot or breach of the peace when he feels there is no alternative means to achieve order. The policies of many police departments are far more stringent, however.

Breaking Into a Building to Arrest

An officer may break into a door or window to gain entry into any place where he knows or believes that a person he has legal cause to arrest is sheltered. In most situations, he must first demand admittance and state his reason for the demand, and this must be followed by a denial or no response. However, this rule should be bypassed if you believe at the time that to demand such entry, and to wait out the time it takes to explain the reason for the entry, would jeopardize a life or would frustrate the arrest.

Resistance to Arrest a Crime

When you are making an arrest, be sure to identify yourself so that there can be no question as to your authority, then make it clear to the person you intend to arrest what you are going to do and for what charge. If he knows that he is being arrested, according to law he must submit to the arrest without offering resistance. If he claims innocence of the crime, or positively knows that he had nothing to do with a criminal matter that would lead to his arrest, he should present his case at a more appropriate time. It is your responsibility to act on valid information and good faith, assuring yourself that the arrests you make are valid.

Warrant Arrests

A warrant is usually directed to any peace officer with jurisdiction in the state. One of the most important aspects of a warrant arrest is to make sure the warrant is valid. The warrant must state the specific charge for which the person is to be arrested, such as "Criminal Code Section 123, Loitering." There must be a description of the person to be arrested. Generally, a person's name is considered his identification, but there is room for error when arresting by name only. You must be sure that you are arresting the individual for whom the warrant is intended. The warrant must also bear the signature of the issuing judge or magistrate. If the warrant is for a felony, the arrest may be made at any time. In the case of misdemeanors, however, the warrant must specifically state that it is for nighttime service, or it can be used as a basis for arrest only during daytime.

The warrant requires that the person named be taken to the judge who issued the warrant, or the court of issue. In your own jurisdiction, it may be a standard procedure to take the arrestee directly to jail to go through the "booking" process. He then posts bail and receives a specific time to report to the court. In these cases, the arrestees are not generally taken directly to the judge unless they demand it. Once the subject named on the warrant has been arrested and processed according to its instructions, the officer signs the document and it is returned to the court.

Arrests Without a Warrant

Except when it is obvious that you are arresting the subject for a crime that he is committing at the time of arrest, or arresting him immediately following a pursuit, it is mandatory that you identify yourself, that you announce your intention to arrest him, and that you state the crime for which you are arresting him. Review the facts that you have and make sure that your justification for the arrest is valid.

Prepare for the arrest by arranging for adequate manpower to back you up, if time permits. Use common sense and distinguish between bravery and foolhardiness. A single-handed arrest accomplished by a brave officer looks good in the personnel jacket, but do not risk it at the expense of possibly losing the suspect or causing yourself to sustain an injury or death because of your failure to call for assistance. Charisma, or command presence, is essential. Make it clear to the suspect you are arresting by your actions, your appearance, and your command voice. Give clear and concise orders. Use only that force which is necessary. Maintain constant visual and physical control of the arrestee. If the situation is serious enough to call for his arrest, it should be standard procedure to consider the possibility that he may try to attack you or attempt to escape. Never turn your back on him, and always "keep on your guard."

Search the arrestee very carefully, and never consider the finding of a weapon as indicative of the fact that he has only one weapon. Many officers have been seriously and and fatally wounded by people in custody who had been "thoroughly searched." As an additional precaution for the protection of the arrestee and yourself, consider the use of handcuffs for all arrest situations.

APPROACH, SUSPECTS IN VEHICLE

Assuming that all persons to be arrested could well be felons, use extreme caution when making an approach in any situation in which you anticipate making an arrest. When possible, wait for the follow-up unit to arrive. One-man patrol was never intended to include one-man arrests.

The driver officer alights from the left side of his unit and pauses at that location. The passenger or follow-up officer goes up to the right and rear of the back window of the suspect vehicle and stands by. The driver officer shouts commands from his vantage point behind the door. The command should be: "*Police officers.* Stay inside the car and do not move. Driver, turn off the ignition and drop the keys out through the window. Move very slowly." Once the driver has done this, then order the peole to continue moving very slowly, and to do the following: "Driver, place both of your hands on the steering wheel with your palms up. You in the front seat, put your hands up against the windshield with the palms against the glass. Up in the back seat. Move very slowly and place your hands on the back of the seat in front of you with the palms up. Remain in that position until I tell you to move." The exact text may vary, but the instructions should be essentially the same. The reasons for slow movements are obvious, and the hands on the windshield, steering wheel, and the back of the front seat are all where they can be seen. The reason for not instructing them to simply raise their hands up is that they may have concealed weapons in the headliner of the car, or above the sun visor.

Figure 10.2   When the felony suspect has his hands outside the vehicle you may maintain visual control with more ease. Courtesy of the Police Department, Scottsdale, Arizona.

During this process with occupants of a car suspected of crimes, it is your decision as to whether you will hold your revolver in your hand. If you do, be sure that it is not cocked, and that you keep it close to the body and trained on the suspects at all times. Some officers are so proficient at drawing and firing their revolvers that it may be more to their advantage to keep the revolver in its holster until it is needed, thereby leaving the hand free. At nighttime, one hand will already be full of flashlight. Another alternative is to have the back-up officer work with revolver in one hand and flashlight in the other, while the driver officer leaves his revolver in his holster until he needs it.

REMOVING THE OCCUPANTS FROM THE CAR

A cardinal rule is: never put your hands inside the suspect car while anyone is inside. If you want the driver to stop the car, tell him to stop, then tell him to drop the keys outside. Avoid, also, the natural tendency to stoop over and pick up the keys. Leave them on the

Figure 10.3   Order felony suspect to step out and place hands on back of head. Courtesy of the Police Department, Scottsdale, Arizona.

ground. Once you have accomplished the stop and the occupants are under your control, the driver officer approaches the left side of the suspect car and order the occupants to leave one by one. Tell them to leave from the right side of the car. If it is a four-door car, have the suspects exit from the back seat first, then the front seat, in this order: right rear, left rear, right front, driver. If it is a two-door car, it may be easier to have the right front passenger get out first, followed by the people in the back seat, and then the driver. As they exit, line them up in a standing position with their backs to the car. While the back-up officer holds them under his control, the driver officer should come around the car and roll up the windows of the suspect car. The officers should then proceed with the search.

The search may be accomplished in a variety of ways, but I recommend that in situations when the suspects outnumber the officers, particularly, the suspects be instructed to assume a kneeling position with their legs crossed, or to assume a prone position with faces down. Their hands should be above their heads or behind the backs of their necks. The latter pose may cause a problem, because one of the suspects may have a weapon placed under his coat at the neck. It is best to have the hands up high at least until you can check the back of the neck. When this check is completed, have them lock fingers with their hands behind their heads.

Officers who sustain injuries while searching persons are apt to be men with several years of experience. They have probably made hundreds, or thousands, of arrests without incident and have grown confident that they are doing everything right. Actually there is a possibility that those men are developing bad habits without realizing it. One way to counteract this development of bad habits is to approach each arrest and each search as an entirely new experience, and strictly according to an established procedure.

There are two essential aspects to search and seizure: law and procedure. The following section covers the procedure. It is extremely important that an armed and potentially dangerous suspect be disarmed as quickly and efficiently as possible.

Types and Methods of Search

The patrol officer conducts three basic types of searches: the frisk, the field search, and the strip search. Each has its own distinct procedure.

Figure 10.4   Position for the wall search using a vehicle for support. Courtesy of the Police Department, Scottsdale, Arizona.

FRISK, OR "PAT DOWN." The frisk is the cursory search. It generally accompanies a field interview situation and is not considered an exploratory search. The only objects for which you can search during the frisk are weapons. However, if the frisk reveals other contraband and it can be truly shown that the discovery was incidental to the frisk, rather than the frisk being used as an excuse to look for some objects, then the discovery of the contraband is sufficient cause to conduct the more thorough search. Start at the head and work the hands along the outside of the clothing wherever weapons may be found. Do not place your hands inside the clothing unless the outside patting process reveals something that feels like a weapon, in which case you may search inside to verify your suspicions.

FIELD SEARCH. This search may be conducted on reasonable cause to search without an arrest, or prior to an arrest, and it should be routine whenever you perform an arrest.

1. Keep the person off balance. This can be accomplished by three basic methods: the wall search position, the kneeling search position, and the prone search position.

For the wall search position, have the subject stand about three feet away from some solid object, such as a wall or an automobile. If you use an automobile, be sure that the windows are closed. Have the subject face and lean up against the object with the palms of his hands and his arms outstretched. Have him move his feet back and stretch his arms and legs out so that he is not able to move away from the position without difficulty. When searching from the left rear of the subject, place your left foot in a hooked position in front of his left foot. When searching from the right rear, place your right foot in a hooked position in front of his right foot. Place your free hand on the small of his back while using the other hand to conduct the search. The hand on his back will feel any movements that he is making, and your foot under his can be used to pull his foot out from under him if he should become combative.

For the kneeling search position, have the subject kneel on both knees, and cross his legs behind him. As you search him from behind it is possible to exert a slight pressure on the top of the crossed legs to maintain control. Have the subject hold his hands high above his head or lock his fingers behind his head if he is not wearing a bulky jacket or some other item of clothing that may be a hiding place for a weapon.

For the prone search position, have the subject lie face down on the ground or floor surface with arms and legs outstretched. This position of disadvantage makes it very difficult for the subject to assume a combative position.

2. Maintain your own balance on your toes, and always face the subject. If you hold your weapon during the search, hold it close against your side. The outstretched weapon that is sticking into the back of the subject is impressive, but it is in a vulnerable position; the subject could swing around quickly and disarm you. Once you have

him under control, or if a back-up officer assumes a cover position, the best place for the searching officer's weapon is securely fastened in his holster. It is not unusual for a suspect to attempt to attack the officer during the initial phases of an arrest and search.

3. Search with one hand. Use the other hand for defense and to place on the small of the suspect's back during a wall search. You can hold him off-balance with this hand.

4. Start at the head, running your hands through the hair, and watching for straight-edged razor blades that might have been planted for the purpose. (Other places for planted razor blades are inside small trousers pockets and along the inside of the waistband.) While standing to the right rear of the subject, hook your right foot in front of the subject's, and run your hands around the collar of his jacket or shirt, down the front of the shirt, and starting at the shoulders, down the inside of the sleeve up to the armpits. The armpit area of a bulky jacket or coat is a favorite hiding place for pistols or revolvers. Run your hand down the outside of the arm, feeling the sleeve, then around the waistband. At the waistband, feel for any string that may be hanging from the belt and be holding a gun or knife at the other end for easy access. Loosen the belt if necessary.

Search the legs, starting at the crotch area and working down from the outside and the inside. One popular hiding place for weapons is inside the shorts in the area of the genitals, because of the knowledge that there will be a natural reluctance to touch the private parts. Another popular place is on the inside of the calf of the leg, where a garter or elastic part of a sock may be used to hold a weapon. Feel inside the subject's shoes or boots. After completing one side, go to the other side and repeat the operation. If the subject is wearing boots with open tops, consider the advisability of having him remove the boots so that you may make a more thorough inspection.

5. Make all your commands and instructions clear and brief.

6. When you have another officer assisting you in the search, have him stand off to one side opposite the side you are working on. If there is more than one subject, search each one in turn, starting with the one on the left while your "cover officer" is standing at the opposite side of the line. Search the first subject from the left, then move him and yourself to the right end of the line and search him from the right. Repeat this procedure with each subject. By using this method, it is possible to search as many people as there are in the line without ever placing yourself between two of the subjects you are searching. By having the "cover" officer move to the opposite side of the line whenever you move, you are assuring maximum coverage of the subjects during the entire searching process.

7. Never turn your back on a subject.

8. Do not be timid when searching an individual, but do not use abusive methods or abusive language.

9. Do not get too close to any subject before you have him at a position of advantage.

10. Your search is for weapons, tools or implements used to commit crime, evidence relevant to a crime, or the fruits of a crime.

STRIP SEARCH. This search is conducted in the privacy of headquarters, and eventually in jail during the booking process. The most efficient means of searching an individual's person and clothing is to have him remove all of this clothes and then perform a systematic and thorough search of his body and of each item of clothing. Carefully examine the individual's body from head to toe, looking for any item than may be attached to the body by means of tape, a bandage, chains, straps, or various types of jewelry. Favorite hiding places are the hair, bottom of the feet, in the mouth, near the genitalia, and in the body crevices. If necessary to search the interior of the body cavities, call upon the services of a medical doctor to conduct the examination under clinical conditions.

SEARCH OF WOMEN IN CUSTODY

There is no legal distinction between searching a man and searching a woman, and searches may be conducted by police personnel of either sex. However, the propriety of etiquette should prevail unless the life of a person is endangered. In the case when a search is essential for the protection of life, it must be conducted, but it must be justifiable in the eyes of many other persons at a later time. The most acceptable arrangement for a search of a woman is to have a woman conduct it. In the absence of a woman who may conduct the search, handcuff the female suspect with her hands behind her back, and place her pocketbook or purse where she cannot get her hands inside. You may roll the police baton across any suspected bulges to ascertain if they are caused by some hard object such as a weapon. A cursory search may be made by any woman in the immediate area if she is willing, but a thorough search must be made by a female employee of a law enforcement agency who has been adequately trained in the art of self-defense and in searching techniques.

As with the male suspect, search of body cavities should always be made by a medical doctor under sanitary clinical conditions.

VEHICLE SEARCHES

The method for searching vehicles should be as thorough and as imaginative as possible. The most effective means is to begin at the front and work systematically to the back on one side, then work back to the front of the vehicle on the opposite side. If two officers are working together, they should conduct the search independently of each other, with each officer conducting a complete search in succession. This procedure is far more efficient than having each officer search a portion of the vehicle. There arc so many hiding places that it is easy to overlook one, and two complete searches are better than one partial search.

Where to Search

This is a real challenge to the inquiring officer. Evidence and contraband have been found in virtually every place where anything may be concealed. Consider the places where objects have been found by other officers.

In the bumper and grill areas, certain items may be concealed by the use of masking tape or wire. Look for boxes, which may be welded on, that serve no functional purpose for the operation of the vehicle. The area under the hood provides many excellent hiding places, for example, inside the air cleaner, the vents, or the air conditioner. Certain accessories may be inoperable and the housing parts may be used to store items such as smuggled marijuana or other narcotics.

Under the dashboard, there are several places that may hold evidence, for example, the area above the glove compartment, the fuse box, or the underside of the dash. Use a flashlight and a mirror to search this area. Under the floorboard may be a good place for a built-in carrying case. In one smuggling case, an officer lifted the floor mat and found a trap door. Opening it, he found a large storage box welded to the underside of the car. The box was full of narcotics.

Look for torn places in the upholstery, in the headliner, and in the side panels, these may signal the presence of a hidden pocket for carrying a concealed weapon. The area inside the dome lights and similar empty places are accessible for hiding, and they should also be searched.

Move everything that is movable and look inside, behind, and under it. Ask yourself where you would hide a weapon, narcotics, stolen merchandise, or whether you would hide it at all. One rather successful burglar carried his stolen merchandise right out on the seat of the car, and was stopped for routine questioning on several occasions. When asked about the merchandise, he stated that it was his. When asked about his success, he explained that his secret was to remain calm and cool when questioned, because his natural manner did not arouse any of the officer's suspicions. He added that some officers erroneously believe that a thief or burglar will become very nervous in the presence of an officer, obviously for fear of being found out.

Generally, when searching an automobile for evidence, it is good practice to be familiar with the particular body designs, and to look for modifications or deviations from those designs. Conduct a thorough search and use your imagination.

NOTEBOOK ENTRIES REGARDING SEARCHES

Whenever you discover any items of evidence during a search, record in your field notebook an accurate description of the item, and describe exactly where and under what conditions you found it. If the owner or driver of the vehicle is present, ask for a statement of ownership for each item you find, and record his response. Handle the items as you would handle any other evidence.

Figure 10.5   Handcuffing the suspect. Never release your hold on the cuffs and keep the suspect at a disadvantage. Note the officer's foot position. Courtesy of the Police Department, Scottsdale, Arizona.

PRISONER CONTROL AND TRANSPORTATION

Once you have completed the search and have satisfied yourself that the subject is not armed, the next step is to apply the handcuffs with the suspect's hands behind his back, the palms out. To handcuff the subject in this position, stand behind him as you put on the handcuffs. Have him hold his left hand back, or you hold it while applying the cuff, then do the same with the right hand. Tighten the cuffs so that they will be secure, but not so tight that they will cut circulation. Use the double lock mechanism to prevent the subject from tightening the cuffs, then asking for sympathy and a loosening of the cuffs, as a

Figure 10.6   Applying the second handcuff. It is best to
have the palms out, as indicated here. Courtesy of the
Police Department, Scottsdale, Arizona.

possible opening to his escape. If you handcuff an individual, use both
cuffs, and attach them both to the subject.

When you have custody of a prisoner, that custody may not be
turned over to another officer without strict adherence to certain rules
that must accompany the transfer procedure. Without an exchange
of the information concerning the nature of the charge for which
the subject is being held, the officer assuming custody has no way of
knowing whether he has a felon or misdemeanant. If you relinquish
custody of a prisoner to another officer, give him the information he
needs.

Whenever you receive custody of a prisoner from another officer,
conduct a thorough search for your own satisfaction. This should be
a department requirement. It is not a surprise to hear that the second
or third officer who searches a suspect comes up with some weapon
that had been somehow overlooked on the previous searches. In one
case, a subject had been arrested for driving while under the influence
of alcohol. He was a jovial fellow, but he was going to jail because
he had violated the law. He did not resist, and had all the appearances
of a harmless drunk. He was first taken to a local police station to be
held for transfer to the county jail. He was searched in the field by
the arresting officer, searched by the booking officer at the jail, and
searched again when another officer took him out of the cell and
placed him inside a transportation unit to take him to the county jail.

While they were en route down the highway, the suspect pulled a small calibre automatic pistol out of his undershorts and fatally shot the officer. When the officer died, he lost control of the vehicle and the car crashed into a retaining fence. The killer was still in the back seat after the accident, but his gun had been thrown from his hand and had slid under the front seat where he could not reach it. There was a steel mesh cage between the front and rear seat. A passerby discovered the accident. The suspect pleaded to be let out, but the man observed the officer with the bullet wound, the gun on the front floorboard, and presumed that the suspect had committed the murder. He used the police car's radio and called for assistance. Thanks to his presence of mind, the suspect did not get away and was held to answer for his crime. Three complete searches and the gun was not discovered! A terrible price to pay for a slipshod series of searches.

Maintain visual supervision of every subject in your custody until he has been thoroughly searched and securely held in jail or a holding room. Whenever you place a prisoner into a cell containing other prisoners, first instruct the others to step back away from the door. This will prevent any rushing movement by the prisoners inside when you place the new prisoner in the cell.

Female Prisoners

Female prisoners pose special problems. They may attempt to use their charm and femininity on the gullible male officer. They may use tears and attempt to elicit sympathy for their plight, or speak of their importance in the social, political, or economic structure of the community. A woman may also become very sullen and uncooperative. Some females may charge that a male officer has taken improper advantage of them and attempt to bargain to drop their charges of rape in exchange for the officers' dropping criminal charges against them.

Use courtesy and diplomacy with all prisoners, particularly the females. When making an arrest, it should be perfectly clear that any placing of the hands on the person is to accomplish the arrest. If you adopt a policy of handcuffing all arrestees, the female should be handcuffed. In addition to adding to the safety of the situation, the handcuffs will also serve to show other people that the woman is in custody of police officers and that her charges of "rape" are probably false, even though the officers are not in uniform.

Self-defense by the officer against a woman who violently resists arrest, or who attacks him, should consist of the same basic techniques that are used against attacks by men protagonists. "Necessary and reasonable force" is justifiable against an attack by either sex. Be extra cautious that nothing you do while defending yourself and maintaining control of the prisoner can be misinterpreted as an undue amount of liberty taken under the guise of self-defense. Avoid making any injudicious remarks that may later be taken out of context and quoted, or misquoted. Use no statements that have double meanings. A double entendre may sound quite funny at a party or in a barroom under social conditions; but in an arrest situation, it can sound insidious and evil.

TRANSPORTATION OF PRISONERS

At the beginning of the tour of duty, when an officer assumes control of his vehicle, he should search the entire vehicle, particularly that portion that is used for transporting prisoners. When making an arrest, each subject should be thoroughly searched prior to being placed in the vehicle. Additionally, it should become routine for the officer to search the vehicle again after each time a prisoner is transported, to be certain that the subject did not secrete something in the unit. Items such as revolvers and knives are occasionally found, but other items of value to an investigation may likewise be disposed of, such as narcotics, pawn slips, slips of paper containing names and addresses of accomplices, or stolen documents used for false identification.

If the transportation unit is equipped with a screen or shield separating the driving compartment from the rear of the vehicle, the prisoner should ride in that compartment alone or with other prisoners, with the officers in front. If the unit does not have this equipment, place the prisoner in the right portion of the rear seat and the second officer immediately behind the driver. If there is any indication that the prisoner will attempt to kick out the windows or kick at the transporting officers, remove his shoes. For additional safety to the prisoner during the trip, fasten his seat belt. With his hands cuffed behind his back and the seat belt fastened, the prisoner's likelihood of escape is lessened.

If the situation occurs when there is one officer and one prisoner, and the police unit is not equipped with a screen between the front and rear compartments, consider placing the arrestee in the front seat with the seat belt securely fastened and his hands cuffed behind his back. Watch his feet; but if he is securely fastened, he will not be able to reach your feet or the car's foot pedals.

Transporting Female Prisoners

Two officers, one preferably a female, should be used to transport a female prisoner. If a second officer is not available, consider the use of a woman volunteer from the scene of the arrest, who will accompany the officer and his prisoner to jail or headquarters, then be

returned to her home. Seating while transporting a female prisoner
is the same as that when transporting a male prisoner.

At the beginning and completion of each trip involving female
custodial transportation, indicate in your field notebook the exact
time, the mileage to the tenth of a mile, and the location. Radio in
this information to the dispatcher at the same time. The dispatcher
should use a time-stamp machine or some other means to indicate
the time the trip begins and ends, and record the locations and the
mileage readings that the officer calls in. A convenient aid for this
process would be a printed form that the dispatcher would fill out
correctly, time stamp, then forward to the officer at the time he files
his report concerning the arrest. The "trip" card could be attached to
the original of the report and become a permanent record.

POLICE DISASTER CONTROL

Of all the public officials charged with the preservation of lives
and protection of property, the patrol officer is at the forefront in
times of natural and man-made disasters. However infrequently
disasters may occur, the disaster situation is a primary responsibility
of law enforcement agencies. You should always anticipate the unexpected and be prepared for the inevitable.

Natural disasters are to be anticipated in certain sections of the
country because of weather and geological vagaries. Heavy rains or
snowfalls bring their own devastating effects in the form of floods or

Figure 10.7   Underwater rescue team of officers take part
in personal rescue operations. Courtesy of the Police Department, Concord, New Hampshire.

blizzards, but they also lead to rock or land slides. Earthquakes and tidal waves are not unusual in those areas bordering the Pacific Ocean. Tornadoes, hurricanes, cyclones, and other "ill winds" occur in various parts of the country. Other disasters characteristic to specific locales have taken their toll in lives and property, but such losses have been reduced considerably through the efforts of the many public and private agencies involved in disaster and emergency services that have prepared in advance, then carried out their plans when the need arose.

In addition to natural disasters, which may be anticipated because of known natural phenomena, there are many other occurrences that should be included in your plans. Consider the train or ship wreck, the aircraft crash, accidental or caused explosions, broken tanks leaking poisonous gases, forest or grass fires caused by humans, a cracked reservoir resulting in flooding, or any other situation calling for major emergency services far beyond the extent of those emergencies you handle on a regular basis.

Figure 10.8 This sheriff's reserve unit is prepared for various types of rescue. Courtesy of the Sheriff's Department, Orange County, California.

There are several aspects of disaster control that directly involve the patrol officer. They include planning, training, and maintenance of a state of readiness. To some extent, the patrol officer is involved in logistics and public information when there is an impending problem about which advance information is available. Once the disaster occurs, the patrol officer is directly involved in all aspects of the disaster control activities. There is an immediate need for intelligence data to identify the nature and extent of the disaster, to notify persons to be warned and/or evacuated, and to contain the disaster area. Rescue operations, including medical aid for the injured, evacuation of survivors, and care for their property, are all tasks performed by the police in cooperation with the many other agencies similarly involved.

These are a few of the steps and techniques which will concern you as a patrol officer in disaster control.

1. Identify the nature and extent of the problem.
   a. Ascertain if there is an immediate danger of further problems, such as a second explosion or more of the same earth movement.
   b. If possible, determine by the nature of the incident whether there is some immediate action that can be taken to avert a repetition or continuance of the devastation.
   c. Determine the number of persons injured, the approximate nature of their injuries (such as burns, broken bones, or bruises) and their location(s).
2. Communicate your information by radio through your dispatcher.
   a. State the nature and extent of damage.
   b. Indicate which emergency services are immediately needed, and in what quantity, if it can be determined (for example, thirty or more injured persons would call for more than ane ambulance).
   c. If you have ascertained that the nature of the situation calls for a specialist, such as an engineer (who can prescribe corrective action or who can advise on the anticipated rate and direction of a slide), request that such a person be sent to the scene.
   d. Indicate the type of assistance that will be needed, the approximate amount needed, and where it is needed.
   e. Advise the dispatcher how best to gain access to the scene, and whether there are any obstructions via what might otherwise be the most logical route of approach.
   f. Broadcast any other information pertinent to hazards still existing, such as escaping gas or a bridge about to be washed out, to guide assisting units in planning their approach.
   g. Remain near your unit, and return to it frequently, to keep your headquarters and other units informed.
3. Administer urgently needed first aid. Your responsibility to provide first aid to the injured is of prime importance and should not be minimized. However, consider the situation in its perspective. If you were to immediately alight from your unit and begin administering aid before evaluating the scene and communicating your needs to headquarters, you would be tackling the job alone. By taking the extra few minutes to alert headquarters, your quick action will bring dozens or hundreds of other people to the scene to assist.
4. Establish a command post. As soon as possible, attempt to establish a telephone contact with headquarters. If this is not possible, utilize the radio, preferably the secondary frequency that is used for car-to-car transmissions. The word "mayday" is the international distress signal, and by stating the word preceding your broadcast, you will be sure to receive the attention and the clearance you need to broadcast.

   Set up the command post in a location secure from any continuing hazard but close enough to afford you a good view of the scene. Keep communications open and coordinate the police activities from the command post. Although policy varies from department to department, the usual policy is that the first officer on the scene, or the officer assigned the call, will be in command until a higher ranking officer arrives and states his intention of assuming command.

5. Contain the area. Once you have identified the nature of the problem and its extent, established communications, and summoned aid, looked after the immediate first aid needs of the victims that you could assist, and set up the command post, you should set up the perimeters of the area if you have not already done so. Have officers assigned to the outer limits of the perimeter and instruct them to allow no one to enter but those engaged in the rescue operations.

There are several purposes for perimeter control. Chief among them is to keep the number of people exposed to any hazard to a minimum. Any disaster scene almost spontaneously draws crowds of curious people. They should be diverted away from the scene as soon as possible.

6. Maintain open emergency lanes. Certain streets should be kept open and free from congestion to provide for the free flow of emergency and other service vehicles into and out of the disaster area.

7. Evacuate survivors and other persons in the area whose lives are in jeopardy. People must not only be instructed to leave, but also be helped to leave in many instances. Seek the assistance of such organizations as the Salvation Army and the American Red Cross to assist in the movement of the people and their personal effects, and to provide temporary shelter.

8. Provide public information services. People who are directly involved should know of the incident. In addition to making personal contacts, local radio and television stations may broadcast warnings to the people to evacuate. Whatever information there is available should be released to keep residents who have evacuated informed as to the condition of their property.

9. Provide for coordination with other agencies.

10. Arrange for access into the area by authorized people only. Some agencies have prepared for such contingencies by printing color-coded identification cards that are issued at the command post or some central location and collected after the need passes.

11. Record the event. If the event is of some magnitude and continues for a period of time, a scribe or stenographer may be assigned to transcribe all information provided by the various officers, supervisors, and field commanders or other persons. In other situations, the many officers who take part in the action each may prepare a report covering his individual participation. One officer is then assigned to coordinate all of the reports and to prepare one "cover" report, which ties in all of the information and caps it off with a summation. The report provides a permanent chronological record of the event and the department's participation.

Logistics and Mobilization

As an emergency public safety agency, the police department should be equipped to meet the usual and unusual demands of various occurrences. The limitations on what a police department could keep on hand are defined only by the limitations of financial resources and the imagination of the officers who prepare the plans. Every contingency should be anticipated, although requests for sup- plies and equipment must remain realistic.

Local, state, and federal civil defense agencies and their personnel are similarly engaged in preparing for the many disastrous occurrences that inevitably do occur. Any police department planning or training should definitely be in cooperation with those other agencies involved in civil defense or disaster planning.

Once a disastrous event takes place, there is little opportunity for advance planning. Most procedures should be fairly routine, at least during rehearsals, so that when an actual problem arises, mobilization for disaster control occurs almost automatically. Mutual aid plans and coordination with the various other agencies should be implemented immediately.

All available personnel are usually pressed into service and all non-critical operations are suspended. Officers from the various non-emergency functions, such as office assignments, most investigative details, identification, and records details, are re-assigned to the patrol division for field deployment. Off-duty and reserve officers should first be placed "on call" in anticipation of the need for their services. On-duty personnel will have their shifts extended to 12 hours with the first relief starting immediately on a 12-hour shift and the second relief shift coming in later to assure around-the-clock coverage.

EXERCISES AND STUDY QUESTIONS

1. Under what conditions would you decide to abandon a pursuit?
2. What is the danger of more than one police unit responding to a single emergency call?
3. What are some of the problems involved in manpower deployment during disaster control situations?
4. What is your opinion of ramming a suspect vehicle to stop it?
5. Under what conditions would you abandon a pursuit?
6. What is your opinion of warning shots?
7. Demonstrate the method for searching a felony suspect.
8. Describe the procedure for removing felony suspects from an automobile.
9. Which suspects would you handcuff when arresting them?
10. Under what circumstances may an officer use deadly force?

SUGGESTED SEMESTER OR TERM PROJECTS

1. Develop a set of guidelines for pursuit driving situations that could be followed by the members of your department.

2. Prepare a policy statement for your local police department regarding the use of firearms.
3. Set up a set of disaster plans for a natural disaster that might occur in your jurisdiction.

REFERENCES

BRISTOW, ALLEN P., and JOHN B. WILLIAMS, *A Handbook in Criminal Procedure and the Administration of Justice.* Beverly Hills, Calif.: Glencoe Press, 1966.

California Penal Code.

FRICKE, CHARLES W., and ARTHUR L. ALARCON, *California Criminal Law.* Los Angeles: Legal Book Corp., 1965.

KOLBRECK, LEROY M., and GEORGE W. PORTER, *The Law of Arrest, Search, and Seizure.* Los Angeles: Legal Book Corp., 1965.

Los Angeles Police Department, *Daily Training Bulletins,* Vols. I and II. Springfield, Ill.: Charles C Thomas, Publisher, 1954 and 1958.

Trial Law Report: The Police (a report to the President's Commission on Law Enforcement and the Administration of Justice). Washington, D.C.: Government Printing Office, 1967.

WESTON, PAUL B., and KENNETH M. WELLS, *The Administration of Justice.* Englewood Cliffs, N.J.: Prentice-Hall, Inc., 1967.

Crowd Control

and

Riot Prevention Tactics

CHAPTER ELEVEN Civil unrest seems to be indigenous to civilization, though there are times when it is apparent only in isolated situations or among small numbers of people. Certainly now is not such a time in the United States. Since the end of World War II, civil unrest in the United States has become increasingly widespread and open. Laborers, students, and minority groups have been most prominent and dramatic in their efforts to effect immediate changes in social practices and standards. They conduct demonstrations, sit-ins, teach-ins, and nonviolent civil disobedience, which usually begin as noncombative and nondestructive incidents, but sometimes end in violence and bitter combat. Some movements include mass criminal conspiracies for the purpose of interfering with lawful processes. Others produce spontaneous riotous outbursts arising out of ostensibly peaceful assemblies.

The continually recurring conditions of civil unrest and lawlessness throughout the country make it apparent that it is possible for a   **263**

264

CROWD
CONTROL
AND RIOT
PREVENTION
TACTICS

Figure 11.1 At an induction center rally the Oakland police and numerous other agencies demonstrated their ability to effectively cope with a major problem as a team. Courtesy of the Police Department, Oakland, California.

Figure 11.2 Moving large numbers of people requires utilization of military formations and use of a reasonable amount of force. Courtesy of the Police Department, Oakland, California.

major disturbance to occur any place and time there are enough people for a "quorum." Given the right combination of factors, any situation whatever involving large numbers of people may evolve or explode into an unlawful assembly. Without immediate, decisive police action, the situation could quickly evolve into a full-scale riot.

Although reliable intelligence sources for your particular department may report to your command personnel that there is no impending large-scale unlawful assembly or similar confrontation with
your forces, the same intelligence sources will report that the potential
is almost always there. There are certain individuals and organizations
that watch for potential situations with some "promise" for their own
selfish motivation to gain sudden power and wealth under the guise
of some seemingly selfless purpose. If the situation appears as though
it will be newsworthy and they will gain sufficient publicity to serve
their needs, there is little doubt that they will appear on the scene
and make whatever capital they can out of an unfortunate situation.

Most unlawful assembly situations involve local problems. With
quick action, they can be quelled and order can be restored with a
minimum of property damage and injuries. The first portion of this
chapter discusses the warning signals for impending riots or unlawful
assemblies, the purpose and objectives of the police at the scene of a
civil disturbance, psychological considerations in crowd problems and
stages in the formation of a mob, and the procedure for special
problems, such as snipers, arsonists, and looters. To illustrate the
overall problem facing the administrator in such situations, it includes
some background information on mobilization procedures and staff
concepts in crowd control. The next part of the chapter presents crowd
control formations, followed by a discussion of the legal considerations
concerning the police role in crowd control and riot prevention
operations.

WARNING SIGNALS

Sometimes it is possible to determine in advance the potentiality
of a civil disturbance of major proportions. Although it may not be
possible to predict exactly where or when such a situation may occur,
some of the following warning signals should cause you to be more
attentive to any event at which large groups of people gather for
any purpose. The most volatile are those that are attended by groups
of people with a common purpose in mind, such as a rally or advertised demonstration for some single cause.

1. An increase in the recurrence of the same rumor, or the sen-
sationalism of rumors of similar design, such as alleged police abuse of
people in certain neighborhoods, or of students, or other alleged
defenseless persons. The rumor may be an expanded and exaggerated
version of some actual incident in which a police officer may have
used force.

2. An increase in threatening or insulting signs or pamphlets in
commercial or other public places. There may be an attempt to make
it socially acceptable to ridicule or display open contempt for the

266

CROWD
CONTROL
AND RIOT
PREVENTION
TACTICS

field patrol officer, thereby reducing his general effectiveness.

3. An increasing number of incidents of violence or threats of violence. In one incident that occurred during this writing, a self-appointed champion of a cause that was popular with his peers made frequent public statements that "no policeman should get in his way, or that he should expect to suffer the consequences." One night, during a routine field interview situation, a lone police officer was killed by a single bullet. The next day the newspapers carried a story indicating that a suspect had been taken into custody for the fatal shooting. It was the same individual who had earlier made the threats. When certain individuals make bold statements to friends, they sometimes find themselves in a position in which they are committed to doing what they said, or else must suffer the grave consequence of being ridiculed themselves and cast aside because of their lack of courage to follow through. Threats of this nature should not be taken lightly.

4. Disturbances at various locations that appear to be of a similar nature as if designed to test the capabilities of the police department, or the decisiveness in the official in charge of an institution, such as a school, as a prelude to more serious action later. This "testing" process may go on for several weeks or months, sometimes for the purpose of stimulating interest and support. Minor confrontations planned for the purpose of causing an officer to become angry and take some injudicious action may be the object of such confrontations. An unjustified use of the police baton, or excessive force in an aggravated arrest situation, can be used to the advantage of any individual or organization that chooses to point at that incident as a visual aid to prove their claim that *the police* are brutal or abusive. Sometimes it is possible to gain the sympathetic support of a great many unsuspecting and well-meaning dupes in such a movement.

5. More than the usual number of disturbances at places of entertainment or sporting events. Again, the disturbances may be a form of "testing" and "baiting" to keep a cause growing. A "movement" must continually have something, or it dies of lack of interest and has no purpose for its participants.

6. Factional gang fighting or warfare, or a series of raids on parties and places of peaceful congregation. These incidents create a dissipation of the police department's effective strength at a single location.

7. Threats and attacks on private property. Such attacks may be engineered to appear as a popular cause, and they may be used to draw the police into private affairs that are noncriminal in nature, placing the officers in an unpopular position. Sometimes the incidents are designed to appear politically oriented so that the police are condemned for acting as "political oppressors."

8. An increasing need for the use of force in effecting arrests.

9. An accompanying increase in the number of complaints about

abusive practices of the police, and continuing claims that such complaints are receiving no satisfactory action.

10. Public name-calling and a general attitude of contempt and disrespect for police officers.

THE POLICE PURPOSE AND OBJECTIVES

At the scene of a disturbance—major or minor—the police purpose is constant: protection of human lives and personal property, and the restoration of order and peace in the community. The police officer is a *peace officer*, and it is your responsibility to maintain peace where it exists, and to restore peace when there has been a breach. Restoration of the peace is accomplished by persuasion when possible; by force if necessary, but that degree of force that is necessary, no more.

The objectives of the police department at the scene of an unlawful assembly are containment, dispersal, prevention of recurrence, arrest of violators, and operation according to some system of priorities.

1. CONTAINMENT. Unlawful assembly and riot situations are as contagious as the bubonic plague unless they are quarantined from the unaffected areas of the community. Once the specific area is identified, it should be closed off and contained until the problem has passed. Nonresidents and casual onlookers should immediately be advised to leave the area. All other persons who are at the scene should be advised to leave, thereby reducing the number of potential antipolice combatants.

2. DISPERSAL. Any large crowd that has formed that acquires the characteristics of an unlawful assembly must be dispersed. Although the original purpose of the gathering may have been lawful, the current nature of the assembly at the time of the officer's arrival may clearly distinguish it as unlawful. Once that is determined, it is your sworn responsibility to command the people to disperse. Once you have given the order, allow them a realistic amount of time to leave and provide avenues by which they may leave. If necessary, use crowd control formations to expedite their movement. Always use this device for movement of the crowds only, and never as a means of aggression or as a cover for personal animosities.

3. PREVENTION OF RE-ENTRY. Once the people have been moved out of an area and dissipated into smaller groups of individuals, protect the area against their return. Enforce the quarantine. If allowed to regroup and resume their original actions, the crowd's action may be far more devastating than it was in the initial gathering. Maintain a vigilance over the quarantine area and prevent re-entry as long as the emergency exists. Such a situation is not unlike a major fire. Putting out the fire is only part of the action. Sometimes it is

268

CROWD
CONTROL
AND RIOT
PREVENTION
TACTICS

necessary to leave a crew to prevent a flare-up from the smoldering ashes. The containment action should be enforced in a crowd control situation as long as the "smoldering" continues.

4. ARREST OF VIOLATORS. Whenever practicable, one of the first acts of the first officers to arrive on the scene of a disturbance is to locate and isolate the individuals who are inciting the crowd to more positive action and those who are flagrantly violating the law. Once these individuals are removed, the problem is often solved. If you do arrest such violators, immediately remove them from the scene to avoid any attempts by the crowd to rescue them from your custody. If your continued presence is needed at the scene until assistance arrives, maintain visual contact with those violators and have them removed as quickly as possible.

5. ESTABLISH PRIORITIES. Whenever you arrive on the scene of any sizable crowd disturbance, you will be outnumbered considerably. It is always necessary to establish a system of priorities depending upon the circumstances at the moment of the action, then to proceed according to those priorities. Assess the situation to determine the nature of assistance and number of people you need, and communicate that information upon your arrival before you take any immediate action at the scene. There are exceptional situations, however, when such action may not be practicable. Slavish adherence to a rigid and unbending priority system may be a short cut to failure.

PSYCHOLOGICAL CONSIDERATIONS

A variety of factors are involved in the conversion of a lawful gathering of people into a seething, violent mob bent on mayhem and destruction. A crowd consists of a body of individual people with no organization, no single leadership. Each individual's behavior is fairly controlled and ruled by reason. He and all the others have been thrown by circumstance into a crowd for some common purpose, such as observing a sport's event, which may give them at least one thing in common. With the help of a triggering device of some sort, this peaceful crowd of individuals can be converted into a mob.

A mob takes on the semblance of organization with some common motive for action, such as revenge for a heinous crime committed on the scene where the crowd is assembled, some aggravated fight situation, or a confrontation with the police when it appears to the new arrivals that the police action is unwarranted. Leaders emerge and goad the people into violent action. The crowd no longer consists of individuals, but takes on the characteristics of a single body with leadership and a common purpose, and an unbelievable pliability and quick response to emotional whim.

Preconditioning may actually lead to the formation of a mob. For example, an advertised event might attract great numbers of people to a specific location, all with the same purpose in mind. It may be a "grudge" sporting event, a confrontation of opposing gang factions, a civil rights demonstration, a church revival meeting. Any crowd of people that has some single common interest, whatever it may be, has already been preconditioned to some extent. The mob, once in full bloom, is characterized by homogeneity, emotionality, irrationality, anonymity, and universality.

The homogeneity of a mob is characterized by the similarities that they adopt as members of this new spontaneous organization. They share common attitudes and opinions, experience the same dissatisfactions, and their conflict seems to take on the appearance of a communion of people. Of course, to some extent, they may share this homogeneity before they gather for some common purpose.

The mob's emotionality is easily recognized. A high degree of emotional tension and excitement prevail. To keep the mood at such a high pitch, which is essential to the perpetuation of a mob, manipulators in the crowd may provide loud, high-pitched sounds, such as extremely loud up-beat music, with constant beating on drums and continual physical activity. Once the activity begins to lag, or is stopped abruptly, the state of emotionality runs down.

There are two pecular and dangerous aspects of the mob's irrationality. One is an almost immediate narrowing of perception, a "tunnel-vision" effect of seeing only what one is intent upon seeing, and as accompanying lack of rational judgment. The second peculiar aspect of the irrationality is its strikingly regressive character evidenced by childlike—or animalistic—unsophisticated, usually violent, behavior, as if it were a compulsive release of pent-up emotions. Otherwise totally rational and intelligent people will behave under mob conditions in sharp contrast to their normal pattern.

Anonymity is a very important factor in any mob action. Under the temporary loss of rationality in a mob situation, the individual loses inhibitions and is not likely to think much about whether he is recognized or not. The person may believe that he can "lose himself in the crowd," or he may simply not think. This anonymous state provides for the mob member a haven from apprehension and punishment for his crimes, and he may actually feel as though he is on a "moral holiday." One way to counteract the anonymity factor is to locate individuals in the mob and identify them by calling their names, which may bring them at least to the realization that they are not as anonymous as they may have thought.

Universality is another factor in mob psychology. As a matter of fact, it can weigh heavily on the perception of people even under rational conditions. The mob member who lives the part long enough may actually grow so nearsighted that he projects his immediate surroundings to encompass the entire world. Simply because he has a few

270

CROWD
CONTROL
AND RIOT
PREVENTION
TACTICS

hundred excited and incited people in his immediate vicinity who seem to approve of his actions under mob conditions, he may actually believe that the same feeling is shared by everyone else. Consider the statements of many spokesmen for revolutionary groups who profess that their feelings are shared by the "majority."

The phenomenon of universality should also be guarded against by the police officer, who may gauge his opinion of "all students" or all persons of a certain organization, or nationality origin, or racial background, or sports interest, on his experiences with a few persons who behave as animals in a mob situation. "Everyone" simply does not encompass *everyone*.

The Mob's Leaders

Take a look at the people who emerge as leaders in civil disorders or riots. They are usually characterized as dominant, persuasive, or opportunistic. The dominant leader is usually coldly aloof from the others, and demands immediate action without thinking of either the processes or the consequences involved. The persuasive leader is one who maintains a personal rapport with each individual of his group, and they identify with him. He is seemingly a sincere individual who reshapes their thoughts in such a way that those who follow him will believe that he is to receive the credit for any good that may come out of the holocaust. The third leader, the opportunist, is one who sees an opportunity to seize control of a mob that is already bent on a single action, such as destruction of some object. He manipulates the mob so that he will get the recognition for the action as if he had planned the entire event for the purpose of some transcendent goal. Through the sacrifices of others, the opportunist emerges as some sort of "sainted" figure. Any one or more of these leaders may go to the scene of a disturbance or riot for the specific purpose of involving themselves, or they may emerge as indigenous leaders in the crowd. Under conditions when their actions would be applauded, they would be classified "natural leaders."

The People in the Mob

Many different types of personalities make up any crowd, and each plays a part in the formation of a mob. The psychopath is rare, but he may show up at such an event as the "angry man" who has a particular axe to grind, and may be in such a highly polished state of paranoia that he can recruit people to fight his battles for him. The hotheads, or impulsive actors, are there, quick to lose their tempers and their inhibitions. The criminally intent individual may find the riot a convenient cover for his unlawful act; the mob will take the blame for his crime while he harvests the fruit.

These are some of the mob's more impressionable "followers," who will willingly and impulsively sacrifice their moral values for any cause that immediately presents itself to them in their immature state of development. They comprise many of the "sheep," or the "cattle," for the manipulators to use in achieving their nefarious goals. And then there are the "also there's." These are the many people who just happen to be on the scene and, unless diverted away from the scene before the crowd converts into a mob, become so enraptured by the "mob psychosis" that they, too, become sheep and unwittingly become involved in the panicky, "stampede-like" activities of a riot.

Psychological Influences

The agitator, or leader, who attempts to incite a riot, or who assumes control of a riot already in progress and directs it to serve his purposes, has several factors working for him in such a situation. He may use rumors and propaganda techniques that will give the lagging riot impetus by passing the word that someone has been killed by a policeman, or that some reprehensible act has been committed by the opposing faction. In the mass confusion that is taking place, the "inciter" may actually create his own incidents; for example, he might bait an officer to use force upon him, then point to his injuries as "visual proof" of police brutality. Gaudy bandages or self-imposed wounds on the head, which are often superficial, but which bleed profusely, are not unusual in some riotous situations.

The novelty of the situation works for the inciter, as the new and strange circumstances become a "fun thing" or a "happening" for the thrill-seeker. The anonymity works equally well for the agitator, or inciter, because he may remain in the background and make his shouted suggestions for action that others will carry out for him in the "everyone is doing it" atmosphere. Under the guise of group behavior, the riot allows the individual to release inhibitions that he would maintain under normal conditions. Consider the testimony of suspects in cases where brutal gang killings have occurred in mob actions. The suspects interviewed say such things as: "I hit him on the head too. . . . Everyone else was doing it. . . . Besides, he was probably dead already. . . . If I didn't hit him, somebody would'a hit me."

There is always the feeling in a crowd disturbance situation that there is strength in numbers, and even the timid individual sometimes assumes the posture of the ferocious beast when backed up by his several protectors. Suggestibility works to the advantage of the inciter in a crowd; they are more likely to accept his ideas as their own and act on them when in a crowd than when they are alone. Consider the situation when a child molester is arrested after a chase, and a tense neighborhood scene is created. The victimized child is screaming,

272

CROWD
CONTROL
AND RIOT
PREVENTION
TACTICS

the enraged parents are loudly demanding action, the officer is attempting to talk to the suspect rationally and the suspect's obscene epithets are reaching the ears of the people in the crowd; suddenly, someone shouts, "Get that b — — — — — d!" This is an example of a situation that could quite easily evolve into a riot.

STAGES IN THE FORMATION OF A MOB

Many experts on mob psychology say that there are certain perceptible stages which manifest themselves during the formation of a riot. As a field police officer, I have felt or sensed these stages. They are more subtle than they appear on paper, but they are present and can be recognized. To deal with a crowd effectively, it is imperative that you make an effort to ascertain what point of development it has reached, and determine whether it has reached mob proportions yet. A mob will have to be handled differently from a crowd, since there is little value in attempting to reason or debate with it. Only some sort of dramatic action will jolt the mob members back to the reality that they are individuals, and that dramatic action should not assume the characteristics of an "overreaction" by the police officers.

Mob psychology experts have used various titles to identify the progressive stages in the development of a mob. For the purpose of this discussion, these stages are referred to as Stage One, Stage Two, and Stage Three.

Stage One

At this stage, the crowd is still functioning as a conglomerate of individuals. There is some milling about, but any fighting or pushing taking place occurs in independent and unrelated events. The atmosphere is charged with some common feeling of impending activity that seems to act as a form of gravity that pulls the people together, but at this stage it is difficult to define the source of the feeling. It may be some widely spread rumor that a specific event, such as a gang fight, is about to take place. In one of their bulletins dealing with the problem of riot prevention, the Federal Bureau of Investigation refers to this as the "bristling" stage, and the term implies that the people are "bristling." When you approach a disturbance at this stage, some of the "bristling" occurs when the "electricity" in the air of the situation literally causes the individual to feel the "chill in his spine," or to feel the hair on the back of his neck "stand on end," yet there is no spectacular event to which the feeling can be attributed.

At this stage, it is possible to move spectators and disinterested bystanders away from the scene, and to begin counteracting the problem by arresting individual law violators, removing them from the scene, and generally taking effective and decisive enforcement action. If you locate any anticipated agitators, divert them from the scene.

Stage Two

In the second stage, the crowd loses its atmosphere of individualities and takes on the appearance of a single unit. The agitators have assumed their positions and they are beginning to see the results of their suggestions. Opportunists or confederates of the leaders may be circulating in the crowd, getting it moving and thinking as a single unit. Rumors begin to spread and there may be considerable "baiting" of the officers on the scene in an effort to precipitate a cause for action on the part of the crowd. The crowd is well on its way to becoming a cohesive unit at stage two.

The most effective action at this point may be to move in with squad formations, removing the leaders and dispersing the people, and making an effort to return the gathering to its earlier state as a collection of individuals who can be dealt with in an intelligent and rational manner.

Stage Three

By now, the mob is functioning as a single unit and its leaders are in control. Any event is likely to precipitate violent action. Some officers have appropriately referred to stage three as the "riot just waiting to happen."

At this stage, the most effective action is decisive police movement in a show to force to move the people out of the area and to cause them to break down into small groups. Little reasoning, if any, is likely to be effective at stage three. All three of these stages could probably be classified as unlawful assembly. Fortunately, it is possible to deal effectively with the majority of crowd control situations and thus prevent devastating riots.

PROCEDURE FOR HANDLING AN UNLAWFUL ASSEMBLY

1. ASSESS THE SITUATION. One of the first things to do is to determine whether the original purpose of the gathering was lawful or not, and then determine its lawfulness at the time of your arrival. Look at the people in the crowd, and determine their state of intoxication, their attitude, their emotional state, and general condition. Attempt to determine whether the crowd has taken on any of the characteristics of the mob and what stage of development it has reached. Locate the

274

CROWD
CONTROL
AND RIOT
PREVENTION
TACTICS

Figure 11.3 Dogs are trained for riot duty. This and following photo courtesy of the Police Department, Salt Lake City, Utah.

Figure 11.4

cause of the problem, if possible. Locate and identify the leaders, and agitators, if any. Look for signs of organization.

2. SURVEY THE SCENE. Except for cases in which there is an extreme need for immediate action, as when an individual is under direct and violent attack at the moment of your arrival, this "surveying" process has greater value to the overall department effectiveness than a lone officer attempting to handle the situation by himself. Determine as soon as possible the best location for the command post, and locations from which observers away from the immediate scene may have the best vantage point. The command post will be the center of operations and, once set up, may be difficult to relocate.

The observation post should be nearby so that motion picture and videotape equipment may be set up to make a visual as well as audio record of the event. It must be in a location that is reasonably secure from attack.

While surveying the scene, consider the geographical factors, such as natural barriers, buildings, and the wind and weather conditions in case it should become necessary later to use tear gas and riot formations. Note the best methods of approach for your support units.

3. COMMUNICATE. As soon as possible after your arrival and evaluation of the situation, *communicate!* Report on your assessment, keeping the report brief, but concise, giving your superiors and communications personnel sufficient data with which to proceed with their plans for action. The operations officer in charge will make a decision as to the needs for mobilization and additional support units, and any other long-range planning that may be necessary. The dispatcher will assign support units based upon the information that you provide.

When you communicate your needs, indicate whether it is *help* or *assistance* you require. Indicate how much and where you need the help or assistance. If there is a specific location away from the scene where you have reason to believe that an officer could be assigned to expedite the movement of people away from the area, his assistance at that point might be as valuable as the other units that you are going to request directly at the scene. If you believe it will provide a tactical advantage for your units to use a specific method or avenue of approach, communicate that information to the dispatcher. Be brief, and be mindful that some people monitor the police radio frequencies.

During the first few minutes of your presence at the scene of a civil disturbance, your attention to the matter of communicating your findings and providing your headquarters personnel with adequate information is critical. Remain as close to the radio as possible until additional units arrive, so that you can answer any questions that may arise and communicate any new developments.

4. WATCHFUL WAITING. Observe the action and make your presence known to the people in the vicinity. A single police car and a lone officer or two can do little to quell a major disturbance, but there are some individuals who will take heed of the fact that you are using the radio to call for assistance, and some of them will be impressed with the knowledge that the officer on the scene is making preparations for decisive police action.

If the crowd is too much to handle alone, stay near the unit and wait for the support units. If there is need for some immediate action, do it, but be sure to distinguish between bravery and foolhardiness. In one beach city not too long ago, two officers approached a hostile crowd, so the story goes, and decided to take some quick action. They radioed in that they were going to be off the air for a few minutes at

276

CROWD
CONTROL
AND RIOT
PREVENTION
TACTICS

the beach, then they waded into the crowd to disperse the people. Seizing upon the opportunity of the moment, with anonymity completely assured for all the participants, the people in the crowd surrounded the officers, removed their clothing and passed two disarmed and undressed officers over their heads back out to the edge of the crowd. They were ridiculed and mocked by the crowd, and were powerless to arrest a single person for the embarrassing situation. To move slowly but surely with no retreat is a better method of action than to rush in, with the possibility of having to make a strategic withdrawal. To retreat is to lose face for the strength of law enforcement. Much of that strength is symbolic and it should not be jeopardized by an impetuous and foolhardy officer.

5. RESCUE AND SELF-DEFENSE. Until help arrives, take care of the immediate needs of the situation, such as rescue of people under attack, administration of first aid, and self-protection. The *primary* objectives are to protect lives and property and to restore order.

6. MAINTAIN AN OPEN LINE OF COMMUNICATIONS. Keep your dispatcher advised on the progress at the scene. If you are able to handle the situation satisfactorily before help arrives, be sure to cancel the call for assistance. In a time of need in a civil disturbance situation, there are probably many officers who are risking their lives in heavy traffic to respond to your aid as quickly as possible, and they should be advised that they may discontinue their response as soon as you realize that they are no longer needed. Continue directing the support units to the scene, and to the perimeter area, for traffic control, diversion of people from the scene, and general perimeter control.

7. ESTABLISHED A COMMAND POST. In your own department, there should be a designated plan for action in civil disturbance situations. In most normal police incidents, it may be the department policy for the assigned officer to be in command until a higher ranking officer relieves him of the authority by telling him that he is assuming control. It may be an established procedure for the senior officer present to assume command in the absence of supervisory personnel. Whatever the policy, it should be established and made known to every officer who will be affected by the policy.

Set up the command post, which will probably be the first police car on the scene, at the edge of the crowd. It should be located in a position where it can be seen by the greatest number of people in the crowd, yet not where it can become the object of attack. If the unit has an outside public address system as part of its standard equipment, you will have ready-made means of communicating with the people with the help of an amplifier. In the absence of any special sound equipment, the radio in the car will serve as a public address system. Turn up the radio volume as loud as possible, switching to an outside speaker if the unit is equipped with one, and from another radio transmitter, such as another nearby police car, transmit the message intended for the crowd. The command post radio will amplify the message.

At the command post, the ranking officer will be in charge according to the procedure specified in department regulations. If manpower from neighboring jurisdictions is provided, the authority rests with the department in whose jurisdiction the problem exists. Under normal operating conditions, the commander in the office is usually in charge of field operations through the headquarters communications personnel. In situations such as this, however, the field officer in charge on the scene should have command, subject to the administrative supervision of the higher ranking officers on duty, but without any interference except by their specific direction. The field commander is assured authority commensurate with his responsibility for taking decisive action, which may not allow time for conferences.

8. TAKE IMMEDIATE ACTION FOR SERIOUS VIOLATIONS. Arrest the perpetrators and immediately remove them from the scene. If such arrests will drain off strength of manpower from the scene, wait until sufficient manpower is available to make arrests and then take the prisoners to jail immediately. In judging manpower strength, consider the possibility that some individuals on the scene may decide to take advantage of the opportunity; some may be there as a result of lengthy preparation. What would be a better way to sap the strength of the police department than to use a few individuals to "bait" the officers into arrest situations, causing them to divert some of their strength to the custody and transportation problems resulting from the arrests? Once enough officers are removed from the scene, a major confrontation with those who are remaining might prove too much for them, and the result could be an embarrassing—possibly devastating —breakdown in the police strength.

9. THE DISPERSAL ORDER. Assuming, for the purpose of this guide, that the disturbance has not yet reached riot proportions and that there is still the need for removing the remaining people from the scene, the following few steps describe the recommended procedure for handling an unlawful assembly. If the situation has deteriorated beyond that point, then move on to the next stage and meet the problem head-on, without exceeding your authority in what could be described as an "overaction," a term which eludes precise definition.

When preparing to give the order to the people to disperse, position yourself so that you will be seen and heard by the greatest number of people you intend to disperse. In most states, the legal codes require that this action be performed by some official, such as a magistrate, a mayor, a sheriff, a prosecuting attorney, or some other person, usually the police officer. The police officer is generally the man to whom the task is relegated because of his immediate response to the situation.

278

CROWD
CONTROL
AND RIOT
PREVENTION
TACTICS

In the absence of more strictly defined procedures in your own department, use the following tactical guidelines to assure the greatest likelihood of convictions.

a. Assign witnesses at strategic locations who can testify that they saw and heard you issue the command to disperse. Use reliable witnesses for this purpose, including newsmen, judges, and public officials. Television crews and news photographers are ideal for witnessing the event, and their assistance should be solicited.
b. Order the crowd to disperse. Use amplification equipment, if available. The order should be in accordance with the laws of your state, and should include a statement of your identity and the authority for the order. It is an order, not a threat. Give the crowd a realistic time limit within which to disperse.
c. Order all assigned officers to stand ready, guarding the perimeter, but making its possible for the people to leave as directed. Officers who are carrying batons should hold them with both hands at port arms position, never in a menacing manner, such as in a waving position.
d. Expedite the departure of the people who are commanded to disperse.
e. Repeat the order at least three times so that as many people as possible can hear you. If there are people who do not speak your language, use an interpreter.
f. Wait until the expiration of the time limit. Do not use a "countdown," or "baiting" technique, with the people. Merely wait the stated time.
g. At the end of the time limit, arrest the offenders. If the crowd is complying but for some reason there is a slowdown in traffic, it may be necessary to use a "long count" for the time limit, but do not make a game of it.

10. ARREST PROCEDURE. The charge for which you arrest the violator obviously depends on the statutes in your own jurisdiction. For this type of situation, you have been arresting individuals throughout the action for specific law violations only indirectly related to the unlawful assembly. What we have done in this procedure is to build a case for the arrest of people who fail to disperse from an unlawful assembly when ordered to do so. It provides you with a uniform charge and uniform procedure, but still requires that each individual be arrested and held to answer as an individual member of the crowd.

a. Arrest the violators. The law will specify which persons are exempt from arrest under unlawful assembly conditions. In order to identify those persons who are authorized by your department to be at the scene, some departments have prepared color-coded plastic badges for issuance right on the scene.
b. Arresting officers should work in teams of two officers each. In large crowd situations when many officers have responded to the call for assistance, consider having the officers who form the arrest teams re-

move their weapons and other equipment that provide bulk for the
officer, and also provide means of attack for any arrestee who is
successful in wrestling something such as a revolver from the holster
of the officer whose hands are full of prisoner. Under sufficient cover
by other officers, the arrest team can concentrate on the physical
custody problems. There will, no doubt, be people with cameras on
the scene, and it is not unusual for them to focus their attention and
cameras on the close contact confrontations between officers and
arrestees. Close-ups of such scenes are often misleading and lead to
frequent and long-lasting misunderstandings.

Field booking procedures may prove most effective for an unlawful assembly—non-riot—situation directly at the scene. The jail bus or
van can serve as the mobile jail, and a short booking process can be
set up as each prisoner is placed on the bus. The members of the
arrest team can take their arrestee to the booking station outside the
bus, pick up a numbered card, use marking pencil and inscribe their
names and the name of the arrestee on the card, then have their
photograph taken with the arrestee. As the arrestee is placed in the
bus, a card carrying the same number can be filled out with the name
of the subject, the charge, and a thumb print or simultaneous four-
finger print of each arrestee.

Another arrest technique is to place three or four arrestees in a
police car, then remove them from the immediate scene by driving
to a temporary holding area several blocks away from the scene. At
this area, the arrestees may be handled in larger groups, and when the
booking requirements have been met, they can be transported to jail
in larger numbers. Whatever method you use, immediately remove
them from the scene.

    c. Do not engage in conversation with the people at the scene. This is
no time to attempt to justify your actions or to explain the circumstances that led to this action. Any discussions can be referred to an
information officer, who should be located at some location remote
from the problem area.

    d. Maintain a businesslike and professional manner, moving curious on-
lookers from the scene, and continuing to arrest the violators for failure to disperse, or whatever specific crimes they commit in your
presence.

    e. Once you have cleared the area and have arrested all of the violators,
remain and continue to move curiosity-seekers out of the area until
all signs of the unlawful assembly have dissipated.

11. GENERAL GUIDELINES.

    a. Preplanning must be high on the agenda whenever your department
anticipates any disorder or major disturbance. Although the purpose
for the gathering may be publicized as a lawful one, never assume

280

CROWD
CONTROL
AND RIOT
PREVENTION
TACTICS

that the meeting will continue in a peaceful and lawful manner. The very nature of the situation may stimulate counterdemonstrations or similar action by opposing factions or individuals with different views. Plan for the civil disturbance, then hope that it does not occur.

b. Meet with responsible leaders. Prior to any planned incident or meeting at which there is a possibility of a disturbance developing, meet in advance with the people who will be in charge. Discuss the situation with the property owners and the leaders who will be at the scene. Express your concern for assuring them of their constitutional guarantees of the First Amendment, and explain to them your purpose for being on the scene to assure that freedom. Explain to them also what their responsibilities will be to make sure the assembly continues as a lawful one. Secure a commitment from the property owners as to what type of support they will give in asking law violators to leave and in signing criminal complaints against those violators.

c. If they can be located, and if they respond to rational requests, ask the leaders to disperse the crowd before attempting to take police action.

d. Maintain order and attempt to quell the disturbance without attempting to punish any of the violators.

e. Use only that force which is necessary, but take positive and decisive action. Immediate action with an unlawful assembly will often deter the occurrence of a major riot, which will take far more serious action.

f. If the situation appears to be growing worse, possibly because of perceptible organized resistance to your efforts to restore order, consider the possibility of evacuating the area of residents, businessmen, and other people who could either become victims of violence, or who could add to the numbers of people who are causing the disturbance.

g. Post the quarantine area with signs and barricades, if necessary, and have officers patrol the perimeter to keep out unnecessary vehicles and pedestrians.

h. Keep the traffic lanes open for emergency and support vehicles.

i. Arrange for off-street parking and protection of the vehicles of the assisting agencies.

j. Consider the use of a field dictating unit or tape recorder for "debriefing" yourself and other officers who respond to the situation to record impressions and other random expressions for later evaluation of the overall situation.

k. Consider the fact that the most impressive police action at the scene of any type of major disturbance is the expeditious removal of the leaders by a well-disciplined squad of officers who give the appearance of knowing what they are doing, and who demonstrate their ability to get to work and get the job done.

SPECIAL PROBLEMS

At any unlawful assembly of major proportions, there is a strong possibility that the assembly will flare up into a riot. Consider the following problems, which often accompany such an occurrence.

There are certain psychopathic individuals who will attempt to take advantage of the mass confusion and excitement at a riot scene by taking concealed positions and shooting at people with some type of weapon, usually a military or hunting rifle. These individuals are potential murderers—if they have not killed already—and must be taken into custody as quickly as possible. The first step in handling such a situation is to clear the area of innocent bystanders. Isolate the area and guard against the suspect's escape. Move in, and use whatever force is necessary to take him into custody. Assignment of antisniper teams of officers may be necessary in aggravated situations.

Arsonists

The arsonist with a torch in his hand is another potential killer, and he must be taken into custody immediately. If he is about to throw a fire bomb, consider the lives of the people inside the buildings that he is about to set afire and act accordingly. It may be necessary to use deadly force to save the lives of countless innocent people. Again, use only that force which is necessary, but do not hesitate at the risk of many more lives that may be lost by your indecisiveness.

Looters

Under even the most serious riotous conditions short of martial rule, a blanket order cannot be given as to how looters should be dealt with. Looting may consist of acts of simple misdemeanor thefts, or it may consist of burglary, or breaking and entering. Take the suspects into custody by whatever means are necessary. Consider the circumstances and the individuals involved. As a police officer, it is your awesome responsibility to avoid getting "caught up" in the feeling of mob psychosis. You must continue to operate as a *thinking individual police officer whose responsibility it is to protect lives—* including those of your suspects—*and property.* Handle looting situations individually, as you would any other police incident.

Riot

There is always the possibility that a major unlawful assembly may erupt into riot. When that happens, the police action must be forceful and dramatic, aimed at destroying the mob organization and restoring order as quickly as possible. Consider the following guidelines for riot control.

a. Surprise offensive. The police action in its initial stages at a riot must

282

CROWD
CONTROL
AND RIOT
PREVENTION
TACTICS

be dramatic. It must have shock value in order to effectively arrest the progress of the riot's development, and the element of surprise may enhance its effectiveness.

b. Security of information. Plans for action and communications regarding the movement of personnel and equipment should be kept confidential. For highly confidential information, consider using direct telephone lines, or radio frequencies separate from the normal police bands. Some types of "scrambler" devices have been manufactured for use with radios, and they may be used for security purposes, although they are rather expensive and have limited value.

c. Maximum utilization of force. A show of police force should be made in a well-organized, military manner. With the combined forces of your own department and support units from agencies of nearby jurisdictions, there is little likelihood that you will have the number of officers actually necessary to handle the situation. Make the best use of the force that you do have by assigning the officers in fast-moving, compact, and efficient military-type squad formations.

d. Flexibility of assignments. Officer teams should be flexibly assigned to various places where the need is greatest, and where they will create the impression that there are more officers on the scene than there actually are.

e. Simplicity. Keep the plan and the instructions simple and direct. Avoid mass confusion among the officers.

STAFF CONCEPTS IN CROWD CONTROL

There are many staff considerations involved in crowd and riot control. Two immediate problems are scheduling, and police coverage of the rest of the city. Logistics, organization, and coordination all play their respective parts in the operation.

Mobilization

The first step to mobilization is to discontinue all nonessential police tasks, such as the routine patrolling and response to miscellaneous calls for service. Adequate personnel will have to be assigned to two locations at the beginning: the site of the event, and the site of the complaint board. There will probably be a considerable increase in telephone and radio communications, and many of the nonessential calls will have to be postponed or "counseled out" by diplomatic desk officers. These officers must make it possible for all available field officers to respond only to emergencies in addition to the disturbance scene. On-duty personnel will probably also be extended an additional four hours, making it possible to assign the entire department to two 12-hour platoons which will alternate on duty as long as the need exists.

Figure 11.5 Crowd dispersal by means of tear gas. An innovative method for dispensing tear gas, this device is extremely effective for dispersing a large crowd. Courtesy of the Police Department, Oakland, California.

Figure 11.6 The correct firing position for the aerosol tear gas (ATG) dispenser. Accuracy and target selectivity are advantages of the ATG. Courtesy of the Police Department, Oakland, Caifornia.

284

CROWD
CONTROL
AND RIOT
PREVENTION
TACTICS

Figure 11.7 The underhand roll for gas grenade. Pull the pin then hold down the lever until you throw the canister. There is a two to five second delay before the explosion and the release of gas. Courtesy of the Police Department, Oakland, California.

Off-duty officers and reserve forces should then be called to duty. In order to effect this process with the minimal interference with headquarters telephone operations, there should be some form of emergency call system with a pyramid-type procedure. Office clerical personnel should be assigned to begin the call-up with a few initial calls to off-duty officers or their families. The call system should continue from those strategic outside phone locations. This system will free both the department's lines and the people who would otherwise have to be making the calls. When mobilizing off-duty officers, it may be wise to have the officers report in uniform to a staging area some distance away from the police headquarters building, possibly nearer

to the location where the disturbance situation is taking place, and in
a location where the officers' private vehicles will be safe. Using this
staging area will keep the movement of the force of officers confidential, and it may add to the element of surprise when the officers arrive
on the scene. If there were any organization to the agitation at the
crowd scene, it would not be impossible for someone with a small
two-way radio or telephone to watch police headquarters for personnel movement. In the absence of such organization, this remote
staging process at least reduces confusion at the headquarters building.

Mutual Aid Agreement

Since the World War II years, many contiguous jurisdictions have
had rather elaborate machinery for immediate coordination of combined forces under mutual aid compacts and agreements. In California,
for example, the entire state is divided into mutual aid zones, and
most of the cities in each county have mutual aid pacts. Whenever
there is an alert of "limited peril," and the local police forces cannot
adequately handle the problem, the alert is broadcast, and officers
from the contiguous jurisdictions respond to assist. The jurisdiction
having the problem maintains the authority for coordination and
supervision. When the situation involves a larger area, such as two or
more cities, coordination is assumed by a predesignated administrator,
such as the county sheriff. If the problem calls for more assistance than
the county's police forces can provide, the authority and responsibility
for coordination then goes to a zone commander, who is probably one
of the sheriffs of the several counties in the zone. The chain of rein-
forcement continues to expand until the situation obviously calls for
statewide coordination. At that point, the governor declares martial
rule.

Martial Rule

Martial rule is a military state, and during its existence all constitutional provisions are suspended. There is no local control, and the
objective of putting down the riot becomes a military objective for the
National Guard, or state militia, under the control of the commander
in chief, who is the governor, and his adjutant general. Because the
condition of military rule is alien to a free society, the decision to
impose martial rule is an extremely grave one, and the governor must
use this power only when the local forces cannot handle the situation.
Requests for the imposition of martial rule must come from the chief
executive officer of the local government, or from some other official

286

CROWD
CONTROL
AND RIOT
PREVENTION
TACTICS

source, such as a magistrate or the sheriff. The governor may also make the decision himself. The mechanics for the request and imposition of martial rule depend on the various state laws.

Once the local government officials see the need for additional assistance beyond the forces that they may utilize within their own jurisdiction, it is advisable to alert the governor's office and the National Guard so that they may plan for the contingency of martial rule. In the meantime, it is wise to activate the mutual aid plan, and to proceed according to the needs dictated by the situation. When the governor authorizes the use of the National Guard, the first step in the military assistance is to place this force under the supervision of the local police administrator in an assisting capacity.

The governor imposes martial rule only when he sees no alternative. During that time when martial rule is in existence, the military commander is in complete charge of the situation. His objective is to restore sufficient order to enable the local police to reassume control of the situation. The minute that objective is achieved, the governor orders the martial rule at an end. The National Guard then reverts to its "support" role until the governor and the local officials determine that it is no longer needed.

Federal Troops

If the riotous situation reaches such proportions that the local police must relinquish control to the State National Guard, the state martial rule is not sufficient. The governor must then request assistance from the President of the United States. The President then goes through a process similar to that the governor went through, and he may impose federal martial rule. The State National Guard becomes federalized, and federal military troops are sent into the jurisdiction. Once the President determines the need for federal martial rule, he makes the determination and proclaims it to be in effect. In the absence of presidential order, the military troops may be placed at the disposal of local law enforcement administrators when there is a grave need for such assistance. Actually, this determination of grave need may be made by local military commanders and the assistance rendered, but it must then be followed by satisfactory justification to the President through the appropriate levels of command.

The entire system of mutual aid and martial law is designed to provide for local control until all possibilities of quelling the disturbance have been attempted and have failed. Only then may the governor step in and impose martial rule, and he may keep it in effect only as long as the immediate need exists. The same procedure applies to the President of the United States. Local law enforcement has long ben recognized as the *primary* law enforcement body in the country, and the laws have been passed with that concept in mind.

Assignment of Responsibility

If there is any advance warning about an impending civil disturbance of major proportions, and if planning may be accomplished in advance, such planning should include some serious consideration of which officers will be given the initial assignment to attempt to control the crowd and prevent the riot. The following factors should influence the administrators in selecting the officers for this duty: The officers should be young men who are in perfect physical condition. They should be among the taller men on the force, and they should maintain an immaculate uniform appearance. In addition to being physically capable of doing an excellent job, the men for a special enforcement detail should also "look the part." They should be cool and reflective, mature, and emotionally stable under stress conditions. They must have a certain degree of social sensitivity and be optimistic about their goal of restoring order through persuasion if possible, force only if necessary.

Intelligence Assignments

A staff officer should be assigned to independently define and measure the field problem in a detached manner, free of the emotional strain of making immediate decisions. This officer should report to the police chief and other command officers so that they may make their decisions based upon his evaluation and the reports from the field commander. To assist him in this information gathering operation, the intelligence officer may use a team of "scouts," who enter the field to observe and report on everything that comes to their attention from their points of vantage. When making intelligence assessments, the assigned officer will consult with various specialists to aid the staff in making judgment decisions about situations such as natural disasters, floods, earthquakes, hurricanes, or forest fires, that may accompany the civil disturbance.

Logistics

An officer should be assigned to plan in advance for the accumulation and proper dispensation of supplies and equipment, and to

288

CROWD
CONTROL
AND RIOT
PREVENTION
TACTICS

handle distribution details during times of actual need. If a sudden need should arise to feed and provide rest areas for two thousand officers, for example, this officer should be ready to act at once to meet the emergency. A logistics officer must be ready for any contingency.

Public Information

An officer with sufficient rank to make judgments concerning information releases under various circumstances should be assigned to man a post somewhere removed from the immediate scene of the disturbance, and also far enough away from the center of communications and headquarters operations to avoid interfering with those operations. The information officer should be the only one authorized to release information concerning the event. All units should be required to keep the information officer posted on changing events. The information officer will actually be the best informed of the noncritical operating personnel, and in his location he can keep the news media informed on events as they happen. If such an officer is assigned, and the policy for "no news except through the information officer" is enforced, the press and other people who have a need to know about the situation will go to the information center to satisfy their needs, and remain outside the critical operating areas.

Staging Area

The staging area may be at the headquarters building or, to reduce confusion and add to the elements of secrecy and surprise, it may be at some high school or shopping center in the general vicinity of the event.

Operations

Once the mobilization of officers and the enactment of the plan for special action occurs, the senior patrol officer on duty must serve the dual purpose of attacking the disturbance problem, and assuaging the people in the rest of the city by restoring some semblance of police patrol in those nondisturbance areas as quickly as possible. In some departments, the patrol commander will turn authority and responsibility over to an operations officer, who will then coordinate the police control of the special problem. The patrol commander can then adjust to the situation, and provide continuity in patrol coverage throughout the rest of the city as best he can with the resources he has remaining. The operations officer should be an officer who is completely familiar with the overall planning and training for the problem, so that he is in the strongest possible position to implement the emergency operations. He must also have sufficient rank to command the immediate cooperation and compliance of all other involved personnel.

CROWD CONTROL FORMATIONS

To Assemble Squad. (Detail, Platoon, etc.)

The command is: *SQUAD–FALL IN*

At the command "Fall in," the members of the squad form a line according to height. The tallest man, referred to as the "point man," falls in at the right. On falling in, each man except the one on the left (end man), extends his left arm laterally at shoulder height, palm of the hand down, fingers extended and joined.

Each man except the one on the right turns his head and eyes to the right and places himself in line so that his right shoulder touches lightly the tips of the fingers of the man on his right. As soon as proper intervals have been obtained, each man drops his arm smartly to his side and turns his head to the front. In a platoon formation; the squads again dress right, but also position themselves one arm's length from the rank in front.

If the officers you wish to assemble are widely separated or are too far from you to hear your command, attract their attention by using a whistle or other sound device and use a prearranged signal. At the same time wave your hand above your head in a circular motion and then point to the location where you intend for them to assemble.

To Align Squad

The command is: *DRESS RIGHT, DRESS*

At the command of "Dress," each man except the one on the left extends his left arm and aligns himself to the right. The squad leader places himself on the right flank at the end of the line and facing down the line. From this position, he verifies the alignment of the men and orders individual men to move forward or back as necessary. Alignment checked:

290

CROWD
CONTROL
AND RIOT
PREVENTION
TACTICS

The command is: *READY-FRONT*

At the command "Front," arms are dropped quietly and smartly to the side, and heads are turned to the front.

To Count Off

The command is: *SQUAD–COUNT OFF*

At the command of "Count off," each man except the one on the right flank turns his head and eyes to the right. The squad leader (sergeant) calls out "One." The point man calls out "Two." Each man in succession calls out "Three," "Four," etc., turning his head and eyes to the front smartly as he calls out his number. This command may be given whenever it is desired that the men know their position in the body.

The Squad

For police purposes, the size of the squad may be seven to twelve men under the command of a sergeant who, in the following diagrams, is designated number "1"; the assistant squad leader is the last man. If there is need for a gas man or special weapons man, he is always included as the next to the last man in the following diagrams.

The squad leader will take a position from where he can best control the squad, moving about freely as the situation demands.

Squad, Single File. (Squad Column or Line.)

The command is: *SQUAD–FALL IN–SINGLE COLUMN*

The hand signal is: Index finger extended from a closed fist held above the head, arm vertical.

(Single file formation is used to move the squad through narrow openings. It should not be used at the point of contact with the mob.)

2 3 4 5 6 7 8 9 10 11 12

1

⟵——— Line of movement

Squad, Column of Twos

The command is: *FALL IN–COLUMN OF TWOS*

The hand signal is: Two fingers extended from a closed fist held above the head, arm vertical.

(As a rule, a crowd formation is commanded from a column of twos.)

2 4 6 8 10 12

Note: Odd numbers to the left.

3 5 7 9 11

1

←—————— Line of movement

Squad Column Changes, Squad Column to Column of Twos.

(Squad line on the march.)

Marching in a squad column, the squad leader may change the body to a column of twos in the following manner:

The command is: *COLUMN OF TWOS—MARCH*

At the command of execution, the even numbered men will "mark time." The odd numbered men will move one step to the left and one step forward and then also "mark time," dressing down immediately. The squad will continue to "mark time" until the squad leader commands a halt or another movement.

Squad Column Changes, Column of Twos to a Squad Column.

(Squad line on the march.)

Marching in a column of twos, the squad leader may change the body to a squad column in the following manner:

The command is: *SQUAD COLUMN—MARCH*

At the command of execution, the squad will continue to move in the normal pace; however, the odd numbered men will move to the right in an oblique movement and integrate into the even numbered column in their respective positions. Upon integration, the squad will dress down immediately and continue to march in quick time.

Squad Diagonal

The command is: *SQUAD DIAGONAL—MARCH*

The squad leader moves his hand in a circle above his head in a manner similar to that used for the assemble signal, then points in the direction he wishes the diagonal to go. The number two man moves to the location designated by the squad leader, and the other men follow him in that direction. Each assumes a position one-half step to the rear and left (or right) of the man in front of him.

CROWD & RIOT CONTROL
FORMATIONS

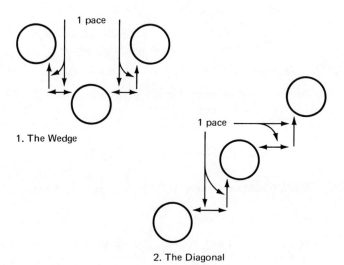

1. The Wedge

2. The Diagonal

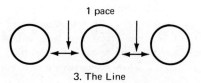

3. The Line

Fig. 1 The Wedge, Diagonal & Line

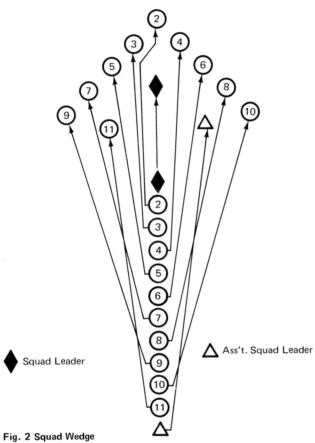

Squad Leader ◆

Ass't. Squad Leader △

Fig. 2 Squad Wedge

CROWD
CONTROL
AND RIOT
PREVENTION
TACTICS

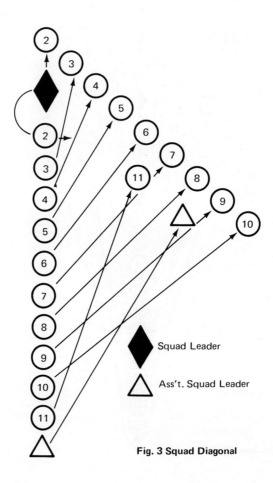

Squad Leader

Ass't. Squad Leader

Fig. 3 Squad Diagonal

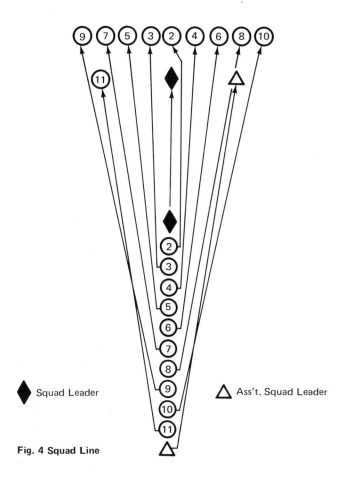

Squad Leader ◆   △ Ass't. Squad Leader

Fig. 4 Squad Line

The command is: *SQUAD WEDGE—MOVE*

The squad leader extends his hands above his head in an inverted V, with the fingers of both hands meeting. The number two man moves to the position designated by the squad leader.

Drawing Batons

Batons should be drawn prior to moving the squad into a crowd formation. Generally speaking, the most effective position for batons in a crowd control formation is at the *port* position.

The command is: *PORT—ARMS*

The hand signal is: The squad leader draws his baton and holds it at port arms.

At the preparatory command of "Port," the squad members adjust the leather thong of their batons on their hands in the prescribed manner and prepare themselves to draw batons at the command of execution, "Arms."

To attain simultaneous execution, sufficient time should be allowed between the preparatory and execution commands for proper adjustment of thong.

LEGAL CONSIDERATIONS

There are many laws that are enforceable at the scene of a major disturbance as individual violations, and they encompass the entire text of the penal codes of any state. Other laws that deal specifically with the problem of unlawful assemblies enable officers to arrest individuals who participate in an unlawful assembly, a rout, or a riot, or who remain at an unlawful assembly after being ordered to leave. This last law is an excellent one if used with discretion and only for special needs.

Federal Law

Title Ten of the United States Code includes the following laws that specifically deal with conditions of violence within the states.

Sec. 331 *Federal Aid for State Governments.*

"When there is an insurrection in any State against its government, the President may, upon the request of its legislature or of its governor if the legislature cannot be convened, call into Fed-

eral service such of the militia of the other States, in the number
requested by that State, and use such of the armed forces, as he
considers necessary to suppress the insurrection."

Sec. 332 *Use of Militia and Armed Forces to Enforce Federal Authority.*

"Whenever the President considers that unlawful obstructions,
combinations, or assemblages, or rebellion against the authority of
the United States, make it impracticable to enforce the laws of the
United States in any State or Territory by the ordinary course of
judicial proceedings, he may call into Federal service such of the
militia of any State, and use such of the armed forces, as he considers necessary to enforce those laws or to suppress the rebellion."

Sec. 333 *Interference with State and Federal Law.*

"The President, by using the militia or the armed forces, or both,
or by any other means, shall take such measures as he considers
necessary to suppress, in a State, any insurrection, domestic violence, unlawful combination or conspiracy, if it—
"(1) so hinders the execution of the laws of that State, and of
the United States within the State, that any part or class of its
people is deprived of a right, privilege, immunity, or protection
named in the Constitution and secured by law, and the constituted
authorities of that State are unable, fail, or refuse to protect that
right, privilege, or immunity, or to give that protection; or
"(2) opposes or obstructs the execution of the laws of the United
States or impedes the course of justice under those laws.
"In any situation covered by clause (1), the State shall be considered to have denied the equal protection of the laws secured
by the Constitution."

Sec. 334 *Proclamation to Disperse.*

"Whenever the President considers it necessary to use the
militia or the armed forces under this chapter, he shall, by proclamation, immediately order the insurgents to disperse and retire
peaceably to their abodes within a limited time."

Supreme Court Opinions

In a 1965 decision, Cox v. Louisiana (33 L. W. 4105, 4109, 4110),
the United States Supreme Court expressed its views on the importance of keeping the public peace:

"Nothing we have said here . . . is to be interpreted as sanc-
tioning riotous conduct in any form or demonstrations, however
peaceful their conduct or commendable their motives, which conflict with properly drawn statutes and ordinances designed to pro-

298

CROWD
CONTROL
AND RIOT
PREVENTION
TACTICS

mote law and order, protect the community against disorder, regulate traffic, safeguard legitimate interests in private and public property, or protect the administration of justice and other essential governmental functions.

"Liberty can only be exercised in a system of law which safeguards order. We reaffirm the repeated holdings of this Court that there is no place for violence in a democratic society dedicated to liberty under law, and that the right of peaceful protest does not mean that everyone with opinions or beliefs to express may do so at any time and at any place. There is a proper time and place for even the most peaceful protest and a plain duty and responsibility on the part of all citizens to obey all valid laws and regulations. There is an equally plain requirement for laws and regulations to be drawn so as to give citizens fair warning as to what is illegal; for regulation of conduct that involves freedom of speech and assembly not to be so broad in scope so as to stifle First Amendment freedoms, which "need breathing space to survive." (NAACP v. Button, 371 U.S. 415,433); for appropriate limitations on the discretion of public officials where speech and assembly are intertwined with regulated conduct; and for all laws and regulations to be applied with an equal hand. We believe that all of these requirements can be met in an ordered society dedicated to liberty. We reaffirm our conviction that 'freedom and viable government are . . . indivisible concepts.' (Gibson v. Florida Legislative Comm. 372 U.S. 539,546)."

CONCLUSION

Any situation involving large numbers of people and the occurrence of the wrong combination of factors may evolve into an unlawful assembly. Without immediate, decisive police action, the situation could quickly develop into a full-scale riot. The key to successful containment and control of civil disturbances by the police department is decisive action by a well-trained and extremely well-organized team of officers.

EXERCISES AND STUDY QUESTIONS

1. List and discuss the five police objectives at the scene of an unlawful assembly.
2. Define "mob psychology."
3. How does a mob differ from a crowd?
4. In what way is *anonymity* related to mob membership?
5. What is "universality"?
6. What crowd control formation would you use to remove a mob leader from the center of a large mob?

7. What are the three progressive stages in transformation of a crowd into a mob? Define each of the three.
8. Recount the recommended procedure for handling an unlawful assembly.
9. Where would you set up a command post at the scene of a riot?
10. What is your department's policy toward (1) arsonists, (2) snipers, and (3) looters during riots?
11. What are some of the steps the staff would take in mobilizing for a riot?
12. What steps has your department taken in planning for a mobilization of all your officers in case of a riot?
13. What is *martial rule?*
14. Under what conditions may federal troops be called into a local police problem?
15. Of what significance is the Supreme Court ruling in Cox v. Louisiana?

SUGGESTED SEMESTER OR TERM PROJECTS

1. Compile a list of all the laws of your state and city, or county, that may be related to unlawful assemblies or riot conditions.
2. Set up a tactical plan for use by your department in handling an unlawful assembly situation.
3. Establish a mobilization plan for calling the officers of your department to duty in case of a major disaster or civil disturbance.

REFERENCES

ADAMS, THOMAS F., "Civil Disturbances Tactical Plan 'A'," Unpublished report prepared for the Santa Ana, California Police Department, August 1968.

FEDERAL BUREAU OF INVESTIGATION, *Prevention and Control of Mobs and Riots.* Washington, D.C.: Government Printing Office, 1965.

FRICKE, CHARLES W., and ARTHUR L. ALARCON, *California Criminal Law.* Los Angeles: Legal Book Corp., 1965.

INTERNATIONAL CITY MANAGERS' ASSOCIATION, *Training and Equipping Police Crowd and Riot Control Officers and Units.* Chicago: International City Managers' Association, 1966.

LOS ANGELES COUNTY SHERIFF'S DEPARTMENT, *Crowd and Riot Control Instructional Guide.* Los Angeles: Sheriff's Department, 1963.

————, *Supervisor's Role in Emergency Operations.* Los Angeles: Sheriff's Department, 1967.

LOS ANGELES DISTRICT ATTORNEY, *Civil Disturbance Manual for Law Enforcement.* Los Angeles: D. A. Evelle J. Younger's Office, 1967.

LOS ANGELES POLICE DEPARTMENT, *Daily Training Bulletins,* Vol. I.

Springfield, Ill.: Charles C Thomas, Publisher, 1954, Chaps. 17 and 18.

MOMBOISSE, RAYMOND M., *Crowd Control and Riot Prevention*. Sacramento, Calif.: State Printing Office, 1964.

SUTHERLAND, EDWIN H., and DONALD R. CRESSEY, *Principles of Criminology*, 5th ed. New York: J. B. Lippincott Co., 1965.

Community Interaction

CHAPTER TWELVE   The patrol officer cannot separate himself from the community he serves, or set himself apart from it as if he were on one side and the people on the other side of some invisible barrier. The policeman is an integral part of his community and it is an integral part of him. In many respects he *is* the community. He reflects its habits, cultures, social pressures, and prejudices, as well as its permissiveness, or its strict adherence to the laws of the city, the state, and the United States. The officer lives in the jurisdiction where he works, or within commuting distance. He shops, seeks recreation, raises children, attends school, goes to church, visits with his friends and neighbors, and functions as just another member of the community he serves most of the time when he is not working. When he is on the job, he fills the role of the police officer, but he does not lose his identity as an individual and as a part of the community. As with any other occupation, the policeman must play a role, and there are certain requirements of the role that set him apart from   301 those who do not fill the same role. So it is with the doctor, the attorney, the plumber, the taxi driver, the grocer, the college professor, and all of the other life roles.

Figure 12.1 Santa Ana Chief Edward J. Allen and his community relations officers map out strategy for meaningful police-community interaction. Courtesy of the Police Department, Santa Ana, California.

The police department is not generally looked upon as a single unit. It is many individuals who are viewed by other individuals in a variety of ways. To the mayor or the city manager, the police department is the police chief, possibly also his captains or deputy chiefs. To the service club member, the police department is his fellow club member who just happens to be a policeman. To the lodge fellows, the policeman is one of their brothers. Each individual in the community perceives the police department through a different set of eyes, and the police department is no stronger or greater than the officer who is its weakest link. The police department may be the married man with two teen-age children, who sits in the backroom of the neighborhood tavern after closing hours and drinks beer while on duty, and makes passes at the divorcee who works in the doctor's office down the street. To the average person, the police department is the patrol officer, who patrols the streets and performs the many hundreds of police services in his own quiet, efficient manner. The police department is what the people see it is, and what the policemen are, not what the city charter says it is. The police department must be above reproach, which means that every single one of its members should likewise be above reproach.

The policeman must have impeccable manners, he must be unquestionably honest, his moral standards must be almost cherubic, his bravery must be undaunting, and he must have all of those qualities

that are promulgated in his code of ethics and the laws that describe
his job. More important than merely having all of those attributes,
he must have them *in the eyes of others.* Yet, he lives and works, plays
and prays in the same community in continuous interaction with all
of the other people in the community in his role of policeman and
whatever other role of the moment he is playing. Let us approach the
police-community interaction from the viewpoint that the police officer
is involved in this interaction virtually all of the time, and almost
without exception he is never separated from his policeman role.

THE OFFICER AS AN INDIVIDUAL

The police officer's authority is actually little more than that of the
average citizen, but his responsibilities are far greater. He is compelled by law, by court decisions, and by his department's policies to
take decisive enforcement action whenever a criminal law violation
comes to his attention. He is limited in that he may arrest for misdemeanors only when they are committed in his presence, and he
may make suspicion arrests for felonies based upon reasonable cause,
which is narrowly interpreted by the courts to assure the accused of
his constitutional guarantees of the "due process" clauses. Every arrest
or law enforcement action that the officer makes must be justified in
the eyes of his superiors, the prosecuting attorney, the courts, and
eventually the U.S. Supreme Court.

The officer must develop considerable skill in using the correct
choice of words at all times, according to the situation. Sometimes a
poorly—or accidentally—chosen word may cause unexpected conflict.
Words are spoken by attitude and innuendo as well as by actual
utterance. Choose them wisely. Any antagonism that arises during a
citizen-officer contact should not be a reflection of the officer's poor
attitude. Virtually every ethnic and religious minority has at least one
nickname that is considered insulting when it is directed by some
nonmember toward a member of that minority in a disdainful manner.
It is the responsibility of every police officer to learn what those words
are, and then to make it a point not to use them even during friendly
locker room kidding.

Overfamiliarity with the people in his district may result in difficulties caused by a lessening of respect for the officer. There should
certainly be friendliness injected into the officer's field contacts with
the people in his district, but not to the point where an officer loses
his police "image." Consider the "good Joe" officer who was such a
nice guy and wanted everyone to like him. He would drive through a
certain neighborhood and smile and wave at the kids, and sometimes
even stop awhile and "chew the fat" with them before going on about
his patrolling. The young children loved him. So did the young delin-

quents and some of the young adults, who were in the habit of playing poker for money on the street corner, and who committed various types of minor crimes without having to worry about "good old Joe." When asked about how they were able to get away with such obvious law violations, several of the people questioned replied: "Oh, good old Joe? He wouldn't arrest us. We weren't hurting anyone, and Joe didn't mind as long as we were minding our business and not hurting anyone."

Personal appearance and grooming must be acceptable to the majority of the population. Fads in facial and head hair may be acceptable for motion picture and television personalities, and for the "average guys" as well as the local Lotharios, but most of the people want their policemen to be "clean-cut" and smooth shaven. The officer's uniform must be immaculate and have a semimilitary appearance. Personal cleanliness must also be above average. The officer must be free of offensive body odors, foul breath, and dirty fingernails, and he must use a handkerchief to deal with a case of hay fever.

The individual police officer should never limit his organizational membership exclusively to police-oriented clubs. He is part of the larger community and should not isolate himself from that community. When someone finds out he is a policeman, they may want help in "fixing" a ticket, or they may just want to "gripe" about the "bum tickets" they received the last four times they were stopped. A doctor's friends likewise plague him with requests for a free diagnosis, or a tip about what kind of medicine they can buy from the druggist's shelf to avoid the high cost of prescriptions. An electrician is expected by friends to handle free electrical installation jobs. Unfortunately, the nature of the work and the strange hours that usually accompany employment as a police officer preclude an active participation in community organizations. But social interaction as an individual and as family man are important, and the officer should make a deliberate effort to participate.

Youth groups, parent organizations, religious clubs, lodges, and service organizations all have varied memberships from all segments of the population. Participation in these groups yields results, not only for the individual but also for the community. It allows the officer and the people he contacts during his workday to interact as social equals and to gain an insight into each other that could not be gotten otherwise.

The officer's contact with the traffic violator should be pleasant and friendly, yet not overly familiar. There must be a pleasant smile, but not a happy or sadistic grin. The officer should not be a "sourpuss," but he cannot be too flippant because the violator may think he is treating the matter too lightly, and the violator is going to have to pay a substantial fine for the ticket the policeman is giving him. Some time following the experience of receiving the citation, the in-

dividual will see for himself the violation that he committed and
will agree that he should have received it, providing his contact with
the officer was not unpleasant. If there was an unpleasant scene with
the officer, the same individual will relive the experience and build
his own case for his innocence. In addition, he will find good cause
for growing angry over the unprofessional attitude of the police officer.

The police officer may be a member of an ethnic minority, but once
he becomes a policeman he loses some of that identity because of the
predominance of his role as a policeman. He must guard against developing strong prejudices and he cannot allow any of his intense
feelings *for or against* any individual or group of people influence his
decisions to act as an ethical police officer.

Figure 12.2 The police officer's community relations activities involve more than formal prepared speeches to
large audiences. This officer and his friends are participat-
ing in a "code seven" or "lunch bag" program. Photo courtesy of the Garden Grove Police Department and the
Orange County Evening News.

When dealing with young people in any type of police action, the
officer should always avoid attempts at intimidation through his language or his attitude. The juvenile should be dealt with positively and
with respect if the officer is to expect any respect in return. Kindness
and understanding are sometimes received by some youngsters with
contempt and the officer may find it extremely difficult to hold his

temper. In such cases, a positive and firm approach in the manner of a benevolent but strict parent may be the better approach. Never resort to losing your temper or name-calling, thereby denigrating the objective status of the law enforcement officer.

Figure 12.3 The Delaware State Police officer is explaining the police role to an interested audience. Courtesy of the Delaware State Police.

The police officer is gauged by many people on the type and quality of service he performs. One way he can perform a tremendously important crime prevention service for the merchants and businessmen in his district is by making an occasional inspection visit. He should drop in and ask the owner or manager if there is any objection to his making a few observations about his building security. He will probably find the front doors in good shape. However, the back doors, through which burglars would rather enter, are more likely to need improvement. It may be suggested that the merchant put the safe in a location where the patrolling officer can see it from outside, or that he install a silent burglar alarm system.

While patrolling his district, the patrol officer is in an excellent position to develop informants. Contrary to popular belief, the officer's most frequent source of information is not his underworld "fink," or "stool pigeon." Most of the people who give him information are people in whom he has developed a feeling of pride by keeping their particular neighborhood crime-free. The officer has also given them a feeling of confidence that any information they give him about known or suspected crime violations will not immediately get back to them as a source of the information. By the officer's own courteous service, he creates in the people he contacts a feeling of obligation to help him continue to perform an exemplary job.

Figure 12.4 These school safety patrol boys are visited by a friendly trooper. Courtesy of the Delaware State Police.

One of the community interaction programs that many police departments have established on a more formal basis during recent years has been the "brown bag," or "adopt-a-cop," or "officer-on-campus" program. This is an assigned function, established in cooperation with various schools, colleges, or organizations, at which one or two officers meet with several people in an informal setting while having lunch or refreshments together. The meeting is generally an unstructured affair with the officer attempting to "break the ice" with some of the people he may meet on the street under different conditions. While they are "breaking bread" at the same table, so to speak, they develop a rapport and the conversation usually gets around to the little and seemingly unimportant problems that each of the people have had with police officers at one time or another. Many of the group's questions are answered in such a way that the rapport extends far beyond their informal meetings. It is not uncommon for the officer to find that a great many of the questions asked of him are based on misinformation or complete lack of information about the police role in the community.

POLICE DEPARTMENT COMMUNITY
RELATIONS ACTIVITIES

Every police department in the country is involved in community relations, or police-community interaction. The police department is a service organization and its service involves a direct interaction with the community it serves. During recent years, the trend has been to formalize many of the functions that had previously been conducted on an informal basis. Some departments have created special bureaus or divisions with staff responsibility and full-time, assigned personnel to coordinate the community relations activities of the department. Others have added this function to the list of responsibilities of one or more of the staff officers, to be handled along with various other assignments. Often the various programs of interaction with the public that are not directly related to law enforcement or crime repression activities are cataloged, and an effort is made to measure their effectiveness in terms of public acceptance and changes in crime and accident trends. The following deals with some of the police department's community interaction programs and activities.

Figure 12.5 The police officer makes the community relations unit work by going into the community instead of waiting for it to come to him. Courtesy of the Police Department, Lexington, Kentucky.

Community Relations Unit

Someone within the organization should be charged with the responsibility for the department's community relations activities. He should possess commensurate authority to implement techniques and programs, both formal and informal, that will create and maintain a

308

better community understanding of the police role and a better police understanding of the various peoples and their cultural backgrounds and respective roles in the community. The program must have the complete endorsement of the police chief, because some of the activities break with years of tradition, and they may be rejected at the level of execution without such backing. This community relations unit may function as a rumor control center in times of turmoil. At all times it should operate as a communications vehicle between the people and their police department whenever and wherever there is a need for the communicating process.

309

POLICE
DEPARTMENT
COMMUNITY
RELATIONS
ACTIVITIES

Community Relations Policies

The police department must have a set of workable, and *working*, community relations policies. While assigned to the Staff Services Bureau in the Santa Ana Police Department, I assisted in the preparation of the department's statement of policy in the area of human relations. In that statement, we wrote:

> The mutual advantages of a friendly relationship between the people of a community and their police force should be widely understood and more fully appreciated. The success of a police department in the performance of its duties is largely measured by the degree of support and cooperation it receives from the people it serves. It is of paramount importance, therefore, to secure for this department the confidence, respect, and approbation of the public. The cultivation of such desirable attitudes on the part of the public is dependent upon reciprocal attitudes on the part of this department. These policies are designed to enhance good public relations and [we] anticipate active participation therein by every member of the department.

This statement is based on three major premises: the attitude of the people in the community is affected by the degree of efficiency demonstrated by their police officers in the performance of their duties; there must be a mutual understanding between the people of all backgrounds and ethnic origins and the officers who comprise their police department; and there must be a continuous, free flow of information about the activities of the police department to the public through the news media. The information must be honest and frank.

Fair and Equal Treatment for All Persons

Selection of the men and women who comprise the ranks of the organization is significant in setting the tone for a department that operates free of bias or prejudices. Everyone has the constitutional right to be prejudiced, but the police officer relinquishes the right to let any prejudices he may have reflect in his official actions. If he is so colored by prejudice that he loses his objectivity in his personal contacts with people, he will not be effective as a police officer. Police action should be dictated by the circumstances, and the officer's discretion in taking police action must be without regard to the individual's ethnic, religious, or moral characteristics.

Understanding the People in the Community

Seminars and conferences may be specifically programmed to bring together in educational debates police officers and people from various minority groups or philosophical organizations, political or religious. The aim of such debates is to promote a free exchange of views on various community concerns. They allow the police officer to explain the purpose and intent of the laws and the philosophy of his particular department, thereby reducing the amount and degree of misunderstanding of the police role.

Community Leadership Participation

Someone once said that a camel is a horse put together by a committee. I agree, particularly if the committee is formed to accomplish a specific job. However, committees do serve an excellent purpose if their goal is to develop a broader base of understanding among the people in the community of the many problems confronting their police department. A committee could be established, for example, for the purpose of disseminating information about the juvenile laws of the state and the community, and the police department's enforcement attitude toward those laws. The committee could present their opinions and representative views as citizens of the community at a meeting with the police chief and juvenile officers, and the police department would establish its own policies using the committee's suggestions as guidelines rather than mandates. The police department would then disseminate to the general public, through the committee and the press, the department's policies and enforcement program. This procedure could be effective in dealing with various major problems confronting law enforcement and the community.

Police Reserve Corps

There are many outstanding ladies and gentlemen who might have been excellent police officers or other police department employees, but who decided to enter other lifetime pursuits. By establishing a reserve program, it may be possible to create in a segment of the population a greater sense of involvement in their police department's activities through actual participation. Under normal conditions, the reserves could train and serve alongside the regular officers once or twice weekly. Then, in case of a sudden emergency calling for manpower far in excess of that which the department could provide, the full complement of the reserves could be called into action to handle the immediate problem. Men and women could be used for a variety of functions, including actual field duties, such as operating a patrol unit, protecting a crime scene, directing traffic at the scene of an accident, or handling an unruly crowd. There are many other functions that need equal attention during times of emergency, such as preparing meals for officers who cannot leave their posts, manning telephones and radio equipment, maintaining radio and automotive equipment, and sketching robbery suspects. These and myriad other functions could be performed by people from a variety of occupations and professions.

311

POLICE
DEPARTMENT
COMMUNITY
RELATIONS
ACTIVITIES

Public Information

There should be some means for keeping the public informed about new laws and procedures, enforcement policies, and crime statistics. It is no secret that the police department cannot survive as an effective instrumentality of the government without the cooperation and support of the people, as we have already stated, but the public's support should be based on knowledge gained from accurate information. The department should neither ask for, nor expect, blind faith. Through the medium of personal appearances before every organization that will listen, the police chief and his direct representatives must appear and discuss frankly the actions and intentions of the police department. It is essential that we overcome some of the apathy which is expressed by lack of intercourse with the people. The people and their police department should be discussing the important problems of today and the ways in which these problems can be solved through mutual cooperation.

Press Relations

Whenever anything in the field occurs that appears to be newsworthy, such as an accident or a human interest story, it should be standard operating procedure to call it to the attention of the press media. The "exclusive" should be avoided by adopting a standard department procedure for news releases, and sticking to the procedure. An information officer may be assigned on a permanent, full-time basis, or one should be assigned each time a newsworthy situation occurs. If the department utilizes this practice, it should then be a department policy for all members of the department to adhere to it by referring any inquiring reporters or newsmen to the single individual who is responsible for releasing the information. Such a procedure reduces the disparity between stories emanating from several officers about the same case, and avoids what might be a legitimate complaint of "reliability gap."

The department philosophy should be one of complete cooperation with the press. All information that will not directly hinder the ongoing progress of a case currently under investigation should be released. Withholding information concerning some cases is essential, but in most cases it is not. As a matter of fact, it may be wise to discuss even the confidential information with the press representatives, explaining to them why the release of such information is harmful to the case. They then will act as responsible people should and refrain from releasing the information. This candid approach may be wiser than withholding certain facts and running the risk of their discovering the information through other means and inadvertently releasing their "inside" or "exclusive" that may ruin the case. If the news reporters are truly serving the public as they claim, they will respect the request and withhold printing of certain details until given clearance from the department. As a result, both the police and the press will improve their efficiency.

EXERCISES AND STUDY QUESTIONS

1. If you are not a policeman, what is your opinion of the "average policeman"?
2. What are some of the dangers of overfamiliarity with the people in your district?
3. What is your opinion about the officer's "right" to wear his hair and to groom himself as he pleases?
4. Outline what you believe a "safety inspection" of a liquor store, or some other type of establishment, should include.
5. Who is the policeman's best source of information, according to the author?
6. What should be the purpose of a community relations unit in a police department?
7. What are the basic premises underlying the community relations policy of the police department discussed in this chapter?
8. What are the limitations of prejudice allowed a police officer?
9. What is the value of a reserve program in times of natural disasters?
10. What should be the police department's policy toward cooperation with the press?

SUGGESTED SEMESTER OR TERM PROJECTS

1. Set up a reserve program for the police department where you live, if one is not now in existence.

2. Outline a ten-point community relations program for your police department.
3. Set up and participate in at least three "brown bag" sessions and report on the meetings.

REFERENCES

ADAMS, THOMAS F., *Law Enforcement—An Introduction to the Police Role in the Community.* Englewood Cliffs, N. J.: Prentice-Hall, Inc., 1968.

BRANDSTATTER, A. F., and LOUIS A. RADELET, *Police and Community Relations—A Sourcebook.* Beverly Hills, Calif.: Glencoe Press, 1968.

HOLLINGSWORTH, DAN, *Rocks in the Roadway.* Chicago: Stromberg-Allen, 1954.

INTERNATIONAL ASSOCIATION OF CHIEFS OF POLICE AND ANTI-DEFAMATION LEAGUE OF B'NAI B'RITH, *The Police and the Civil Rights Act.* New York: International Association of Chiefs of Police and Anti-Defamation League, 1959.

KRETCH, DAVID, RICHARD S. CRUTCHFIELD, and EGERTON L. BALLACHEY, *Individual in Society.* New York: McGraw-Hill Book Company, 1962.

LOS ANGELES POLICE DEPARTMENT, *Daily Training Bulletins*, Vol. I. Springfield, Ill.: Charles C Thomas, Publisher, 1954, Chap. 2.

PARKER, WILLIAM H., *The Police Role in Community Relations.* New York: National Conference of Christians and Jews, 1962.

Index